The New Chinese Leadership: C
Opportunities after the 16th Pa

The New Chinese Leadership: Challenges and Opportunities after the 16th Party Congress

The China Quarterly Special Issues
New Series, No. 4

Edited by

YUN-HAN CHU, CHIH-CHENG LO AND RAMON H. MYERS

CAMBRIDGE
UNIVERSITY PRESS

Published by the Press Syndicate of the University of Cambridge
The Pitt Building, Trumpington Street, Cambridge, CB2 1RP
40 West 20th Street, New York, NY 10011 4211, USA
477 Williamstown Road, Port Melbourne, VIC 3207, Australia

A catalogue record for this book is available
from the British Library

Library of Congress Cataloging-in-Publication Data applied for

ISBN 0 521 600588 (paperback)

Printed and bound in Great Britain by Infotype Ltd, Oxfordshire

Contents

Cover illustration: members of the new Standing Committee of the
CPC Political Bureau at their first public appearance, 16 November
2002. From left to right: Hu Jintao, Wu Bangguo, Wen Jiabao, Jia
Qinglin, Zeng Qinghong, Huang Ju, Wu Guanzheng, Li Changchun,
Luo Gan. Photo courtesy of Wu Ching Teng

Notes on Contributors

RICHARD BAUM is director of the Center for Chinese Studies and professor of political science, University of California at Los Angeles.

YUN-HAN CHU is distinguished research fellow of the Institute of Political Science, Academia Sinica and professor of political science at National Taiwan University. He serves concurrently as president of the Chiang Ching-kuo Foundation for International Scholarly Exchange.

LOWELL DITTMER is professor of political science at the University of California at Berkeley and editor of *Asian Survey*.

GERRIT W. GONG is assistant to the president at Brigham Young University in Provo, Utah, with responsibility for planning and assessment. He is also senior associate at the Center for Strategic and International Studies (CSIS) in Washington, DC.

JOHN W. LEWIS is William Haas professor emeritus of Chinese politics at Stanford University. He currently directs the Project on Peace and Cooperation in the Asian-Pacific Region.

KENNETH LIEBERTHAL holds several positions at the University of Michigan: distinguished fellow and director for China at the William Davidson Institute, professor of political science, William Davidson professor of business administration, and research associate of the Center for Chinese Studies.

CHIH-CHENG LO is associate professor of political science at Soochow University and executive director at the Institute for National Policy Research. He is also the secretary-general of the Taiwan–Russia Association.

RAMON H. MYERS is senior fellow at the Hoover Institution and also the curator of the East Asian archives.

JEAN C. OI is the William Haas professor in Chinese politics, director of the Center for East Asian Studies, and professor of political science at Stanford University. She is also the Chair of the China Inner Asia Council of the Association of Asian Studies (2002–2003).

DAVID SHAMBAUGH teaches about China and international affairs of Asia in the Elliott School of International Affairs at George Washington University. He is also a non-resident senior fellow in the foreign policy studies program at the Brookings Institution.

DOROTHY J. SOLINGER is professor of political science at University of California, Irvine, and senior adjunct research associate at the East Asian Institute, Columbia University.

YU-SHAN WU is director and research fellow at the Institute of Political Science, Academia Sinica, professor in political science at National Taiwan University, and convener of political science at the National Science Council of Taiwan.

XUE LITAI is a member of the research staff of the Center for International Security and Cooperation, Stanford University.

SUISHENG ZHAO is associate professor at the graduate school of international studies, University of Denver and executive director of its Center for China–US Cooperation. He is the founder and editor of the *Journal of Contemporary China*.

The 16th Party Congress: New Leaders, New China*

Yun-han Chu, Chih-cheng Lo and Ramon H. Myers

The 16th Chinese Party Congress, representing the most sweeping leadership transition in the history of Communist China, marked a shift of power to the "fourth generation" of Chinese leaders, to be represented by the 59-year-old Hu Jintao. Mao Zedong, Deng Xiaoping and Jiang Zemin respectively represented the first three generations.

The power transition is not complete because Jiang Zemin, the outgoing chief, retains his chairmanship of the Central Military Commission (CMC) and has placed his protégés in the new, nine-member Politburo's Standing Committee. China's new leaders hold all top offices at the national and provincial levels and over 80 per cent of the newly elected 168 seats of the Chinese Communist Party's (CCP) Central Committee.

Although jockeying for power by Party factions had been intense, the CCP's leadership succession was more orderly and peaceful than in any previous Party Congress. The fourth generation of leaders, now in their late 40s and 50s, lived through the Cultural Revolution (1966–76). They hold enormous power and will steer China through its most difficult period. This unprecedented leadership turnover is bound to carry far-reaching implications for China's ongoing economic, social and political transition as well as its engagement with the outside world.

Can this leadership and the 66 million-member CCP[1] realize the goals of the 16th Party Congress, which are to revitalize the CCP, modernize the country, provide a modest living standard for the great majority of the Chinese people, unify the mainland and Taiwan, protect China's national security and elevate the nation's international standing? Are these leaders able to promote economic development and distributive justice, reduce regional economic disparity, harness new and powerful social forces having diverse interests, implement incremental political reform, manage US–China relations, deal with the Taiwan issue, and minimize the negative effects of globalization while channelling its benefits to help China?

To answer these questions, the Hoover Institution on War, Revolution and Peace, in co-operation with Taiwan's Institute for International Policy Research, invited several dozen leading scholars to a conference at the institution in January 2003. The conference examined the backgrounds and capabilities of the new leaders and their willingness to use Jiang Zemin's legacy to solve future problems. The Jiang era includes the

* We thank the Institute for National Policy Research for financial sponsorship, and its chairman, Dr Hung-mao Tien, for his support and encouragement. We also thank the Hoover Institution, and in particular Dr Larry Diamond for his important role in the development of the volume.

1. CCP membership in June 2002 totalled 66 million, 5 million more than in 1997. See *The China Quarterly*, No. 172 (December 2002), p. 1110.

14th and 15th CCP Congresses and the institutional changes that followed them. Will the little-known Hu Jintao rely on Jiang's legacy or introduce innovations of his own, as Jiang did? The chapters that follow try to answer these questions.

China's New Generation of Leaders

Some new political norms that owe much to Deng Xiaoping's leadership came into play at the 16th Party Congress, including that Politburo members should not serve more than two consecutive terms of five years each and not be more than 70 years old. (An important exception was former CCP secretary general Jiang Zemin, who, like Deng Xiaoping before him, chairs the CMC after giving up all Party posts. Jiang is informed of Politburo deliberations, and, with Party elders Zhu Rongji, Li Peng and others, advises the new leadership.)

The new leaders are young; except for the Politburo member Luo Gang (formerly in charge of internal security) and People's Liberation Army (PLA) general Cao Gangchuan, both born in 1937, all were born in 1940 or after. As Suisheng Zhao's chapter notes, they have little memory of the pre-1949 era and were spared the brutal leadership struggles that characterized the Party until Deng Xiaoping became the paramount leader in 1978. All the new Politburo members graduated from college, with nine graduating from China's top universities and only Luo Gan studying abroad and graduating from a university in the former Democratic People's Republic of Germany. Most trained as engineers, many at Qinghua University in Beijing. They all came from families who encouraged them to acquire a higher education and professional expertise; many of those same families during the Cultural Revolution had been accused of being "too bourgeois."

Thus, these new leaders feel that, for the CCP to win the hearts and minds of the people, China must avoid chaos and maintain social stability. Moreover, Chinese citizens must have the opportunity to enhance their "life chances."

These young leaders also believe in Deng Xiaoping's dictum that China can be saved only through reform that is compatible with Chinese culture, ideology and institutions. Just as Jiang followed in the footsteps of Deng but established his own legacy, these leaders, many of whom owe their careers to Jiang Zemin's patronage, will build on Jiang's legacy and create their own.

In his chapter Suisheng Zhao points out that the new Politburo leaders all served in high provincial or ministerial positions or both during the 1980s and 1990s (see his Tables 1 and 2), which gave them the skills to solve problems produced by the ongoing reforms. Respected by their colleagues, their official behaviour mimics that of the modest general secretary Hu Jintao, a team player and deferential to superiors. Like Hu, they loyally serve the Party and state, comfortably participating in a collegial process of consensus building using the principle of democratic centralism. In China's political life, personal networks and their institutional underpinnings are as important as the collective leadership's vision of China's future.

Gerrit W. Gong emphasizes that in the past five years these top leaders have had firsthand observation of China's changing role in the international order. Like Deng and Jiang, they believe that China must rely on diplomacy and trade, build friendly relations with other nations, and participate in international organizations to expand alliances. They have travelled widely, taking 42 foreign trips to 197 countries, including Asia and Africa, with fewer trips to South America, the Middle East and Oceania. Hu Jintao – the most widely travelled among the group – has visited 23 different countries, nearly twice as many as that of his new colleagues. Although they have not been educated abroad and are not fluent in foreign languages, they are carefully briefed about foreign visitors and well informed about significant foreign policy changes taking place in the world. Some, including Hu Jintao, have sent their children abroad to study.

The relationship of Hu with his predecessor Jiang Zemin shows that the new leaders can effectively work with their elders to realize CCP goals. Whether such a mentor relationship between Jiang and Hu is in the best interests of the Party remains to be seen, as Yu-Shan Wu notes in his chapter. Wu suggests that such a relationship can intensify the fears and prejudices shared by Party elders and produce leadership gerontocracy. In the past, Hu had been content to remain in the shadows and publicly said little until being made CCP secretary general. When he came to power Jiang deferred to Deng, kept a low profile and worked hard, and Hu has done the same while maintaining a high-quality performance and building relationships with Party, provincial and government officials. Moreover, Hu endorsed Jiang's leadership and ascended to power without threatening him.

Some China watchers hint at tensions between Hu and Jiang's trusted colleague Zeng Qinghong, but there is no reliable evidence to confirm the reports. Zeng helped Jiang design the "three represents" theory, now leads the Central Party School, and is a Standing Committee member. Hu endorsed the "three represents" theory and vowed to "unswervingly" and "persistently" carry out the policy objectives set out in the political report of the last Central Committee (Suisheng Zhao's chapter). When speaking to the Party's Central Commission for Discipline Inspection (CCDI) on 3 February 2003, Hu referred six times to the "three represents" theory, reminding his audience that corruption must be eradicated from within the CCP. So far, collegiality, not tensions, characterizes the new leadership.

David Shambaugh's chapter observes that, before the 16th Party Congress ended, Jiang and his Politburo colleagues had retired all senior officers of the PLA and installed a new team of young, professional officers. In 2000, the CCP had ordered PLA officers to give up their chairmanships of defence-related industries and ordered them to the barracks to train as an even smaller, professional military leadership. Although the government spent substantial funds to modernize the PLA, a policy that will continue for the foreseeable future, the spending increase of this year was below previous years. As chairman of the CMC, Jiang Zemin keeps a watchful eye on the Party's new leaders and the military establishment as well.

The Jiang Zemin Legacy

Lowell Dittmer's chapter points out that in 1990–91, Jiang aligned himself with the central planning team under Chen Yun, Bo Yibo and Li Xiannian, but then in 1992 supported Deng's call at the 14th Party Congress for a socialist market economy with Chinese characteristics. Jiang went on to reform the command economy, reorganizing enterprises by "grasping the large firms and relinquishing the small ones" and restructuring their friendly ministries. The state encouraged the formation of new private, public and joint venture enterprises; in 1993–94 a new foreign exchange rate was instituted and a value-added tax on enterprise production introduced. The results were stunning. By 2002, the non-public economy accounted for more than 50 per cent of industrial output and employed more than that share of the workforce. In 1999 China gained entry to the World Trade Organization.

According to Dittmer, Jiang first reduced the administrative staff in central and provincial administrations by nearly half and by 20 per cent for county and township administrative posts. He then discouraged factional struggle in the Party and government and extended civility to opposing faction leaders while encouraging them "to retire honourably without ideological recrimination if eased out of the leadership." After Deng died, Jiang continued reforming the Communist Party. He instructed the Central Party School to encourage new thinking about how to transform the CCP into a dynamic, creative political force. The school examined how political parties such as the Kuomintang and Mexico's Institutional Revolutionary Party (Partido Revolucionmario Institucional) were able to survive for so long. The school also studied how European social democratic parties governed and coped with opposition parties. In 2003 Mao Zedong's secretary, Li Rui, was allowed to write an essay outlining how direct elections might be designed for the CCP. The Party also encouraged research on the progress of villages holding direct elections, whether townships should have similar elections, how rural taxation had developed and the factors influencing farmers' living conditions.

CCP leaders have always referred to a "comprehensive doctrine," or *tixi*, as articulated in Marxism-Leninism and Mao Zedong's writings. By the late 1980s Deng Xiaoping's thought also had become a "comprehensive doctrine." Jiang Zemin hopes that his efforts to transform the CCP will place him in the pantheon of creators of a new "comprehensive doctrine."

Lewis and Xue's chapter argues that Party reforms during the 1990s divided society into winners who benefited from the reforms and losers who did not. In the last few years, the number of losers has been catching up with the numbers of winners and their living standards declining.

Many losers – the unemployed, the aged without social welfare, and those treated unjustly by the Party and state – perceive the CCP as corrupt and blame it for the sudden increase in their numbers.

To restore the public's trust in the CCP, the Party had to clean up its act. To do that, Jiang conceived the "three represents" theory that he introduced in February 2000 during a tour of Guangdong and Shanghai cities. Just as Deng had during his 1992 tour of the south, Jiang called for new thinking in the Communist Party (Deng had urged the Party to promote a socialist market economy with Chinese characteristics). In his speeches Jiang urged the Party to use science and technology to transform Chinese society. He then called on it to admit capitalists; self-employed, financial and technical-skilled professionals; managers and technical staff of foreign-funded enterprises; and entrepreneurial-technical staff in the non-public sector. Finally, he called for innovative ideas from all segments of society to meet the challenges of the times. Jiang warned Party members that society was rapidly changing and that, if they did not champion those changes, the CCP would be left behind in the dustbin of history. New ideas must replace old ways of thinking. After the CCP Politburo affirmed Jiang's "three represents" theory, on 1 July 2001, Jiang again called for reform in a speech at the Central Party School to celebrate the 80th anniversary of the Communist Party.[2]

According to Zheng Bijian, former executive vice-president of the Central Party School, the CCP should not become a party of all the people. He said that "only a party representing the interests of the most advanced class [the workers, redefined to include intellectuals and entrepreneurs] can reconcile divergent interests on the basis of the fundamental interest of the broad mass of the people." Zheng said that the former Soviet Union had failed to create a party of all the people: "We definitely cannot copy Western concepts and include all of the broad mass of contemporary Chinese intellectuals, including science and technology workers, cultural workers, and economic managers, in the category of the so-called 'middle class.' This denigrates, weakens, and even obliterates the working class."[3] In her chapter reviewing recent urban economic changes that now challenge the CCP's new leaders, Dorothy Solinger contends that if the "three represents" theory signals Party support for a new urban-elite constituency, the CCP will move in the wrong direction because it will be ignoring a growing segment of uneducated, poor and unemployed that could undermine urban social stability and de-legitimize the CCP.

After the 14th Party Congress in 1992, when the CCP began re-

2. Jiang Zemin, *Quanmian jianshe xiaokang shehui: kaichuang Zhongguo tese shehuizhuyi shiye xin jumian – zai Zhongguo gongchandang di shiliu ci quanguo daibiao dahui shang de baogao* (*The Complete Construction of a Society of Modest Living Standards: New Breakthroughs for Our Task of Opening-up and Creating Socialism with Special Chinese Characteristics – A Report Given at the National Congress of the Chinese Communist Party by Jiang Zemin*) (Beijing: Renmin chubanshe, 8 November 2002) p. 15.

3. Quoted from Joseph Fewsmith, "Rethinking the role of the CCP: explicating Jiang Zemin's Party anniversary speech," *China Leadership Monitor,* No. 1 part 2, p. 5. See http:/www-hoover.Stanford.edu/publications/default.html, Hoover Institution Publications, *China Leadership Monitor.*

configuring the command economy, many state enterprises began closing because they could not cover costs. Unemployment increased as managers and workers lost their jobs, receiving only partial salaries as they awaited new job assignments or tried to find work. Farmers also protested against increases in rural taxes. Corruption scandals rocked several famous state banks. These developments increased society's losers, but winners also increased as the market economy continued to grow.

As complex economic expansion and contraction continued, the state tried to establish a public finance system that fairly distributed both tax burden and services to villages, townships and counties. But Jean Oi's chapter illustrates that some tax burdens declined and others unexpectedly rose. Why?

According to Oi, some villages successfully entered the market because of lower transaction costs and because they switched from low value-added to high value-added products such as manufactured goods. Villages that produced low value-added products earned little, but after officials imposed user fees and raised the land tax, their tax burden rose. Thus, some rural areas experienced economic pain but others did not because of different comparative resource advantages and different transaction costs. Moreover, where tax rules for village land were vague, local officials had strong incentives to readjust those taxes upward. Until officials can design a simple public finance system based upon clearly defined property rights and equitably tax those properties, the state will tax some villages more heavily than others, thus encouraging rural tax protests.

After the mid-1990s, unemployment soared in the urban sector because of lay-offs in manufacturing and the increasing difficulties that migrant workers have in finding jobs. Solinger's chapter cites surveys of household income and employment showing that, as the urban middle class expanded, another group emerged with low income and low employment. At the same time, public opinion polls revealed that many thought the reforms were taking place too quickly. One 1997 survey of six large cities found a larger share than in previous surveys unhappy with their jobs, incomes and degree of freedom of speech as compared to 1987. This same poll also revealed, however, that "Chinese urban residents showed not only relatively strong support for the current political system and a rising sense of nationalism, but also an unwillingness to challenge the authorities, at least not through institutional channels such as the workplace."[4] But that attitude might have changed in 2002, when urban disturbances erupted in many bankrupt and failing state enterprises.

As early as 1978, at the 11th Central Committee's plenum, the CCP began emphasizing the building of a peaceful international environment. When Jiang became CCP secretary general, he strongly affirmed a new foreign policy rule that China should not seek superpower status and its officials should not speak of catching up with the West (a phrase often

---

4. Wenfang Tang, "Political and social trends in post-Deng urban China: crisis or stability?" *The China Quarterly*, No. 168 (December 2001), p. 907.

uttered by Japan's officials more than a decade ago). Jiang emphasized creating a stable regional and international environment for China's security. His visits to Russia, Japan, South Korea and South-East Asia, as Gerrit Gong's chapter reveals, were directed at improving relations and heading off crises before they worsened. As a result, those countries now view China as more friendly and are benefiting from China's rapid economic growth and expanding market economy.

Jiang had hoped his eight-point proposal in 1995 would facilitate a dialogue with Taiwan's leaders, but both the Lee Teng-hui and the Chen Shui-bian administrations rejected such discussions because they were based on the one-China principle. Thus, dialogue between the two sides has been frozen since 1999. Yun-han Chu's chapter points out that, after 2002, Beijing's leaders modified their stance, suggesting that each side could agree that Taiwan and the mainland are part of China, and that, with such an understanding, all topics were open for discussion. The Taiwan authorities never responded to Beijing's concession, and neither side suggested that the sovereignty of one China might be shared.

Among the topics Beijing was willing to negotiate were the "three links" (direct postal, airline and ship connections) between Taiwan and mainland China (see Yun-han Chu's chapter). Finally, in the late summer of 2002, Beijing dropped its one-China demand and invited Taiwan to discuss how to improve relations across the Taiwan Strait. Beijing's leaders also appealed to all Taiwanese (except those who had publicly championed Taiwan independence) to visit the mainland and confer with Beijing's leaders. Meanwhile, in an effort to improve Taiwan's economic growth, the Taiwan government relaxed its rules blocking Taiwan businesses from investing on the mainland.

Although the Jiang and Bush administrations got off to a bad start, when two of their aeroplanes collided over international waters near Hainan Island in early April 2000, the two states were able to arrive at a resolution (see Kenneth Lieberthal's chapter). After 11 September 2001, the two nations began sharing intelligence and working together to block the transfer of money funds to international terrorists. In late 2002 and 2003 China's leaders gently urged the United States to enter bilateral negotiations with North Korea, and even persuaded North Korea's leader Kim Jong Il to agree to send representatives to Beijing where multilateral negotiations between North Korea, China and the United States were to take place in spring 2003 to resolve the nuclear crisis that had erupted in late 2002. Lieberthal describes how, through these and other methods, the Chinese government is dedicated to shoring up its co-operation with the United States.

New Leadership, Institutional Change and a New China?

To summarize, the new CCP leadership that came to power at the 16th Party Congress is dedicated to strengthening and modifying the new institutions that have evolved in the past 15 years. These young, experienced and educated leaders – following in the footsteps of Deng Xiaoping and Jiang Zemin – will promote the market economy and reconfigure the command economy of the state bureaucracy and state enterprises. They will continue to experiment with taxation, monetary and foreign trade reforms as well as with social welfare programmes for the aged, the ill and the unemployed. As Richard Baum's chapter shows, they are willing to build upon the many political reform experiments taking place in several of Guangdong's largest counties and elsewhere. In foreign affairs, they will work with their neighbours and the United States to resolve disputes and engage in co-operative efforts for mutual interests. In particular, they will work to align the CCP with the new groups rising in the new economy.

Can China's new leaders reverse the trend of the number of losers catching up with the winners in China's economic reforms? Can they ameliorate the corruption in the CCP and build honest, effective governance. The contributors to this volume believe that the prospects for doing so in the next five to ten years are fair to good provided Party leaders hold themselves accountable for mistakes and promote incremental institutional reforms that can offer incentives for people to modify their behaviour to address their problems. Why such optimism?

First, China's new leaders seem to be addressing the widening gap between the losers and winners; within the last few months Party leader Hu Jintao conducted a televised visit to some wretchedly poor areas and expressed his Party's commitment to improving such conditions. Secondly, these leaders must be willing to admit mistakes and replace officials who are corrupt and incompetent. In spring of 2003 the CCP's top leaders finally admitted the government had badly responded to the SARS (severe acute respiratory syndrome) epidemic and sacked the government health minister Zhang Wenkang and the mayor of Beijing, Meng Xuenong, who at first had downplayed the epidemic. But good intentions are not enough. China's leaders must not only be creative and open to new thinking but honest and admit mistakes to rectify them quickly before government is severely discredited.

The chapters that follow suggest that the exiting generation of leaders not only learned by doing and performed capably before retiring, but that the new leaders might very well do the same. Although the new leaders reject Western-style democracy, they are trying to use competitive mechanisms to solve problems and establish feedback mechanisms to re-adjust policies and rules. Opting for change or reform also means creating new rules, either formal or informal, to enhance the effectiveness of organizations and their leaders to solve their problems. It was gradual institutional reform in the CCP, as cited in many of the chapters, which created the incentives for ensuring the smooth transition to the fourth generation of Party leaders. China expert Andrew Nathan agrees, claiming that the 16th Party Congress was "the most orderly peaceful, deliberate, and rule-bound succession in the history of modern China outside of the recent institutionalization of electoral democracy in Taiwan."[5]

5. Andrew J. Nathan, "Authoritarian resilience," *Journal of Democracy*, Vol. 14, No. 1 (January 2003), p. 7.

The new leaders want experienced, qualified officials selected by merit, who will, by taking responsibility for their actions in public life, be held accountable and eradicate corruption. China's leaders also realize they must transfer more authority to lower Party and state levels, but finding loyal, capable officials to use that authority wisely is difficult. Many Chinese trust that their leaders can solve China's problems, but some intellectuals, students and workers do not agree and in 1998 tried to establish the China Democracy Party.[6] Predictably, they were arrested, tried and sentenced to prison, because the CCP will not tolerate any unapproved solo interventions into political life.

If the CCP intends to use force repeatedly in the future to eliminate political competition, that strategy will be counter-productive. China's leaders seem to realize that, and they are already discussing how to design electoral rules to elect their local and central government leaders. Experimenting and selecting appropriate rules, while educating Party members and citizens to adopt rule-complying norms, is the political path for China's future.

These are daunting challenges for a country with a population of more than a billion. Rick Baum's chapter suggests that the CCP is inching toward a "soft authoritarian" style that, if successful at promoting gradual institutional reform, might be able to create a "new China." Just as soft authoritarian governance characterized Taiwan under the Kuomintang for nearly four decades, China's current authoritarian government tries to change the way its people live and think to create a new China.

It will have a larger, modern market economy but still be unable to narrow the gap between rich and poor, with monopolies and segmented markets continuing to generate even more losers and winners. If the Party and state can persevere in their reforms and creatively adapt by taking advantage of new opportunities, the regime and its people might turn the corner in their titanic struggle to reduce poverty. As winners ascend to elite status, they could serve as role models for the young, making the CCP less adverse towards corruption.

This new China will be involved in international problems, especially in foreign trade. As the global economy increasingly influences who loses and who wins in China, the Party and state will need to adhere to rules to gain market access to other nations while allowing its trade partners to expand their share of the China market. If the Chinese demonstrate their competitive skills, they can balance declining market shares with expanding ones, both at home and abroad. China's goal of unifying Taiwan and the mainland will probably not be realized, but the continuation of their market integration might facilitate establishment of a co-operative framework to enhance mutual trust. In this changing new China, the tensions between losers and winners will determine the stability and efficacy of China's new path.

6. Teresa Wright, "The China Democracy Party and the politics of protest in the 1980s–1990s," *The China Quarterly*, No. 172 (December 2002), pp. 906–926.

Leadership Change and Chinese Political Development*

Lowell Dittmer

ABSTRACT This article has three goals. The first is to characterize the nature of the current Chinese political system, culminating at the 16th Party Congress, as a combination of economic, domestic political and foreign policy reform. Economically, it represents a continuation of marketization, privatization and globalization under more centrally controlled auspices. Politically, it represents a continuation of Dengist emphases on elite civility and administrative institutionalization. And in foreign policy, it brings China to the threshold of great power status, as the old ambivalence between overthrowing the international system and assuming an important role within it nears resolution. The second purpose, viewing "Jiangism" in comparative developmental terms, conceives political development in terms of both state-building and nation-building: the greatest emphasis has been on the former. The third goal is to subject Jiangism to immanent critique by pointing out the most conspicuous emergent contradictions. These seem to include gaps between rich and poor and between east and west, a largely unsuccessful attempt to reform the nation's industrial core and its attendant financial system, and a paradoxical inability to police the state even while increasing state capacity.

Viewed as a developmental process, the 16th Party Congress, held after a two-month delay in Beijing on 8–14 November 2002, marks essentially the efflorescence and consummation of "Jiangism," that is of the political thinking and policy line of Jiang Zemin. Clearly Jiang's own political power has reached unprecedented heights, coinciding paradoxically with his long anticipated "retirement." But by Jiangism we refer not to Jiang the individual leader (who has in fact been less personally dominant than either of his two main predecessors), but to the entire Chinese reform regime or *tixi*, denoting a comprehensive doctrine that sets out clear goals for society to achieve, obstacles to be removed, and the appropriate set of institutions to lock the PRC on to a given developmental path. Just as "Maoism" has conventionally been applied to the 1948–76 period, so might "Jiangism" be coined to characterize Chinese politics from the mid-1990s to the present, acknowledging that Jiang has in fact had greater political impact on this time than anyone else.[1] He stepped down as general secretary at the 16th Party Congress in November 2002 and subsequently yielded the state presidency at the Tenth National

---

* I wish to thank Mike Lampton, Ramon Myers, Chu Yun-han, Lo Chih-cheng and other commentators for their perceptive comments on an earlier draft of this paper, and Chung-min Tsai for his research assistance.

1. Thus many aspects of Jiang's policy line were implemented by Zhu Rongji, for example, just as many "Maoist" policies were in fact implemented by Zhou Enlai or Liu Shaoqi. However for the purposes of this analysis such distinctions are not relevant. The "Jiang regime" can claim credit for all policies implemented under its aegis.

People's Congress (NPC) in March 2003, but it would be premature to write Jiang Zemin's political epigraph. He has made clear that he is not eager to fade from the scene, although whether he stays on to transform, adorn or besmirch his historical legacy is an enigma only time can unravel.

An appraisal of the Jiang Zemin *tixi* presumes some basis for comparison. Since the advent of the regime in 1949 ("Liberation"), the conventionally accepted basis for comparisons has been systemic, comparing China with other socialist regimes under the rubric of "comparative communism." That this is still an informative basis for comparison is demonstrated in Yu-Shan Wu's penetrating essay. But China, by self-designation as well as by more objective indicators, has also been from the outset a developing state, a member of the Third World. With the sharp reduction in the number of consciously socialist states since the end of the Cold War in the early 1990s, and with the fading credibility of Marxist-Leninist ideology, the relevance of this international reference group may be said to have increased. Yet any attempt to evaluate Jiangism from a developmental perspective must necessarily rely upon a body of literature that is vast and at best fragmentary and elliptical. For the purposes of this article, political development is here defined in terms of three dimensions. First is the development of state capacity, as ultimately measured in its ability to foster rapid and reasonably equitable economic growth, and divided primarily into extractive capacity, regulative capacity and redistributive capacity.[2] Secondly, although growth is primary, it can easily run out of control and damage or temporarily derail the developmental process. Thus in addition, institutionalization is required, giving rise to an oscillation between political development and political decay.[3] Finally, the concept of political culture was introduced to bring mass publics into the political equation, showing on the one hand how they are moulded or socialized by the state, and on the other how their evolving desires contribute to the nation-state's collective identity.[4] This process involves a dialectic between the emancipation of the masses to participate more actively in politics and the restraint of that activity to accord with certain rules of civility, ultimately leading towards some form of "democratization."

What, then, does Jiangism stand for? To some extent it is an extension of Dengism, but at the same time Jiang has attempted to refine and adjust

2. See Gabriel Almond, "The return to the state," *APSR*, Vol. 82, No. 3 (September 1988), pp. 853–874; Robert Jackman, *Power Without Force: The Political Capacity of Nation-States* (Ann Arbor: University of Michigan Press, 1993; and Kjeld Erik Brødsgaard and Susan Young (eds.), *State Capacity in East Asia* (New York: Oxford University Press, 2000).

3. Samuel Huntington, *Political Order in Changing Societies* (New Haven: Yale University Press, 1968); Robert Scalapino, Seizaburo Sato and Jusuf Wanandi (eds.), *Asian Political Institutions* (Berkeley: Institute of East Asian Studies, 1986).

4. See Lucian Pye and Sidney Verba (eds.), *Political Culture and Political Development* (Princeton: Princeton University Press, 1965); Gabriel Almond and Sidney Verba, *The Civic Culture* (Boston: Little, Brown, 1965); Lucian Pye, *Politics, Personality and Nation-Building* (New Haven: Yale University Press, 1962); and Pye, *The Spirit of Chinese Politics* (Cambridge, MA: Harvard University Press, 1992 ed.).

Deng's *tixi*. Though not a brilliant policy innovator, Jiang has shown skill as a compromiser and synthesizer, integrating aspects of Maoism and Dengism into a novel composite. Economically Jiang might be said to represent the "deepening" of reform, imposing greater central direction on the economy while at the same time pushing China's opening to the outside world. In the realm of politics the Jiang regime has been associated with the slogan "stability over all" (*wending ya dao yiqie*), to use the term coined by Deng in his 1989 meeting with Kissinger. Although it is true that Jiang has placed greater (at least more successful) emphasis on stability than either of his main predecessors, that characterization is not entirely fair. He has taken sizeable risks, including the mobilization of mass nationalism against his primary trade partner and security threat, and the acceptance of Draconian economic reforms prerequisite to entry into the World Trade Organization (WTO). But Jiang seeks to minimize risk by ensuring stability: no stability without change, but no enduring, positive change without stability. With regard to China's relations with the outside world, Jiang's era represents not only China's re-emergence from the ostracism imposed after Tiananmen Square but a cautious rise to great power status. This article considers each of these achievements in turn, juxtaposed with the contradictions that have recently emerged and will conceivably affect the future tenability of Jiang Zemin's current political high tide. Finally, it compares the concluding characterization of the Jiang legacy as the sum of its triumphs and flaws with the developmental schema adumbrated above.

Political Reform of the Economy

Jiang's first and most basic contribution was the continuation of reform, at a time when this was in some doubt. The political atmosphere in the wake of the crackdown at Tiananmen Square and the subsequent collapse of socialist regimes in Eastern Europe and the Soviet Union in 1989 to 1991 was that of "new cold war," precipitating a defence of surviving socialist economic institutions such as the state-owned enterprises (SOEs) and central dirigisme against "peaceful evolution" and the "capitalist road." We now know that Jiang Zemin's primary patron when he was selected as Party secretary in late May 1989 was not Deng Xiaoping, whose first choice was Li Ruihuan, but the central planning clique under Chen Yun, Bo Yibo and Li Xiannian. Jiang presumably knew this and accordingly tilted rightwards during his early years, forming a strong coalition with Li Peng and the elders, to the extent that Deng apparently toyed with the idea of dumping Jiang and rehabilitating Zhao Ziyang. When Deng made his tour to the south, however, joining forces with provincial leaders who were resisting the economic retrenchment and centralization favoured by the central planners, Jiang shifted to the right, and under the circumstances his conservative supporters could not but shift with him. Had he opted otherwise, as one can easily imagine a more "principled" character doing, the left just might have prevailed, forcing Deng's fourth and last retirement and returning the economy to more orthodox lines. Even had it failed, this would have opened yet another leadership split, necessitating another reshuffle of the line of succession.

Deng's resuscitation of the forces of reform in 1992–93 unleashed another capital investment binge, shooting the annual GDP up to about 13 per cent, thereby unleashing another round of double-digit inflation. When Deng at the 14th Congress promoted Zhu Rongji as executive vice-premier and economic "czar" to bring the runaway economy to heel, Jiang promptly embraced him. For the next decade Jiang played high-level triangular politics, tilting between Zhu and Li Peng depending on the issue in focus. The result was a continuing but deepened reform quite different from the reform of the 1980s. On the one hand, marketization continued, dominating price formation in the commodity sector, and thanks to ruthless reform of small and medium SOEs, marketizing labour allocation as well[5] (capital alone remains essentially unmarketized and inefficiently allocated).[6] And for the first time under Jiang, despite initial hostility in the wake of the collapse of the communist bloc, privatization began to make significant headway. True, there had been some movement in this direction in the 1980s (the "responsibility fields," for example, are very close to private ownership), but the township and village enterprises are "owned" by local government agencies, and private entrepreneurship was for the most part limited to small peddlers, merchants and restaurants. In the 1990s the entire urban housing stock was sold at very low prices to residents, and the combination of "grasping the big, dropping the small" (*zhua da fang xiao*) and the ideological legitimization of private start-ups resulted in a burgeoning private sector. In 1998 China collected 46 per cent of total tax revenues from the private economy, reducing its long fiscal dependency on SOEs. With SOEs downsized, private firms have become the major source of new jobs. In recent years, private capital has accounted for 35 per cent of total capital investment and contributed 60 per cent of China's GDP growth; at the end of 2000, the non-public economy accounted for 50.8 per cent of industrial output, and it is estimated that by 2004 it will contribute more than 60 per cent of industrial output and employ 75 per cent of the workforce.[7]

Distinguishing Jiang more sharply from Deng is his greater emphasis on the role of central government apparatus in regulating and managing the reform. The decentralization of authority initiated under Deng was arrested and to some extent reversed. Whereas in the early 1980s the

---

5. E.g., from 1998 to 2002, state-sector employment in China's cities fell by 34 million jobs, or 30%.

6. See Thomas G. Rawski, "China's move to market: how far? What next?" in Ted Galen Carpenter and James A. Dorn (eds.), *China's Future: Constructive Partner or Emerging Threat*? (Washington, DC: Cato Institute, 2000), pp. 317–340.

7. "Feigong jingji nashui zhan Zhongguo banbi jiangshan" ("Tax payment by the non-public sector makes half off China's total tax revenues") *Qian Shao* (*Frontline*), No. 104 (September 1999), p. 135; Wang Jiahang, "Minying qiye chenwei; ziben shichang xin liangdian" ("Private enterprises have become the new spotlight in the capital market"), *Renmin ribao* (*People's Daily*), 10 September 2002; as cited in An Chen, "The new inequality," *Journal of Democracy*, January 2003, pp. 51–59.

leadership shifted from "two down" to "one down" in the central appoint-ment of provincial and local officials, central control of nomenklatura appointments has now been reasserted, and under Zeng Qinghong the Organization Department (*zuzhibu*) has further strengthened its role in personnel selection and management.[8] The 1993–94 comprehensive re-form of China's financial and banking system included shifting from the particularistic, negotiable fiscal contract arrangement between centre and province to a tax assignment system (assigning specific categories of tax collection to each level of government) in which the central government also established its own separate tax administration. This greatly strength-ened the fiscal power of the centre, whose share of budgetary revenue relative to the provinces rose from 33.7 per cent in 1993 to 55.7 per cent in 1994, with 52.4 per cent in 2001. After a long period of declining total governmental revenue, from 31.2 per cent of GDP in 1978 to a low point of 10.9 per cent in 1995, revenue collection seemed to make a modest turnaround, rising to 17.1 per cent in 2001 (though still low in relative and historic terms).[9] Central subsidies to the provinces and the SOEs were curtailed to constrain the money supply and curb inflation. The banking sector was reorganized to reassert central control over fixed capital investment, thereby facilitating the nationalization of fiscal policy and an effective countercyclical mechanism. The number of provincial subsidiaries and supra-regional subsidiaries of the People's Bank of China and the four major commercial state banks was reduced, in order to limit the power of local cadres in the allocation of credit. For the same reason, those in charge of these supra-regional subsidiaries are no longer appointed by the local authorities but by their head offices in Beijing. Aggressively tackling the old problem of an inefficient SOE sector with a "grasp the big, drop the small" policy, the leadership made clear its priorities: the centre would retain control of the "commanding heights" of the economy, the large-scale, modern SOEs (reportedly modelled after the South Korean *chaebol*) would be redesigned to thrive in the inter-national market competition, and only the small-scale, inefficient SOEs would be privatized. And, in at least some industrial sectors, this strategy seems to have borne fruit.[10]

The third major facet of the Jiangist economic strategy has been an acceleration of China's opening to the outside world. The trade-to-GDP ratio has risen from 18.9 per cent in 1980 to 30 per cent in 1990, to 49.3

    8. See John P. Burns, "Strengthening central CCP control of leadership selection: the 1990 *nomenklatura*," *The China Quarterly*, No. 138 (June 1994), pp. 458–491. The process of strengthening central control became further evident in 1995, when "Interim regulations on selection and appointment of Party and government leading cadres" was published. It was reinforced in 1998, when the personnel office (*renshibu*) under the State Council lost much of its personnel management authority to the CC Organization Department (*zuzhibu*), and further by the ten-year programme published in 2000 on deepening the cadre personnel system.
    9. Dali Yang, "State capacity on the rebound," *Journal of Democracy*, January 2003, pp. 43–50.
    10. See Kun-Chin Lin, "Divergent responses to oil price collapse, 1986 vs. 1998: central state and subnational actors between the plan and the market," paper presented at the Annual Meeting of the AAS, Washington DC, 4–7 April 2002.

per cent in 2000; which is very high trade dependency for a country with a large internal market. As trade has risen, so has foreign direct investment (FDI), rising from US$3.5 billion in 1990 to $41.7 billion in 1996. When the FDI stalled in the late 1990s (declining from $45.25 billion in 1997 to 40.3 billion in 1999) in response to the Asian financial crisis and ensuing international recession, the Jiang regime, making major negotiating concessions at considerable cost to its economic interests (such as approximately 40 million urban unemployed by the turn of the millennium), successfully negotiated entry into the WTO in 2000, with a resulting upsurge of FDI: China negotiated over US$100 billion in 2002, surpassing the United States as the world's leading FDI recipient. FDI helped make China an export juggernaut, which in turn, since the devaluation, elimination of the dual-currency system and adoption of a managed float in 1994, has resulted in a perpetual current account surplus, swelling foreign exchange reserves to $268 billion by the spring of 2003. China's export sector has become increasingly dominated by foreign investment, forming an enclave insulated from the domestic economy and hence with limited multiplier effects (for example, since the 1980s Guangdong has attracted on average more than a third of China's FDI).[11] In 1985, foreign invested enterprises (FIEs) produced only one per cent of China's exports; by 2000, they produced nearly half. Trade servicing the export sector has also come to predominate among China's imports: by 2002, 80 per cent of China's imports were capital goods for the FIEs. And China's advanced technology sector is also being built largely by FDI, as domestic capital allocation continues to flow into old investment channels. The high-tech crash in the West has only accelerated the plunge of high-tech enterprises into China, responding to intensified price competition. WTO compliance, by forcing (*inter alia*) tariff reductions to an average of less than 10 per cent by 2005 and an opening of the telecom, banking and insurance sectors to foreign competition, can only reinforce China's economic globalization. Yet in some ways globalization subverts some of the regime's other priorities, such as the reassertion of central control over the political cultural and economic subsystems.

Political Institutionalization

China's momentous shift of emphasis from revolutionary revitalization to institutionalization, from leadership by a proletarian vanguard to a ruling party, began of course with Deng Xiaoping at the Third Plenum of the 11th Party Congress in December 1978. But Deng's efforts at political institutionalization were less effective and well-integrated in practice than in theory, marred by a vicious business cycle and by recurrent political turmoil. The major contribution of the Jiang regime to the ongoing institutionalization of the political arena has been to consolidate Deng's

---

11. Kjeld Erik Brødsgaard, "Regional disparities in China," in Werner Draguhn and Robert Ash (eds.), *China's Economic Security* (New York: St Martin's Press, 1999).

ideas rather than to add bold new initiatives. It may be divided into three categories: formal politics, informal politics and ideology.

Formal politics. Formal politics may be subdivided into two aspects – structural reform and personnel policy – both of which focused on efficiency-enhancing reforms rather than democratization. Structural reform included early signs of interest in a larger margin of elimination (*cha'e*) when delegates to the 16th Congress elected CC members, or for some such margin when the CC elected members of the Politburo. But there has been little headway in electoral or other democratic reforms (such as the 1998 suggestion that village-level elections be extended to townships/counties) since the 15th Party Congress.[12] Instead, the Jiang leadership has agreed to introduce "elite democracy," that is, inducting "trustworthy experts" from a broader cross-section of society into the top echelons, recruiting officials into the mid-ranking bureaucratic levels through "public exams" and other such adjustments. More recently, there have been hints of a possible renewed interest in political reform among such members of the fourth generation as Hu Jintao and Zeng Qinghong, though whether this survives the two congresses remains to be seen.

Structural reform of the central economic apparatus has been ambitious and systemic. Zhu Rongji, with Jiang's implicit support, energetically implemented a "little state, big society" downsizing in 1998–2002, reducing the administrative staff in central and provincial administration by nearly half, and county and township by 20 per cent. Were this merely a reiteration of the periodic personnel reductions that characterize bureaucratic authoritarianism (as in 1982, 1988 and 1993)[13] it could not really be considered structural reform, but the thrust of this reorganization is to make the state not only "leaner" but more suitable for a regulatory role. By 1998, most industrial ministries of the State Council had been abolished, their macreconomic regulatory functions repackaged into the new MITI-like superministry, the state Economic and Trade Commission, and the SOEs formerly attached to the ministries reassigned to the localities or set up as independent corporations. The size of the personnel of the State Council was reduced by 47 per cent, provincial administrative personnel by 50 per cent, and county and township personnel by 20 per cent. Three ways were designed to marketize the industrial ministries (*bumen*) at both the central and local levels: to turn them into business entities (corporations, enterprise groups, holding companies and so on) that are stripped of their government administrative functions; to turn them into semi-official trade associations or business councils (*hangye zonghui*); and to turn them into macro-regulatory agencies. The first group can incorporate non-state enterprises. The second group draw their

12. *Wen wei po* (*Wenhui bao*) (Hong Kong), 31 December 2001, A3; *Ming bao*, 17 January 2002, B14; Si Liang, "China makes earnest preparations for 16th Party Congress to be held in second half of this year," Zhongguo tongxun she (China News Agency) (Hong Kong), 7 January 2002.

13. See David Shambaugh, "The post-Mao state," in D. Shambaugh (ed.), *The Modern Chinese State* (New York: Cambridge University Press, 2000), pp 161–187.

membership from the whole industry regardless of the ownership classification. And the third group are supposed to treat all firms – state-owned, collective, foreign invested and private and so on – as equals under the same market rules of competition.[14] Part of the rationale for this reorganization is simply to divest the state of unprofitable SOEs, whose average margins of return, after remaining quite high (above 25 per cent) through the 1980s, sank precipitously in the 1990s (less than 5 per cent in 1997, for example).

Jiang's personnel administration, like Deng's, focused on ingress and egress, creating vacancies and improving turnover through increasingly rigorous enforcement of term and age limits, resulting in a relatively young elite with the highest educational attainments in the history of the PRC. But despite repeated rectification campaigns and "strike hard" (*yanda*) crime crackdowns, resulting in impressive conviction statistics (and the highest execution rate in the world), the regime has been rather less successful at stemming cadre corruption. Relevant to a consideration of personnel policies is an overview of the outcome of the 16th Congress, undertaken in greater detail here by Suisheng Zhao. In broad outline, though this is no longer referred to as a "generational succession," the 16th Congress has seen perhaps the most extensive transformation of China's leadership since reform was initiated 25 years ago. More than half of the CC members and alternate members were phased out in accord with age limitations, 14 of the 24 full Politburo members are new faces and only one (Hu Jintao) of the nine Politburo Standing Committee members has remained. The professional backgrounds of the new officials, albeit primarily technocratic at the Politburo level, are increasingly diverse within the CC and at lower levels. Also striking is the increasing decentralization of the leadership, with a third of the CC membership now hailing from provincial bases, 50 per cent of the Politburo and 44 per cent of the Standing Committee; though the correlation is informal, every province now has two CC "delegates" save Xinjiang and Tibet which have more.[15] The Secretariat, now led by Zeng Qinghong, had a sweeping turnover: new members include Liu Yunshan (propaganda), He Guoqiang (replacing Zeng as head of the organization department), Wang Gang (in charge of the CC General Office), General Xu Caihou (political work in the PLA) and He Yong (Party discipline).

---

14. Lowell Dittmer and Lance Gore, "China builds a market culture," *East Asia: An International Quarterly*, Vol. 19, No. 3 (Fall 2001), pp. 9–51.

15. Four provincially based members of the Politburo Standing Committee are Wu Guanzheng, Party secretary of Shandong province, Huang Ju, Party secretary of Shanghai, Li Changchun, Party secretary of Guangzhou province and Jia Qinglin, Party secretary of Beijing. In the Politburo, in addition to these four, are Wang Lequan (Xinjiang), Hui Liangyu (Jiangsu), Liu Qi (Beijing), Zhang Lichang (Tianjin), Zhang Dejiang (Zhejiang), Chen Liangyu (Shanghai), Zhong Yongkang (Sichuan) and Yu Zhengsheng (Hubei). Though provincial representation on the Central Committee has statistically declined from the CR period to the reform era, the 16th Congress may represent a reversal of this trend. Zhiyue Bo, *Chinese Provincial Leadership: Economic Performance and Political Mobility since 1949* (Armonk, NY: M. E. Sharpe, 2002), pp. 19–32.

Informal politics. Informal politics consists of the use of non-official or even quasi-illegitimate means to accomplish legitimate political objectives. Its strong point has always been its superior means-ends efficiency, while its weak point has been its lack of public legitimacy.[16] While in Western sociology such informal politics as the Kaffeeklatsch is generally considered functionally conducive to formal organizational objectives, in CCP history there has often been a sharp disjunction between formal and informal politics, such that the latter were used to circumvent and undermine the formal rules of the game. Two aspects of informal politics generally considered prime suspects from this perspective – elite factionalism and leadership succession – are worth reviewing during the Jiang era.

In both areas, there is evidence that informal politics has shown greater mutability than formal politics, but that the pattern of change has generally been adaptive to modernization objectives: informal arrangements are not simply institutionalized into formal ones, but adapted and transformed. Informal change has thus become a leading indicator of later organizational formalization. Take the faction: the internal structure has remained basically unchanged, based on vertical ties of personal loyalty to a patron. But factional loyalty has slackened and become more fungible amid the heightened personnel mobility of the reform era. During the Maoist era, factions were ideologically as well as personally defined, and remained fiercely loyal in what could become a fierce "game to win all or to lose all."[17] During the Deng era, factionalism underwent several changes. Although there was an ideological dimension to the contest between the Deng supporters and the surviving Maoists, the elimination of Hua Guofeng and his followers was followed by an ideological consensus in support of the policy of "reform and opening to the outside world." Factions were henceforth organized around policy lines qua bureaucratic interests rather than ideology, pitting a coalition of radical marketizers against a coalition of bureaucratic gradualists, and with only a few exceptions (the Gang of Four, all of whom died in prison), factional conflict was generally pursued with greater civility. But although there was generally a greater correspondence between factional allegiance, bureaucratic interest and policy preference during the Deng era, the gap between informal and formal organization paradoxically widened. This is because the Deng leadership, caught in a contradiction

16. Consider the informal division of labour between Jiang Zemin and Zhu Rongji, in which Zhu took public charge of government downsizing, SOE and banking reform and other such Draconian policies while Jiang quietly backed him up. This seemed to be working well in 1997–98, but when Zhu drew a blank in his April 1999 visit to the US in quest of a WTO negotiating breakthrough, Li Peng, Zeng Qinghong and others seemed eager to take advantage of this setback to eliminate him, jeopardizing China's whole campaign to join WTO; only Jiang's backing forestalled that. Informal political arrangements are vulnerable to public exposure.

17. See Andrew J. Nathan, "A factionalism model for CCP politics," *The China Quarterly*, No. 53 (January–March 1973), p. 36 ff. and Tang Tsou, "Chinese politics at the top: factionalism or informal politics? Balance-of-power politics or a game to win all?" *The China Journal*, No. 34 (July 1995), pp. 95–157.

between its desire to institutionalize term limits by personal example and a need to retain the power necessary to implement reforms, retained informal power while relinquishing formal office. From their informal positions as factional patrons, Deng and his "sitting committee" could intervene at will and trump any decisions of the Politburo with which they disagreed, as they did most notoriously during the spring 1989 Tiananmen Square protest movement.

Jiang Zemin continued many of Deng's measures to bring factionalism under control. The code of civility was further extended to opposing faction leaders, who have (with the exception of Chen Xitong, who was purged and jailed) been permitted to disagree discreetly with the majority faction and to retire without ideological recrimination if eased out of the leadership. Neither Yang Shangkun nor Qiao Shi was placed under house arrest, but remained free to travel and even make speeches implicitly critical of Jiang's policies.[18] Ideology is no longer a factor in factional showdowns, having been replaced by "corruption."[19] Factionalism has assumed two distinctive features in the Jiang era. First, the gap between informal and formal organization that had opened to such alarming dimensions during the Deng era has been to a large extent closed. The "sitting committee" of retired senior veterans, willing to return to active leadership whenever duty called, has been all but eliminated, by a combination of Jiang's skilful handling of these *eminences grises* and the fact that most of them finally died. And in contrast to Deng Xiaoping, who retired from formal positions while continuing to exercise informal influence, Jiang has avidly pursued as many formal positions as possible in both Party and state hierarchies. Secondly, not only ideology but also policy and bureaucratic interest seem to have dissipated as a basis for factional organization. Factions are no longer identified with distinctive policy platforms; rather, competing factional manoeuvres seem to be oriented exclusively around personnel issues. This is perhaps a result of the attainment of a greater sense of leadership consensus on the package of economic reform and political stability since the purge of Zhao Ziyang and his followers in 1989. Even as the jockeying for position preparatory to the 16th Congress illustrated that factionalism had by no means disappeared, there has been a remarkable vacuum of policy disputes.

What is distinctive about Chinese Communist leadership succession arrangements? First, China is unusual in the amount of anticipatory attention devoted to this particular rite of passage. Throughout CCP history, succession has been a source of inordinate concern and occasional outbursts of concentrated, disruptive strife. The reason elite

18. Thus Qiao Shi, who reluctantly set the precedent for retirement at age 70 at the 15th Congress, toured the country in early 2002 giving speeches against lifetime tenure even as a letter campaign was being waged against Jiang's retirement at age 76. Yet Qiao still served as a member of the preparatory committee for the 16th Party Congress.

19. This might be considered evidence of the growing prevalence of the rule of law, were it not for the capricious way the crackdown has been applied (see the case of Jiang's friend Jia Qinglin, who despite the Yuanhua scandal that exploded under his auspices in Fujian province was promoted to the Politburo Standing Committee at the 16th CC).

fights outnumber completed successions relates to a second feature peculiar to the Chinese case: the marked preference for pre-mortem succession arrangements. Owing perhaps to a political tradition of dynastic succession in the absence of primogeniture, the Chinese leadership has invested a great deal of political capital in the preliminary making and recurrent reconsideration of anticipatory succession arrangements. Thus the Gao–Rao split in the mid-1950s emerged in the context of Mao's express desire to retreat to a less active role and put others on the "first front," and the decade-long Cultural Revolution involved the rotation of first Liu Shaoqi, then Lin Biao, then (more tentatively) Wang Hongwen and finally Hua Guofeng, into the precarious role of heir apparent. Notwithstanding Deng Xiaoping's avowed determination to institutionalize the process, he himself made two abortive selections (Hu Yaobang and Zhao Ziyang) before finally settling on Jiang Zemin. Most other socialist systems have been content to defer the issue post-mortem (such as Stalin's succession to Lenin, Khrushchev's to Stalin, Honecker's to Ulbricht, Gorbachev's to Andropov, via Chernenko).

The history of the CCP succession issue may be divided into three eras: pre-Mao, the Maoist succession and post-Mao. During the pre-Mao era, succession crises were nasty, brutish and short. Succession was pre-mortem and invariably involuntary, consisting of a confrontation between a discredited incumbent and the rest of the Politburo, who would ultimately force him out with the backstage support of the Comintern. The decisive difference of Mao's era concerned the charismatic personality of the incumbent, which derived from the improbable crowning success of his leadership, which against all odds succeeded in banishing the defeated Nationalist regime and establishing uncontested sovereignty over the mainland for the first time since the Qing. Mao's record after liberation was more mixed, but his regime can plausibly claim to have lastingly transformed the Chinese political spectrum and to have established China as a world power. Yet ironically the Maoist succession scenario was the worst in CCP history, consisting of incessant pre-mortem intrigue, coup plots and power struggles, only to culminate in a post-mortem succession crisis anyway, in which Mao's default successor proved too weak to survive. For the first time in CCP history, the incumbent intervened repeatedly in pre-mortem succession arrangements, as a way of manipulating and balancing off would-be rivals.

It was in the shadow of this nightmare that the Deng Xiaoping regime introduced sweeping reforms in succession arrangements. Yet Deng's innovations were to some extent compromised by his own leadership style. Though he eliminated most of the trappings of the cult of personality, working to allay the impression that the paramount leader is indispensable and that his replacement necessarily involves a "crisis," Deng continued to view monocratic leadership as essential, referring to himself as the "core" of the second generation. Deng therefore asserted the right to select his own successor, and like Mao, he used the selection tactically to manipulate the loyalty of the rest of the leadership. To his heir apparent he would assign all the most delicate and high-risk jobs, such as rejuvenation of the central leadership (for Hu Yaobang in 1983–85) or price reform (for Zhao Ziyang in 1988), basking in credit in the event of success but otherwise scapegoating the successor. But Deng did introduce two important innovations. The first was term limits: for all government positions, the revised constitution stipulated a limit of two five-year terms. Secondly, taking into account that his second comeback had been built upon an older generation of officialdom not ideally qualified to lead China into the second millennium, Deng conceived of succession as a generational necessity, attempting to institutionalize the orderly replacement of a whole generation of veteran incumbents.[20] At the provincial and local levels the introduction of term limits and retirement packages has on the whole been quite successful.[21] At the top, the picture has been ambiguous: Deng Xiaoping arranged for his orderly retirement from formal positions of authority but then made a mockery of his own arrangements by intervening to replace his own successor designates. Yet he did then finally succeed in stage-managing the CCP's first orderly pre-mortem succession, ceding all formal power in 1989 and relinquishing informal influence (at the brink of death) in late 1994.

Jiang inherited expectations for a second generational succession, along with the supposition that he would step down from all posts in accordance with the informal rule of an age limit of 70 for Party leadership posts, in the wake of the preparatory meeting for the 15th Congress at which that rule was used to facilitate the retirement of his rival Qiao Shi. Jiang managed the generational succession of his colleagues quite smoothly, but about his own retirement he remained publicly Delphic. Recurrently during the 1997–2002 period Jiang would float organizational proposals apparently designed to perpetuate his influence – a return to the chairmanship system, the introduction of a Chinese National Security Commission, the promotion of his resourceful secretary, Zeng Qinghong – but these proposals were rejected. In the August 2001 Beidaihe meetings, the leadership seemed to have reached a consensus for across-the-board retirement of all over 70, with 68-year-old Li Ruihuan offering to retire along with Jiang. Then in the spring of 2002 a series of petitions and letters from PLA officers and provincial officials began to flood Zhongnanhai, beseeching Jiang to stay on. But Jiang's colleagues maintained that if any stayed all should stay. Perceiving that his own retirement was his strongest card, Jiang skilfully played this to induce his colleagues to step down with him. He proceeded first to accept Li Ruihuan's offer to retire at a special Politburo meeting on 26 October. At the Party Congress on 13 November, it was then announced that the only member of the Standing Committee who would stand for re-election to the CC would be Hu Jintao. Jiang then appointed five of his

20. A good synopsis of Deng's reforms of the succession process may be found in Peter N. S. Lee, "The informal politics of leadership succession in post-Mao China," in Lowell Dittmer, Fukui and Peter N. S. Lee (eds.), *Informal Politics in East Asia* (New York: Cambridge University Press, 2000), pp. 165–183.

21. See Melanie Manion, *Retirement of Revolutionaries in China: Public Policies, Social Norms, Private Interests* (Princeton, NJ: Princeton University Press, 1993), passim.

protégés to the new nine-man Politburo Standing Committee (Huang Ju, Wu Bangguo, Jia Qinglin, Zeng Qinghong and Li Changchun), ensuring that he would continue to command a majority. Then, to the surprise of congressional delegates who had just learned of the Standing Committee's collective retirement, he allowed himself to be nominated (by General Zhang Wannian, a retiring member, in a highly irregular "special motion") as continuing chair of the CC Central Military Commission (CMC), because of alleged risks of allowing an untested leadership to deal with the delicate Taiwan and Sino-US issues. This would allow Jiang to attend Poliltburo meetings in a non-voting capacity, and Hu subsequently promised in (leaked) internal leadership briefings that Jiang would preview all "important" Politburo decisions. In subsequent visits with foreign visitors Jiang indicated that he intends to serve the entire five-year term.[22] That should ensure his continuing prominence in the national security arena even after his March 2003 retirement as chief of state, dropping to second in the protocol ranking.[23] While this can in fact be justified by the current dearth of high-level diplomatic experience, it gives rise to the old "two centres" problem that has long bedeviled the CCP, in this case putting the military beyond the control of the leader of the CCP. It also violates the rules of retirement imposed on other officials (including all other members of the CMC) with increasing uniformity, and leaves China's leadership-watchers waiting for the other shoe to drop.

Ideology. Although foreign China-watchers have long discounted the importance of ideology and many CCP leaders have obliquely confirmed this in their concern about a "crisis of faith," Jiang obviously considers ideology a useful mechanism for public agenda setting as well as legitimation and has striven to make his own contribution to the canon. Jiang's contributions have been inspired by a conviction that for ideology to regain credibility it must bear some plausible relationship to the economic transformation of China. Jiang introduced the "three represents" (*san ge daibiao*) – that the Party should represent the advanced culture, advanced relations of production and the interests of the broad masses of the people (with no explicit mention of the proletariat, let alone class struggle) – in February 2000 during a trip to Guangdong, and expatiated on this formula in a series of talks, culminating at the Fifth Plenum of the 15th Congress in October, which ranked it among the guiding doxa: "The Communist Party should stick to Marxism-Leninism, Mao Zedong Thought and Deng Xiaoping Theory, and follow the "Three Represents," the official Xinhua news agency declared in its report.[24] In his speech on the 80th anniversary of the Party's birth on 1 July 2001, Jiang spelled out the political implications, proposing that the criteria for

22. Susan V. Lawrence, in *Far Eastern Economic Review*, 28 November 2002.
23. Tokyo *Kyodo*, 20 November 2002; Chinese Newsnet (*Duowei*), 19 December 2002.
24. *Agence France Presse*, 17 September 2001. At the 16th Congress, the "three represents" was duly enshrined in the Party statute – albeit without personal reference to Jiang. *Washington Post*, 21 July 2001; *CNN*, 28 July 2002.

recruitment into the Party be broadened to include members of the middle classes, even members of the bourgeoisie.[25] This is not the first time entrepreneurs had gained entry to the Party: taking advantage of the close historical connection between the economy and the party-state, cadres (or their family members) have quite frequently "plunged into the sea" (*xia hai*) of commerce, while retaining their foothold in the Party. But this had never been admitted in such explicit fashion, and Jiang's formula initially raised a firestorm among the left, who not only objected to the Party's abandonment of the working classes but viewed this as a vehicle for Jiang's personality cult, which crested at his retirement.[26]

Yet as John Wilson Lewis has pointed out, it would be myopic to focus exclusively on the power-political implications while completely disregarding Jiang's vision for the Party's future. The ideas he has introduced, though hardly novel (they stand in lineal descent to Liu Shaoqi's "productive forces theory" (*shengchanlun*) and "whole people's state," Deng Xiaoping's repudiation of class struggle, and Zhao Ziyang's "primary stage of socialism"), represent the search for a new basis of legitimacy for a Party that can no longer rely on charismatic leadership or even necessarily on economic performance. The idea of co-opting political, economic and intellectual elites in a new Establishment has deep resonance in Chinese culture, with obvious appeal to a leadership no longer sure of its *raison d'être*. The chief reservation about the "three represents," articulated not only by the New Left but in subtler and more qualified terms by such leading intellectuals as Kang Xiaoguang and Hu Angang, is that this fusion of elites will abandon China's working classes at a time of growing unemployment and economic inequality.[27] To this the Jiangists protest that opening the Party to the middle classes is not meant to be exclusive. The central theme of Jiang's work report to Congress (which makes no mention of Deng's Four Cardinal Principles) is the goal of *quanmian jianshe xiaokang shehui* (build a well-off society in an all-round way), with the emphasis on *quanmian*, or all-round, signalling, perhaps, a leadership consensus that the time has come to adjust Deng's strategy of growth where conditions are most favourable in favour of a more inclusive and geographically dispersed investment pattern. This is suggested not only by the programme to develop the west launched in 1999, but by the visits to less developed regions undertaken

---

25. *Chung Kung Yen Chiu*, September 2001.

26. In April 2000, the Party published a book entitled *Mao Zedong, Deng Xiaoping and Jiang Zemin on Ideological and Political Work*, and in late 1999 the CC Secretariat formed a committee to edit *The Selected Works of Jiang Zemin;* by late 2001, compilation and editing had been completed, followed by publication upon convocation of the Party Congress.

27. Kang Xiaoguang, "Weilai 3–5 nian Zhongguo dalu zhengzhi wendingxing fenxi" ("An analysis of political stability in mainland China over the next three to five years"), in *Zhanlüe yu guanli* (*Strategy and Management*) (Beijing), No. 6 (1 June 2002), pp. 1–15; also see Wang Shaoguang, Hu Angang and Ding Yuanzhu, "Zui yanzhong di jinggao: jingji fanrong beihou ti shehui bu wending" ("Most urgent warning: social instability behind economic prosperity"), *Zhanlüe yu guanli*, No. 4 (April 2002), pp. 1–17.

by Hu Jintao and Wen Jiabao since adjournment of the 16th Party Congress.[28]

It is however legitimate to wonder whether Jiang's attempt to guide China's modernization via a new ideological "line" may not be technologically dated. Deng's opening of the country to the outside world has been accompanied by extensive print and electronic penetration, leading many to express serious doubts about the feasibility of any attempt to isolate a socialist political culture and maintain unanimity (*yiyuanhua*). Media control has been noticeably fragmented by reform: no private ownership is yet permitted, but managements have become fiscally autarkic, and practically every government organ, social group or party now has its own outlet. So far it would appear that fragmentation has resulted in socio-economic but not political liberalization.[29] The byword is that the party-state's monopoly of political interpretation must not be challenged. The social proliferation of non-governmental organizations (NGOs), peaking at 163,000 registered groups in 1998, inspired Western hopes in a rebirth of civil society, but new regulatory laws were passed the same year reducing that number by a fifth and eliminating "redundant" or "badly managed" groups. The prairie fire-like spread of the internet in China, reportedly now exceeding 59 million users and surpassing Japan as the second largest network after the United States, has led to forecasts of a technologically driven liberalization, but again, the regime has shielded the Chinese internet behind a "great firewall" of considerable sophistication.[30] The success of these defensive efforts may be measured in the virtual disappearance of public *falun gong* activities in China, and by the failure of any of the numerous rural and urban strikes and protests now sweeping the country to develop links with one another, in stark contrast to previous such protest movements. As for the internet, some of its most celebrated political incarnations have been as an instrument of intense Chinese nationalism (such as in the wake of the April 2001 EP-3 incident). Can pluralism grow amid this struggle

28. E.g. in November 2002, Hu Jintao made the first visit of a Party secretary to Inner Mongolian Autonomous Region, and gave a speech at Xibaipo emphasizing "hard struggle and plain living," heavily laced with quotes from the works of Mao. In December he convened a Politburo meeting on poverty, and in January convened a Central Conference on rural work. In the same month, revision of the rules for rural household legislation appeared to simplify procedures for peasant migrants to leave their place of residence and to enhance their rights in the cities to which they migrate. Though perhaps largely symbolic, these measures seemed to signal the leadership's resolve to close the widening gap between rich and poor, between the coast and the interior.

29. Guoguang Wu, "One head, many mouths: diversifying press structure in reform China," in Chin-Chuan Lee (ed.), *Power, Money, and Media: Communication Patterns and Bureaucratic Control in Cultural China* (Evanston, IL: Northwestern University Press, 2000), pp. 45–68; Daniel C. Lynch, *After the Propaganda State: Media, Politics, and "Thought Work" in Reformed China* (Stanford, CA: Stanford University Press, 1999).

30. E.g. Edward Yang, "The internet: beyond the great firewall," *China Economic Quarterly*, 11 November 2002; Jonathan Zittrain and Benjamin Edelman, "Empirical analysis of internet filtering in China" (Harvard Law School, Berkman Center for Internet and Society, December 2002); Michael S. Chase and James C. Mulvenon, *You've Got Dissent! Chinese Dissident Use of the Internet and Beijing's Counter-Strategies* (Santa Monica, CA: RAND Corp., 2002).

between technologically driven commercialism and energetic bureaucratic protectionism?

Relations with the Outside World

Jiang Zemin's smooth accession to power was not accompanied by a
crisis forcing the leadership to adapt, nor has Jiang expressed any interest
in foreign policy innovation, claiming only to maintain Deng's line. The
fundamental reform line of peace and development was retained, as was
the primacy of domestic economic construction. Yet Chinese foreign
policy under Jiang's leadership has evinced at least two distinctive
features. First, China for the first time openly pursued great power
diplomacy (*daguo zhanlüe*), cautiously departing from Deng Xiaoping's
1989 advice to "hide our capacities while biding our time" (*taoguang
yanghui*). Secondly, after years of suspicion of "bourgeois" international
governmental organizations (IGOs), China has become an avid participant in multilateral diplomacy.

China's attempt to join the great game of international power politics
has taken two forms. The first is an enhanced interest in military security:
after a decade of spending decreases, the post-Tiananmen military budget
began to increase, according to official figures, by 11 to 23 per cent per
year, outpacing GDP growth, a rate of escalation that has now been
maintained for more than a decade. Much of this money has been spent
on purchasing advanced aircraft, tanks, missiles and other weaponry from
Russia, which in the context of the collapse of its economy badly needed
customers. Coterminous with military modernization has been a quest for
means to exercise that power in the rational pursuit of Chinese national
interests. Since its renunciation of the export of revolution in the late
1970s China had become essentially a status quo power, with the
exceptions of its claim on the Spratlys and the unresolved Taiwan Strait
embroilment. Thus its willingness to assert its military power was demonstrated in its use of naval vessels to fortify the Spratlys, to patrol Diaoyu
Island, or (most notoriously) in the combination of combined arms
exercises and missile "tests" conducted in response to Lee Teng-hui's
July 1995 Cornell visit. Whereas in the heyday of the Sino-Soviet dispute
China welcomed a strong US presence in the western Pacific, the
Japanese–American Security Alliance is now regarded with greater suspicion, though there is no explicit Sino-Japanese security dilemma. Since
the turn of the millennium, China has de-emphasized the provocative use
of force, in the light of the current strategic asymmetry with a more
assertive US. And except for its still solid friendship with Russia, the
pursuit of great power diplomacy via "strategic partnerships" has been
quietly abandoned. The question of how to employ its growing arsenal
rationally may surface more in another decade or so.

China's involvement in international government organizations (IGOs)
was in effect precluded during the first 22 years of its existence, as the
Kuomintang regime, though defeated and driven into exile on a tiny
offshore island, continued to occupy one of the five permanent seats of

the UN Security Council and to represent "China" in all manner of IGOs. During its first decade, the PRC participated in the full repertoire of communist IGOs, but with the Sino-Soviet split these became polemicized and Beijing stopped attending. Estranged from both superpowers in a bipolar world, maintaining membership in a largely self-defined revolutionary Third World, China became something of a hermit kingdom in the 1960s. Upon its admission to the United Nations in late 1971 as an unintended beneficiary of Washington's triangular diplomacy, China's membership in IGOs expanded from one to 21 between 1971 and 1977. With the launching of Deng Xiaoping's reform and opening policy in 1977–89, IGO membership rose to 37. After the end of the Cold War, China affiliated with an increasing range of IGOs (from 37 to 52 in 1989–97), now going beyond the UN framework to include Asian regional organizations. And, as the universe of international non-governmental organizations (INGOs) exploded upon the collapse of the Cold War, China's affiliation with them expanded even more rapidly, rising from 58 to 71 in 1966–77, to 677 in 1989 and 1,136 in 1997. By 1989, China belonged to 12 per cent of all IGOs (300), and by 1997 belonged to 20 per cent of the new total; in 1989, it belonged to 15 per cent of all INGOs, and by 1997 had likewise increased to 20 per cent of a new total of 5,585. By the latter date China, with Russia and Indonesia, ranked eleventh in belonging to the most IGOs in the world, with 45. The United States ranked ninth, with 47.

Of particular note during the 1990s has been China's increased interest in regional organizations, coinciding with the collapse of the strategic triangle and the end of the Cold War, which reduced China's global leverage. In 1986, China became a full member of the Asian Development Bank, for the first time not expelling Taiwan but permitting its continued membership under a name change to "Taipei, China." China joined the Asian Pacific Economic Co-operation (APEC) forum (founded in 1989) in 1989, agreeing to Taiwan's admission under the same formula. Although China initially viewed the launching by the Association of Southeast Asian Nations (ASEAN) of its expanded ASEAN Regional Forum (ARF) in 1994 with some reservations, by 1997 it had become an active participant both in ARF and in the "track II" unofficial dialogue process that complements official deliberations. And when ASEAN launched the Asian European Meetings (ASEM) in March 1996 in Bangkok, Premier Li Peng attended the inaugural meeting. China was represented at all subsequent meetings, donated US$500,000 to the ASEM Trust Fund and offered to host the foreign ministers' meeting in Beijing in 2001. Most recently, the PRC has been a founding member and host of the Shanghai Co-operative Organization (SCO), the only international security organization in which the US is not a participant, involving co-operation between China and Russia and the Central Asian states of Uzbekistan, Tajikistan, Kyrgyzstan and Kazakhstan. Beijing also took a leading role in the formation of ASEAN + 3 (the ASEAN ten plus China, Japan and South Korea), which promises to become the leading IGO in the East Asian region. Thus has China progressed from being a cautious joiner to taking the initiative in multilateral regional diplomacy, striving to bolster its emerging self-conception as a "responsible great power" and regional leader.

Conclusions

It is still too early to say definitively what the 16th Party Congress will signify in Chinese history: in view of the incompletion of the succession, Su Ge may be correct in calling it a relay race rather than a turning point. Bearing in mind Hegel's cautionary dictum that the owl of Minerva spreads its wings only in the dusk, our purpose at this point is not to torture the past into revealing the future but simply to summarize and assess the direction of ongoing trends. We begin with a critique of the past, confronting dominant Jiangist themes with emergent contradictions. In conclusion we return to the developmental schema outlined above, focusing on the development of state capacity, institutionalization and the transformation of political culture.

The great achievement of Jiangism was to continue vigorous reform of the economy, at a time of acute misgivings about the Dengist reform programme. Marketization was driven forward under Jiang to become almost comprehensive in the Chinese economy, while privatization gradually acquired legal sanction and has made substantial headway. This has been done under more centralized political direction than during Deng's period, without any interest in reviving central planning. The financial and fiscal reforms of the mid-1990s made it possible for much more rational, effective and universal ("national") fiscal and monetary policies to be put into effect. Central assertion of control over revenue policies has strengthened the government in its attempts to implement redistributive policies (such as a national welfare policy and unemployment assistance policies)[31] and to allay the growth of the budgetary deficit. It also enabled the state to introduce, beginning in mid-1999, an ambitious plan to develop China's western region (*xibu da kaifa*) to compensate for the lopsided gains made by the eastern seaboard in the wake of China's opening to the outside world. This plan was approved by the NPC in 2001 as part of the Tenth Five-Year Plan and has resulted in several gigantic, centrally funded infrastructure investment projects, including the Three Gorges Dam, the even larger planned central canal between the Chang (Yangtze) River and the Huang (Yellow) River (*nanshui-beisong*), and the world's highest railway system (between Qinghai and Tibet). Continuing central control of capital investment enabled the state not only to achieve a "soft landing" from the post-southern tour hyperinflation but also to eliminate the vicious boom-bust business cycle and put the economy on a path of steady GDP growth averaging around 8 per cent per annum. Economic centralization proved to be a useful preliminary to the massive exposure to international

---

31. E.g. people receiving social security rose from fewer than 900,000 in 1997 to 12.35 million in January 2002, according to official statistics.

markets that began in the early 1990s and culminated at the end of the decade with entry into the WTO, permitting the influx of whole new industrial sectors and the rebuilding of much of China's urban infrastructure with minimal turmoil, despite greatly accelerated population mobility, both lateral and vertical.

The policies that are perceived to have been most successful are likely to be continued, as the Chinese leadership is quite self-conscious about learning from its experience. Marketization is generally felt to have been successful and fair, whereas privatization has aroused more mixed feelings. Housing reform has been an outstanding success, cutting prices to affordable levels and privatizing a majority of urban residential housing by the turn of the millennium, thereby creating a quasi-middle class of satisfied homeowners. But the privatization of industrial assets has proceeded through informal contacts, arousing considerable resentment. While there is a growing class of entrepreneurs, the heights of the industrial economy are still controlled by party-state cadres or their families. Corruption has become a very serious problem, accounting for 10–20 per cent of national GDP, according to various estimates, resulting in some $20 billion in annual flight capital.[32] Yet according to Chinese figures only 7 per cent of all CCP members proved to have been engaged in wrongdoing are criminally prosecuted, and the prosecution of high-level cases is popularly dismissed as a political purge. Corruption could be tolerated when the tide of economic growth seemed to be benefiting everyone, but since the early 1990s reform seems to have become a more zero-sum game, as the gap between economic winners and losers widened.

There has been a quite extensive and effective campaign to eliminate poverty. According to official estimates, the number living on less than US$0.66 per day fell from 260 million in 1978 to 42 million in 1998. But that may represent only marginal improvement, for according to the World Bank, 106 million people (12 per cent of the rural population) still live on less than $1.00 per day.[33] Farmers lost between 300 and 400 million *yuan* between 1997 and 2000 because of an accumulated 22 per cent drop in prices for their products during that period, while at the same time they had to pay increased illegal levies to local authorities; in the cities, 48 million workers were laid off in the context of SOE reform between 1995 and 2000. According to long-term research on income distribution by the Economic Institute of Nankai University, the Gini coefficient rose from 35 to 40 from 1988 to 1997 (where 100 represents perfect income inequality and 0 represents perfect equality). China during the Maoist period had one of the most equal distributions in the world, but reform China is on a par with such countries as the Philippines (Gini 46.2, 1997) or Peru (46.2, 1996).[34] And (with the exception of the unemployed and laid-off workers) that inequality is more inter-regional

32. Minxin Pei, "The long march against graft," *Financial Times*, 9 December 2002.
33. The World Bank, *The World Bank and China* (Washington, DC: World Bank, 2000), pp. 1–2.
34. Wang Shaoguang, Hu Angang and Ding Yuanzhu, "Behind China's wealth gap," *South China Morning Post*; An Chen, "New inequality."

than intra-regional: urban areas are on the whole richer than rural areas, and the east coast is richer than the western interior provinces. Thus for example the per capita income of Shanghai is ten times that of Guizhou, and Shenzhen is 20 times as rich.[35] Normally, inter-regional income inequality can be considered less politically explosive than intra-regional inequality because it can be assumed to be less visible, particularly given the low rates of upward mobility, but in the light of greatly accelerated regional migration of some 100 million former peasants in search of improved life chances this may well be changing, creating a heightened sense of envy and resentment. At least that is what China's urban population seems to infer when they accuse economic migrants of driving up urban crime rates.

Thus reform has become a more socially divisive process. Meanwhile, state capacity to rectify this growing sense of discontent (over the past five years there has been a 30 per cent growth in labour disputes) remains relatively weak, despite attempts to strengthen it during Jiang's period. Even after the 1994 tax reform, governments at all levels collected only 17 per cent of national GDP in taxes, whereas the United States, one of the lowest revenue collectors among OECD members, collects 29.8 per cent. China's four leading state banks, inured by the legacy of central planning to easy lending policies to a fixed set of SOEs, are burdened with non-performing loans amounting to 35–50 per cent of GDP. Zhu Rongji's 1998 pledge to eliminate the debt overhang within three years via Asset Management Corporations has been notoriously unsuccessful, leaving the banking sector vulnerable to a financial panic of the sort that occurred in the summer of 1988. The banks are backed by the sovereign authority of the central government, but during the economic deflation that accompanied the Asian financial crisis the central government's budget grew by an estimated 27 per cent per year, and has now reached 3 per cent of GDP, the internationally recognized danger signal.

The major political contribution of the Jiang administration has been to meet crisis with change, but change braced by stability, with an emphasis on administrative competence and a political culture of consensus and co-operation. After a decade of nearly incessant personnel adjustments the central government has emerged as a more efficient and market-compatible manager of modernization, led by a younger and more educated elite. The 16th Party Congress represents a culmination of these trends. The most serious risk confronting the regime in the foreseeable future is the possibility that the reforms have simply not been radical enough, that "socialism with Chinese characteristics" has been overtaken by a combination of growing regional inequality, elite corruption, bureaucratism and fiscal overload. Although the fourth generation elite may be equal to the challenge, the incomplete succession at the top has the potential to create a cleavage that may prevent a concerted response. In the past, mass mobilization against inequality and corruption coinciding with an elite split was likely to precipitate major crisis. Thus the prospect warrants closer consideration.

35. Brødsgaard, "Disparities," pp. 5–15.

As Yu-Shan Wu points out, the risk is a re-emergence of the old gap between informal and formal politics, with a new regime under the formal leadership of Hu and Wen, while Jiang exerts informal leadership from the position of CMC chair. This type of duopoly first made its appearance when Mao stepped down from his position as chief of state to the "second front" in 1959, leaving Liu Shaoqi and Deng Xiaoping to manage routine affairs; it reappeared when Deng Xiaoping stepped down from the Politburo in 1987 as part of a planned generational succession. Under Deng, the gulf between formal and informal elites became even greater as he was joined by a whole cohort of senior cadres – the so-called eight immortals – prepared to join him to intervene in the decision-making process whenever it seemed to stall. The current arrangement, with only one background string-puller, is redolent of the monarchical regency (such as the Empress Dowager), yet it is by no means without merit, promising to fuse the experience and wisdom of the older generation with the youth, energy and entrepreneurial zeal of the younger. There is some doubt about this regency's tenability, as the power of the "sitting committee" appears to have been weakened by Jiang's own manoeuvres, and Jiang lacks the charisma of either of his successors. Yet his informal power has never been greater, thanks to the retirement of the third generation cohort and to his factional patronage. Hence the developing relationship between the "two centres" will bear careful monitoring. It harbours three structural weaknesses: first, at best, it is likely to be a holding pattern that defers radical reforms, as previous heirs apparent who undertook independent policy initiatives (such as Liu Shaoqi, Lin Biao) have been repudiated by their patrons; secondly, the arrangement is crisis-prone, as unexpected contingencies beg the volatile question of who is to decide; and thirdly, if a split between centres materializes, either because of diverging world-views or in response to crisis, past precedent strongly suggests that the most likely winner is the incumbent, reopening the old issue of succession.

In the realm of foreign policy, the Jiang Zemin leadership has made a quite momentous shift in the past few years from regarding the rest of the world as surrounding and thwarting justified Chinese aspirations to seeing China as a part of the new world order, and indeed in a fairly powerful and satisfied position within it (with the painful exception of Taiwan). This greater sense of maturity is partly in response to China's acknowledged economic and diplomatic primacy in the region, and partly because of China's increasing recognition of its interest in and identification with the economically developed countries of the world since terrorism on behalf of the world's dispossessed became an issue on 11 September 2001. Jiang was China's first leader to tap raw nationalism as a political asset to bolster his support at the beginning of his term when he was still politically vulnerable, and to learn since that time the political risks of doing so. For the time being, his failure to bequeath foreign policy experience to the fourth generation has helped underpin Jiang's aspirations to prolong his role on the world stage. If Jiang agrees (as expected) to yield to Hu Jintao his chairmanship of the Politburo's "small groups," such as the Foreign Affairs Small Group and the Taiwan Affairs Small Group, this may provide ample ambit for the fourth generation to acquire the necessary diplomatic experience for full succession with minimal disruption of China's successful current foreign policy "line."

In conclusion, the 16th Party Congress represents a consummation of the thinking and political set-up (*tixi*) of Jiang Zemin, whose achievement, widely underestimated, has been considerable. To draw up a preliminary balance sheet, based on our previous outline, three main features emerge. First, the development of state capacity has clearly been a top priority of the Jiang regime, as indicated in its improving ability to manage rapid economic growth amid ongoing marketization and privatization. Responding to the sharply reduced extractive capacity that has resulted from industrial devolution and political decentralization, the regime reorganized the fiscal apparatus in 1993–94 to increase that capacity substantially, though it still remains feeble in relative and historical terms. And the ongoing reorganization and restructuring of the State Council has improved the state's regulative capacity, though the regulation of cadre malfeasance remains weak. Surprisingly attenuated is the state's once mighty redistributive capacity: the leadership has been slow to recognize the emergence of regional inequalities and its response has thus far been anaemic. Efforts to alleviate poverty have focused on subvention rather than retraining, giving the needy fish but not fishing poles. And the launching of such infrastructural megaprojects as the Three Gorges Dam can provide a one-shot fiscal stimulus, but whether they represent the best way to enhance the long-term developmental capacity of the western region remains controversial.

Secondly, probably the greatest achievement of the Jiang regime has been in its promotion of political institutionalization. Though the recent focus has understandably been on the smoothness of the generational transition, no less impressive has been the consistently smooth, even masterful management of political and economic change over the past 15 years, marking major progress from previous administrations. Instead of exploiting informal politics to undermine formal political conventions, Jiang typically uses the informal as a leading indicator before institutionalizing change. Factionalism has become less lethal, less binding, and less ideologically or policy dependent. The established stability of tenure arrangements, personnel mobility, meeting schedules and other procedural matters has established a sound baseline for the further enhancement of state capacity and the development of the rule of administrative law, marred only by Jiang's personal exemption.

Finally, the Jiang regime's contribution to Chinese political culture has been relatively modest, though not entirely nugatory. Like Deng, Jiang has lowered expectations from the complete cultural transformation demanded by the Maoists, and even the campaign for a "socialist spiritual civilization" seems to have had modest impact. Amid tacitly accepted ideological decay, the CCP increasingly relies upon a combination of nationalism and Chinese traditional values. The cultivation of civility and legality has made progress, thanks to the suppression of violent dissent and growing market regulation rather than to deliberate ideological socialization efforts. Yet until the regime ventures to allow the opportunity for the masses actually to demonstrate their civility, if not in multi-party democracy then in some other form of institutionalized but minimally spontaneous political discourse, the relationship between masses and elites will remain guarded and latently explosive.

The New Generation of Leadership and the Direction of Political Reform after the 16th Party Congress

Suisheng Zhao

ABSTRACT   With the rise of the new leadership at the 16th Party Congress, the CCP finally completed the transition from the revolutionary to post-revolutionary generations. The world has been looking for the new leadership to open up China's political system. This expectation, however, may be proved too optimistic. The new leadership will certainly continue economic reform and political institutionalization but the change will be more likely to be gradual and hardly deviate from the direction set by Deng and Jiang. This is not only because members of the new leadership have benefited from the current policies but also because the succession arrangement at the 16th Party Congress has set limits for the new leaders to make a drastic policy reorientation.

Although the 16th National Congress of the Chinese Communist Party (CCP) in November 2002 made a massive reshuffle of leadership, many observers have struggled to find out if a generational change has really taken place. The PRC official media have so far referred to the new leadership under Hu Jintao as "a new term of leadership collective" (*xin yi jie lingdao jiti*) rather than a new generation of leadership. Hu, the new Party general secretary, has not been declared the core of the new leadership. Retired Party general secretary Jiang Zemin retained the powerful Central Military Commission (CMC) chairmanship and his name and photograph appeared before Hu's in official media until the conclusion of the Tenth National People's Congress in March 2003. As Hu has been hemmed in with Jiang trying to pull strings from behind, it is not surprising that observers are wondering if the 16th Party Congress has produced a new generation of leadership or no more than a nominal handover of power, and what the impact of the leadership transformation upon the direction of China's political reform actually is.

Defining Generational Change in the PRC

There are certainly many variables to define a new generation of leadership in China. According to the official account, since the founding of the PRC three generations of leadership, represented respectively by Mao Zedong, Deng Xiaoping and Jiang Zemin, had emerged prior to the leadership turnover at the 16th Party Congress. While many observers accept this divide, others believe that "it is misleading to speak of two leadership generations preceding the present third generation leadership with Jiang Zemin as 'the core,' because both of the first two generations drew from the same pool of veteran revolutionaries."[1] According to this view, "the major divide during this time was between the Deng Xiaoping generation the revolutionary generation – and the Jiang Zemin (post-revolutionary) generation."[2] These scholars apparently take collective life experience as the primary criterion to define generational change, while the Chinese official view emphasizes age difference and new policy orientation.

Age is in fact linked with life experience. Major political upheavals that have taken place very often in modern China have certainly given sharply different life experiences to leaders of different ages and made a significant impact upon their thinking of policy options. However, age/life experience does not always correlate with policy orientations. While the leadership shift from Mao (born in 1893) to Deng (born in 1904) brought about a major policy reorientation that was much more dramatic than the 11 years age difference would suggest, the leadership change from Deng to Jiang (born in 1926) ensured the continuity of Deng's reform policy although Jiang was about two decades younger than Deng. In this case, when defining a new generation of leadership it is important to look at both age/life experience and policy orientation variables.

In terms of age/life experience, Mao and Deng belonged to the same generation of the founding members of the PRC. However, Deng clearly set himself apart from Mao by reforming the rigid communist system and opening up China to the outside world. As Lucian Pye suggested, "the essence of Mao's generation was the sovereignty of ideology, Deng's generation was captured by the concepts of pragmatism, reform and opening up."[3] Jiang and Deng were leaders of two different generations in terms of age/life experiences. However the leadership succession from Deng to Jiang was marked by policy continuity. Launching their careers around the founding years of the PRC and benefiting from Deng's policy of rejuvenation (nianqinghua) of leadership ranks, most members of the Jiang leadership were much younger than and certainly had different life experiences and career patterns from members of Deng's leadership and very few of them had any wartime military experience. In spite of the differences in age/life experience, the Jiang leadership became a loyal custodian of the cause of economic modernization and political stability that Deng started. Rising to the top of the CCP leadership after the violent Tiananmen massacre and the purge of Hu Yaobang and Zhao Ziyang (two short-staying Party general secretaries), while doing everything to maintain stability, the Jiang leadership continued Deng's effort to build an economic performance-based political legitimacy by setting economic modernization as its top policy priority. As a result, Jiang presided over

1. H. Lyman Miller and Liu Xiaohong, "The foreign policy outlook of China's 'third generation' elite," in David M. Lampton (ed.), *The Making of Chinese Foreign and Security Policy* (Stanford: Stanford University Press, 2001), p. 126.

2. Joseph Fewsmith, "Generational transition in China," *The Washington Quarterly*, Vol. 25, No. 4 (Autumn 2002), p. 23.

3. Lucian W. Pye, "Jiang Zemin's style of rule: go for stability, monopolize power and settle for limited effectiveness," *The China Journal*, No. 45 (January 2001), p. 46.

13 years of astounding economic growth and political stability with a minimum of intra-Party warfare in spite of Western sanctions after Tiananmen and the Asian financial crisis. Jiang began to make a major policy reorientation only in his last years of power in an attempt to change the Party's founding principles by presenting a new theory of "three represents" and embracing the bourgeois class into the Party.

The 16th Party Congress has been hailed as a historic moment in the development of CCP rule because "the orderly and peaceful transfer of power, unprecedented in the 81-year history of the Chinese Communist Party, marks a new phase in China's politics as its younger leaders grapple with the problems of modernization."[4] Indeed, the power transfer from Jiang to Hu (born in 1942) finally completed the transition from revolutionary to post-revolutionary generations in the CCP as the Hu generation has hardly any personal experiences or memories of the revolutionary war years before 1949. They grew up in the brand-new PRC, completed education in a relatively peaceful environment of the early 1960s, went to factories or the countryside during the Cultural Revolution, and returned to cities and rose to leadership positions during the post-Mao reform years of the 1980s. The rise of the Hu generation reflects the re-invigoration of China's leadership with young blood and the institutionalization of the leadership retirement system that were set in motion by Deng in the early 1980s and advanced during the Jiang years. After the 1982 constitution stipulated fixed two-term limits for top government posts, mandatory retirement age has been set for top government as well as Party posts. All leaders over 70 years old, except Jiang, retired from the Politburo at the 15th Party Congress. Jiang, at the age of 76, stepped down and let 59-year-old Hu take over the post of Party general secretary at the 16th Congress. The entire 15th Politburo Standing Committee – except Hu – collectively retired and handed over to a new Standing Committee (see Table 1). The average age of Politburo members at the 16th Congress was 60, in contrast to 72 at the 12th Congress in 1982 and 63 at the 15th Congress in 1997.

Age limit and term limit were clearly used as the normative rules for the retirement of leaders at the Congress. Everyone above 68 years old and/or having served two terms without promotion (Hu remained because he was promoted to the position of general secretary) retired from the Politburo Standing Committee. The wholesale retirement of the Standing Committee came together with massive reshuffle of the entire Politburo and the Central Committee. Two-thirds of the 24 members of the new Politburo are new faces. The 356-member new Central Committee features 180 new members, with an average age of 55.4 years, almost five years younger than those at the 15th Congress in 1997. One-fifth of the new Central Committee members are under 50 years old. As a whole, these younger leaders are better educated than their predecessors. If Party school training counts as college education, which is the official line, all 24 Politburo members have college education. Even if Party school

---

4. Editorial, "Hu's the new leader," *Straits Times*, 19 November 2002.

Table 1: **Members of the 16th CCP Politburo Standing Committee**

Name	Birth date and province of origin	Education and professional title	Party membership	Other principal posts	Membership in Central Committee
Hu Jintao	December 1942; Anhui province	Water Conservancy Engineering Department, Qinghua University, 1959–64; engineer	April 1964	President of the Central Party School; first secretary, Secretariat of the Central Committee of the Communist Youth League of China; secretary of the Guizhou Provincial Committee and the Tibet Autonomous Region	Alternative member 1982; full member 1987

Wu Bangguo	July 1941; Anhui province	Radio Electronics Department, Qinghua University 1960–67; engineer	April 1964	Vice-premier, secretary of the Central Enterprise Work Commission, secretary of the CCP Shanghai Municipal Committee	Alternate member, 1982; full member 1987
Wen Jiabao	September 1942; Tianjin	Department of Geological Structure, Beijing Institute of Geology, undergraduate 1960–65, postgraduate 1965–68; engineer	April 1965	Vice-Premier, member of the CCP Central Secretariat, secretary of the Central Financial Work Commission	Full member, 1987
Jia Qinglin	March 1940; Hebei province	Department of Electric Power, Hebei Engineering	December 1959	Secretary of the CCP Fujian Provincial	Full member, 1992

Table 1—continued

Name	Birth date and province of origin	Education and professional title	Party membership	Other principal posts	Membership in Central Committee
		College, 1958–62; senior engineer		and Beijing Municipal Committee, mayor of Beijing	
Zeng Qinghong	July 1939; Jiangxi province	Automatic Control Department, Beijing Institute of Technology, 1958–63; engineer	April 1960	Secretary of the General Office of the State Planning Commission, director of the General Office of the CCP Central Committee, deputy secretary of Shanghai Party Committee	Full member, 1997

Huang Ju	September 1938; Zhejiang province	Department of Electrical Machinery Engineering, Qinghua University, 1956–63; engineer	March 1966	Secretary of the CCP Shanghai Municipal Committee and mayor of Shanghai	Alternate member, 1987, full member, 1992
Wu Guanzheng	August 1938; Jiangxi province	Power Department, Qinghua University, undergraduate, 1959–65, postgraduate 1955–68; engineer	March 1962	Secretary of CCP Central Commission for Discipline Inspection, secretary of the CCP Jiangxi and Shandong Provincial Committees	Alternate member, 1982, full member, 1987
Li Changchun	February 1944; Liaoning province	Department of Electric Machinery, Harbin Institute of Technology,	September 1965	Governor of Liaoning and Henan provinces, secretary of the CCP	Alternate member, 1982, full member, 1987

Table 1—continued

Name	Birth date and province of origin	Education and professional title	Party membership	Other principal posts	Membership in Central Committee
		1961–66; engineer		Guangdong Provincial Committee	
Luo Gan	July 1935; Shandong province	Freiburg Institute of Mining and Metallurgy, the Democratic Republic of Germany, 1956–62; senior engineer	June 1960	State Councillor, secretary of the Central Political and Legislative Affairs Commission	Alternative member, 1982, full member, 1987

Source:
Laowang zhoukan (Outlook Weekly), No. 46 (18 November 2002), pp. 20–25.

training does not count, 21 have college education in comparison with 17 out of 24 in the 15th Politburo. In addition, according to official account, 98.6 per cent of the Central Committee members have a college degree or above (see Table 2).[5]

The rejuvenation of leadership did not only take place at the central level. Prior to the Party Congress there had been a reshuffling process, known as *huanjie* (term change), of provincial Party leaders as provincial Party congresses were held in all 31 provinces throughout China. According to the official report, during the period between September 2001 and June 2002, all provincial Party committee secretaries were changed through promotion or reappointment. The result was a group of youngest provincial leaders in PRC history. Provincial Party secretaries averaged 58.16 years old, and the average age of governors was 55.25, both groups about three months younger than their predecessors. Among 62 provincial Party committee secretaries and governors, the number over 60 years old dropped from 26 to 21. The three youngest were under 50: Xi Jinping, 48, governor of Fujian province, Li Keqiang, 46, governor of Henan province, and Zhao Leji, 44, governor of Qinghai province. These younger leaders at the provincial level are as well educated as their cohorts at the central level. Among the 62 top provincial Party secretaries and governors, six have master's degrees and the remaining 56 have bachelor's degrees (see Table 3).[6]

As mentioned above, with the rise of the new leadership, the CCP finally completed the transition from revolutionary to post-revolutionary and post-liberation generations. While some members of the Jiang leadership joined the CCP before the founding of the PRC in 1949 (for example, ten members of the Politburo at the 15th Party Congress), all members of the Hu leadership joined the Party after the founding of the PRC or, more precisely, after the late 1950s. This is "the first generation of leadership in the PRC with no significant personal memory of pre-1949 China."[7]

Without having war or revolutionary experiences, members of this generation had a better chance to complete formal education. Most of them were college students during the relatively normal years of the early 1960s and are known in China as *lao daxuesheng* (university graduates prior to the Cultural Revolution) although others did not get to college before the Cultural Revolution and became members of *laosanjie* (1966, 1967 and 1968 middle-school and high-school graduates). In fact, all nine Politburo Standing Committee members are *lao daxuesheng* and most of them graduated from China's top universities with the most formal and elitist education in PRC history. They were some of the few to have

5. Tebie baodao (Special Report), "Kuayu fazhan de xin zhuiqiu: pingshu Zhongguo gongchandang di shiliu ci quanguo daibiao dahui" ("The new aspiration for development: on the CCP 16th National Congress"), *Laowang zhoukan* (*Outlook Weekly*), No. 46 (18 November 2002), p. 11.

6. Lu Pi, "Younger officials promoted to provincial-level posts," *Beijing Review*, Vol. 45, No. 34 (22 August 2002), p. 13.

7. Fewsmith, "Generational transition in China," p. 24.

Table 2: **Members of the 16th CCP Politburo**

Name	Birth date	Education	Party membership	Other principal posts	Membership in Central Committee
Wang Lequan	December 1944; Shandong province	Central Party School, postgraduate, 1983–86	March 1966	Deputy governor of Shandong province, secretary of the Party Committee of Xinjiang Autonomous Region	Alternate member, 1992, full member, 1997
Wang Zhaoguo	July 1941; Hebei province	Department of Power Mechanics, Harbin Institute of Technology, 1961–66; engineer	December 1965	Governor of Fujian province, director-general of the State Council Taiwan Affairs Office, director of the CCP United Front Work Department	Full member, 1982

Name	Birth date; place	Education	Joined party	Position	Committee membership
Hui Liangyu (Hui nationality)	October 1944; Jilin province	Distant study, Jilin Provincial Party School, 1984–87; economist	April 1966	Deputy governor of Jilin province, secretary of the CCP Anhui and Jiangsu Provincial Committees	Alternate member, 1992, full member, 1997
Liu Qi	November 1942; Jiangsu province	Department of Metallurgy, Beijing Institute of Iron and Steel Industry, undergraduate 1959–64, postgraduate 1964–68; senior engineer	September 1975	Minister of the Metallurgical Industry, secretary of the CCP Beijing Municipal Committee and mayor of Beijing	Alternate member, 1992, full member, 1997
Liu Yunshan	July 1947; Shanxi province	Distant study, Central Party School, 1989–92	April 1971	Deputy secretary of the Party Committee of Inner Mongolia	Alternate member, 1982, full member, 1997

Table 2—*continued*

Name	Birth date	Education	Party membership	Other principal posts	Membership in Central Committee
				Autonomous Region, director of the CCP Publicity Department	
Wu Yi (female)	November 1938; Hubei province	Department of Oil Refining, Beijing Institute of Petroleum Industry, 1956–62, senior engineer	April 1962	Deputy mayor of Beijing, minister of the Ministry of Foreign Trade and Economic Co-operation	Alternate member, 1987, full member, 1992
Zhang Lichang	July 1939; Hebei province	Distant study in Economic Management, Beijing Correspondence School of Economy, 1987–89	February 1966	Secretary of the CCP Tianjin Municipal Committee, major of Tianjin	Alternate member, 1982, full member, 1992

Name	Birth	Education/early career	Date	Position	Central Committee status
Zhang Dejiang	November 1946; Liaoning province	Department of Economy, DPRK Kim Il Sung University, 1978–80; lecturer	January 1971	Secretary of the CCP Jilin and Zhejiang Provincial Committees	Alternate member, 1992, full member, 1997
Chen Liangyu	October 1946; Zhejiang province	Department of Architecture, PLA Institute of Logistics Engineering, 1963–68; engineer	April 1980	Secretary of the CCP Shanghai Municipal Committee and mayor of Shanghai	Alternate member, 1997, full member, 2002
Zhou Yongkang	December 1942; Jiangsu province	Department of Exploration, Beijing Institute of Petroleum Industry, 1961–66; senior engineer	November 1964	Secretary of the CCP Sichuan Provincial Committee, minister of Natural Resources	Alternate member, 1992, full member, 1997
Yu Zhengsheng	April 1945; Zhejiang province	Missile Department, Harbin Institute of Military	November 1964	Minister of Construction, secretary of the CCP	Alternate member, 1992, full member,

Table 2—continued

Name	Birth date	Education	Party membership	Other principal posts	Membership in Central Committee
		Engineering, 1963–68; engineer		Hubei Provincial Committee	1997
He Guoqiang	October 1943; Hunan province	Department of Inorganic Industry, Beijing Institute of Chemical Industry, 1961–66; senior engineer	January 1966	Governor of Fujian province, secretary of the CCP Chongqing Municipal Committee, director of the CCP Organization Department	Alternate member, 1982, full member, 1997
Guo Boxiong	July 1942; Shaanxi province	PLA Military Academy, 1981–83; general	March 1963	Commander of the Lanzhou Military Region, vice-chairman of the Central	Full member, 1997

Cao Gangchuan	December 1935; Henan province	Military Engineering School of the Artillery Corps, USSR, 1957–63; general	July 1956	Military Commission; executive deputy chief of the Headquarters of the General Staff	Full member, 1997
				Deputy chief of the General Staff, director-general of the Commission of Science, Technology and Industry for National Defence, director-general of the General Armament Department	
Zeng Peiyan	December 1938; Zhejiang province	Department of Radio Electronics, Qinghua University, 1956–62; senior engineer	September 1978	Chairman of the State Development and Planning Commission.	Alternate member, 1992, full member, 1997

Table 2—continued

Alternate Member of the Politburo

Name	Birth date	Education	Party membership	Other principal posts	Membership in Central Committee
Wang Gang	October 1942; Jilin province	Department of Philosophy, Jilin University, 1962–67	June 1971	Director-general of the State Archives Administration, director of the CCP General Office, member of the Secretariat of the CCP Central Committee	Alternate member, 1997, full member, 2002

Source:
  Laowang zhoukan, No. 46 (18 November 2002), pp. 25–31.

Table 3: **Secretaries of the CPC Provincial, Autonomous Regional and Municipal Committees (June 2002)**

Name	Place	Birth date	Education	Party membership time	Membership in Central Committee
Jia Qinglin	Beijing municipality	1940	University	1959	Member of CPC Political Bureau (1997)
Huang Ju	Shanghai municipality	1938	University	1966	Member of CPC Political Bureau (1994)
Chu Bo	Inner Mongolia Autonomous Region	1944	University	1969	Alternate member of CPC Central Committee (1997)
Tian Chengping	Shanxi province	1945	University	1964	Member of CPC Central Committee (1997)

Table 3—*continued*

Name	Place	Birth date	Education	Party membership time	Membership in Central Committee
Zhang Lichang	Tianjin municipality	1939	Junior college	1966	Member of CPC Central Committee (1992)
Wang Xudong	Hebei province	1946	Unknown	1972	Alternate member of CPC Central Committee (1997)
He Guoqiang	Chongqing municipality	1943	University	1966	Member of CPC Central Committee (1997)
Wen Shizhen	Liaoning province	1940	University	1979	Member of CPC Central Committee (1997)
Wang Yunkun	Jilin province	1942	University	1966	Member of CPC Central Committee (1997)

Name	Province	Year	Education	Year	Position
Wang Taihua	Anhui province	1945	University	1973	Alternate member of CPC Central Committee (1992)
Xu Youfang	Heilongjiang province	1939	University	1973	Member of CPC Central Committee
Wu Guanzheng	Shandong province	1938	Postgraduate	1962	Member of CPC Political Bureau (1997)
Hui Liangyu	Jiangsu province	1944	Junior college	1966	Member of CPC Central Committee (1997)
Meng Jianzhu	Jiangxi province	1947	Postgraduate	1971	Alternate member of CPC Central Committee (1997)
Zhang Dejiang	Zhejiang province	1946	University	1971	Member of CPC Central Committee (1997)

Table 3—*continued*

Name	*Place*	*Birth date*	*Education*	*Party membership time*	*Membership in Central Committee*
Song Defu	Fujian province	1946	Junior college	1965	Member of CPC Central Committee (1987)
Yang Zhengwu	Hunan province	1941	Unknown	1969	Member of CPC Central Committee (1987)
Bai Keming	Hainan province	1943	University	1975	
Yu Zhengsheng	Hubei province	1945	University	1964	Member of CPC Central Committee (1997)
Cao Bochun	Guangxi Zhuang Autonomous Region	1941	Junior college	1966	Member of CPC Central Committee (1997)
Chen Kuiyuan	Henan province	1941	University	1965	Member of CPC Central Committee (1992)

Qian Yunlu	Guizhou province	1944	University	1965	Alternate member of CPC Central Committee (1997)
Li Changchun	Guangdong province	1944	University	1965	Member of CPC Political Bureau (1997)
Zhou Yongkang	Sichuan province	1942	University	1964	Member of CPC Central Committee (1997)
Bai Enpei	Yunnan province	1946	University	1973	Alternate member of CPC Central Committee (1997)
Su Rong	Qinghai province	1948	Postgraduate	1970	Alternate member of CPC Central Committee (1997)
Li Jianguo	Shaanxi province	1946	University	1971	Member of CPC Central Committee (1997)

Table 3—continued

Name	Place	Birth date	Education	Party membership time	Membership in Central Committee
Wang Lequan	Xinjiang Autonomous Region	1944	Postgraduate	1966	Member of CPC Central Committee (1997)
Song Zhaosu	Gansu province	1941	University	1965	Alternate member of CPC Central Committee
Guo Jinlong	Tibet Autonomous Region	1947	University	1979	Alternate member of CPC Central Committee (1997)
Chen Jianguo	Ningxia Hui Autonomous Region	1945	Junior college	1966	Alternate member of CPC Central Committee (1997)

Note:
All are male and of Han nationality, except for Yang Zhengwu (Hunan), who is from the Tujia ethnic group.
Source:
Beijing Review, Vol. 45, No. 34 (22 August 2002), pp. 14–15.

passed the vigorous college entrance examination, obtained college degrees and become inspired with youthful ideals to become "red experts."

Their elitist education with its emphasis on the academic achievement of mathematics, science and technology, however, was sharply attacked as pursuing a "bourgeois white experts' road" during the Cultural Revolution. The violence of the Cultural Revolution shattered this generation's youthful ideals and imparted a pragmatism and cynicism to their formative experiences. While some of them joined the Red Guard and rebellion movement, many of them became targets of the movement because of their bad family or educational backgrounds. One commonly shared experience is that they were all sent to factories or the countryside for re-education by working as manual labourers during the Cultural Revolution. Most of them had the opportunity to take up technological jobs, move back to the cities and eventually advance to the senior ranks of leadership only after Deng launched economic reform. As a clear indication of their collective experience, all Politburo Standing Committee members climbed to the provincial/ministerial ranks during the 1980s and entered the CCP Central Committee after the 12th Party Congress in 1982 (most of them after the 15th Congress in 1997) (see Table 1). Hu Jintao became the first secretary of the CCYL in 1982. Wu Bangguo was appointed Shanghai's deputy Party secretary in 1985. Wen Jiabao was given the position of deputy director-general of the CCP Central Committee's General Office in 1985. Jia Qinglin rose to the position of Fujian provincial deputy Party secretary in 1985. Zeng Qinghong was promoted to be Shanghai's deputy Party secretary in 1986. Huang Ju took the position of Shanghai's deputy Party secretary in 1985. Wu Guanzheng became Hubei provincial Party secretary in 1986. Li Changchun was appointed Liaoning provincial Party secretary in 1986. And Luo Gan became deputy governor of Henan province in 1981.

The New Leadership and Policy Continuity

The younger age and distinctive life experience of the new leadership, however, will not necessarily translate into a distinctive policy orientation. Deng Xiaoping opened up China's rigid central commanding economic system but left its authoritarian political system intact. Jiang Zemin has continued Deng's economic reform but not launched meaningful political reform and let the authoritarian political system now come to contradict market-oriented economic reform. The world has been looking for the new leadership to open up China's political system. This expectation, however, may be proved too optimistic. The new leadership will certainly continue economic reform and political institutionalization but the change will be more likely to be gradual and hardly deviate from the direction set by Deng and Jiang.

China has experienced enormous and steady transformation from a revolutionary to a post-revolutionary society as a result of the reform in the past two decades. The impressive transformation has come, however, as a result of gradualism and policy continuity. As Susan Shirk indicated, instead of imposing a big-bang transformation, "Chinese reform was gradual and piecemeal."[8] The transformation has been under the guidance of a grand policy consensus built by Deng and advanced by Jiang over the importance of concentrating on economic modernization and the overall need to strengthen market forces and China's interaction with the international economy. The 16th Party Congress reconfirmed this grand consensus in Jiang Zemin's political report, which put forward the goal of quadrupling the nation's 2000 gross domestic product by 2020. In addition, Jiang has also set in motion further policy evolution when he called for establishment of a more inclusive society under one-party rule by enshrining the "three represents" into the Party's constitution to embrace the new business elite. Jiang Zemin's "three represents" came across to most Westerners as communist gobbledygook, just as the concept of the "socialist market economy" once seemed a laughable oxymoron. But both phrases express a determination to push forward China's modernization. Indeed, Jiang's "three represents" has bequeathed a new programme of action with the essence that the CCP "should represent the elite rather than the masses and it should bind the country together rather than dividing it through struggle and class dictatorship."[9] Admitting private business elites into the Party is an approach towards implementing this new idea and transforming the CCP from a revolutionary to a conservative ruling party, more inclusive and relevant to economic modernization objectives.

The new leaders who emerged at the 16th Congress are pragmatic modernists like their immediate predecessors and have advanced their careers by working on China's economic modernization programmes either as local officials or central bureaucrats. As a result, it is hard for them to depart from the grand consensus, which has so far stood the country as well as themselves in good stead. Following this grand consensus, they will be more likely to build upon Deng/Jiang's legacy to liberalize the Chinese economy further in line with the open-door policy, maintain political stability, improve relations with the United States and enhance China's role in world affairs. It is also in their interest to carry out Jiang's new policy of reinventing the Party by embracing the nascent entrepreneurial class if this policy can help the Party to stay more relevant to these modernization objectives. The grand consensus has been aimed at strengthening or improving CCP one-party rule rather than opening political competition. In this case, these new leaders, like their predecessors, will not allow any challenge to the Party's monopoly over political power.

Concerned overridingly with political stability and economic modernization, the new leadership may make some fine adjustments in policy emphasis to balance out reform in the nation's economic and social landscape, so that the rapid progress made to date in some sectors of the

8. Susan Shirk, *The Political Logic of Economic Reform in* China (Berkeley: University of California Press, 1993), p. 129.

9. William H. Overholt, "China's Party Congress: the new vision," *South China Morning Post*, 16 November 2002.

economy and society is matched in others. After taking over the helm of the Party leadership, Hu made his first trips to Xibaipo in Hubei province, a CCP revolutionary shrine, and Inner Mongolia, a relatively poor and inland region. His message is not primarily to distinguish himself from Jiang with different sources of legitimacy and social-economic agenda. Rather, it is to strike a balance between the priority of economic efficiency and the importance of narrowing disparity in society, and between the continuity of opening up along the coast and the development of the remote west areas. These adjustments do not interrupt policy continuity started by Deng, not only because members of the new leadership have benefited from the current policies but also because the succession arrangement at the 16th Party Congress has set limits for the new leaders to make drastic policy reorientation, at least in the near future.

First of all, although the leadership promotion and succession have become more and more institutionalized, almost like business-as-usual, members of the new generation of leadership have advanced their careers not in an open and democratic setting but through bureaucratic ranks based upon their professional ability and political reliability that had been defined by their predecessors. In the Jiang years, so-called political reliability was settled as "persisting in the road of socialism with Chinese characteristics" and to "have a firm faith, earnestly follow the 'three represents' theory, implement Party policies, and be diligent, clean and honest." Professional ability is emphasized as "having broad vision, strategic thinking and an enterprising spirit" as well as "strong career aspirations, professional competence and relatively high education background."[10] To be politically reliable and professionally competent officials, they have climbed the bureaucratic ladders step-by-step within the established system. Except for the short period of sending down to countryside and factories during the Cultural Revolution, their careers have been largely smooth, without the constant drama and excitement that Mao Zedong and Deng Xiaoping experienced. They have worked to govern an increasingly complex polity rather than to strike out in finding a new policy direction. As a result, it is very hard for these leaders to veer far, if at all, from the established political system and policy principles.

Hu's bland public persona and low profile during his climbing up the Party hierarchy exemplifies the system-maintaining characteristics of the new generation of leadership. Selected a decade ago by Deng as heir to Jiang, Hu had spent time building alliances and gaining experience while drawing little attention before taking over as Party chief at the 16th Party Congress. He is best known for being cautious and able to keep his personality and views on politics a mystery to outsiders. Even at the Congress that named him as Jiang's replacement as Party chief, Hu gave no hint he was expecting to lead China for the next decade. As the secretary general of the Congress, Hu didn't utter a public word before the Congress ended. In his opening speech to introduce the new

---

10. Lu Pi, "Younger officials promoted to provincial-level posts," p. 12.

Politburo Standing Committee members after the Congress, Hu only underscored the importance of Jiang's theory of the "three represents" as the compass for the actions of the Chinese Communist Party. As it was reported in official Chinese media, "Hu Jintao, on behalf of the new CPC leadership, has vowed to 'unswervingly' and 'persistently' carry out the policy objectives set out in the political report of the last Central Committee."[11] That is why Susan Shirk believed that "even the most assiduous Beijingologist cannot identify any policy differences between the two."[12]

In addition, it is worth pointing out that most Politburo members were promoted directly from provincial leadership posts. Fourteen Politburo members, including five Standing Committee (Wu Bangguo, Jia Qinglin, Huang Ju, Wu Guanzheng and Li Changchun) and nine other Politburo members (Wang Lequan, Hui Liangyu, Liu Qi, Zhang Lichang, Zhang Dejiang, Chen Liangyu, Zhou Yongkang, Yu Zhengsheng and He Guoqiang), were provincial Party secretaries and governors prior to the 16th Congress. Strikingly, an unprecedented number of the provinces they came from are located in relatively poor inland regions such as Hubei, Sichuan and Xinjiang, whereas most members of the 15th Politburo were associated with coastal cities and provinces. So many leaders from inland provinces in the Politburo may be a reflection of the CCP leadership's greater awareness of the pressing problems in China's inner provinces and an indication of its willingness to develop the hinterland. However, as one study indicates, to an extent, provincial leaders in inland regions have "less experience or expertise in foreign trade, finance, technological development and large-scale urban construction than their counterparts in coastal regions."[13] The increase of inland provincial leaders in the Politburo is related to strained relations between inland and coastal regions as well as tensions between leaders in relatively poor provinces and rich provinces. A central leadership that is full of provincial leaders who can hardly be put on the same page on virtually every policy issue is certainly not in favour of any bold policy initiatives, especially controversial political reform policy initiatives.

Secondly, policy continuity is more likely also because most members of this new leadership were technically trained and by profession technocrats in administrative capacities, similar to their immediate predecessors. Official biographies of central leaders revealed at the 16th Party Congress show none of them with formal training in social sciences or the legal profession. It is striking that the education background of all nine Politburo Standing Committee members is in technical and engineering areas such as water conservancy, electronics, geology and electric power.

11. Commentary, "Torch passing kindles higher hopes," *China Daily*, 17 November 2002.

12. Susan Shirt, "The succession game," in Gang Li and Susan Shirk (eds.), *The 16th CCP Congress and Leadership Transition in China* (Washington DC: Woodrow Wilson International Center for Scholars Asian Program Special Report, No. 105, September 2002), p. 8.

13. Chen Li, "Emerging patterns of power sharing: inland Hu versus coastal Zeng?" in Gang and Shirk, *The 16th CCP Congress and Leadership Transition*, p. 30.

Two of them (Jia Qinglin and Luo Gan) hold the professional title of senior engineer and the other seven hold the title of engineer, in addition to their administrative positions. Among the other 15 members of the Politburo, ten had formal training in various technical fields and hold the title of engineer. Of the remaining five, Wang Lequan, Hui Liangyu and Liu Yunshan were trained in central or provincial Party schools, Zhang Lichang had a distant education background in economic management, and Zhang Dejiang studied economics in North Korea's Kim Il Sung University. Wang Gang, the alternate Politburo member, has an education in philosophy (see Table 2). This education background shows that the new leadership is a continuation of the "technocratization" of the Chinese leadership, or, in Joseph Fewsmith's words, "the Technocratization of Chinese Leadership, Part Two."[14]

Because these younger technocrats were recruited into leadership positions during the years of Deng's economic reform, they are labelled "market technocrats" as distinct from those "socialist technocrats" who entered into administrative/political roles in the Soviet inspired years.[15] Market technocrats may display greater flexibility to economic liberalization but not necessarily to politically liberal alternatives for China than socialist technocrats. The most important similarity is that both types are ideologically agnostic and their policy orientations have nothing, or very little, to do with rigid communist ideology. However, they are ideologically agnostic not only to communism but also to liberalism. These younger leaders have "experienced ideological disillusionment twice. The first time was with Marx's communism and Mao's socialism. The second time was with economist Adam Smith's 'invisible hand.' ... As a result, new leaders are more interested in discussing issues than defending 'isms'."[16] Both socialist and market technocrats are believers in Deng's "cat theory" and tend to be very pragmatic. Trained as engineers, they "see political issues as problems to be solved based on hard data and hard interest, not as conflicts driven by ideological principles."[17] They experienced the cruel reality of China during the Cultural Revolution and struggled through bureaucratic hierarchy in the reform years, so they are anything but idealists. "They had learned how to serve new bosses without rejecting old ones; when to pay lip service to ideologues and when to keep mum; and when to duck power struggles and when to form new alliances."[18] Lucian Pye's description of the operational characteristics of the Jiang leadership could be readily applied to the Hu leadership. That is, these pragmatic leaders "want governing to be a normal, routine matter, nothing dramatic or extreme. They want government to be just the

14. Fewsmith, "Generational transition in China," p. 24.
15. Richard Baum, "To reform or to muddle through: the challenges facing China's fourth generation," in Gang and Shirk, *The 16th CCP Congress and Leadership Transition*, p. 43.
16. Li Chen, "Mystery behind the myths," *South China Morning Post*, 11 June 2001 (http://china.scmp.com/lifestyle/ZZZXXELDPNC/html).
17. Miller and Liu, "The foreign policy outlook of China's 'third generation' elite," p. 136.
18. Jonathan Ansfield, "Mao's sent-down youths to rise at China Congress," Reuters English News Service, 10 October 2002.

practice of management, not of politics, for that would involve contending over values. In contrast to the constant drama and excitement over new departures that characterized the Mao and Deng eras, public affairs under Jiang have become a prosaic, almost colorless activity."[19]

The third aspect of succession arrangement that helps policy continuity is Jiang's heavy shadows over the new leadership team after the 16th Congress. The fact that Jiang stayed on as chairman of the CMC for more than just a few, transitional months has made him the de facto commander-in-chief to remain as a major force in Chinese politics after relinquishing the post of the Party general secretary. It is revealing that although Hu was ranked first at the line-up of the new leadership presented after the 16th Congress, in the list of the official biographies and photographs by *Renmin ribao* (*People's Daily*) the next day, the name and photo of Jiang were still the first in his capacity as the chairman of the CMC, followed by Hu Jintao and eight new members of the Politburo Standing Committee. State television news also gave prominence to Jiang at a meeting he held after the Congress with military representatives. Hu walked behind Jiang. This protocol sent the message that although a new leadership emerged at the 16th Party Congress, Jiang has not retired from a position of political influence. This is not only because Jiang loves power but also because he wants to ensure the continuity of his policy initiatives. Staying on in an influential position as long as he can, Jiang "will be able to lend his support to China's moderate policies toward the US and Taiwan. He also will be able to help ensure that China's new leaders follow through on promises by the departing leadership to level the playing field for private businesses and to open China's markets to other countries following the country's entry into the World Trade Organization."[20]

With Jiang in de facto command, Hu will not have much leeway to dictate policy as he pleases. He must work with Jiang to complete the power transfer gradually. It is important to remember that Hu, like Jiang, does not have the mandate of a democratically elected leader nor the charisma of a revolutionary or reform leader. Mao Zedong founded the PRC and hence established his personal charisma as symbolizing the communist state. Deng Xiaoping was the architect of China's reform and opening-up and became a paramount leader. They both ruled China and made arbitrary decisions. Jiang Zemin was given the position as the core of his leadership by Deng Xiaoping and prevailed over his rivals such as the Yang brothers and Li Peng with the support of Deng. Jiang finally consolidated his core position only after the death of Deng in 1997. Hu was also selected by Deng to succeed Jiang and was made vice-president of China in 1997 and first vice-chairman of the CMC in 1999 under the auspices of Jiang. It is not hard for Hu to understand that Jiang may topple him if he offends him or makes mistakes. After all, Hu took the

19. Pye, "Jiang Zemin's style of rule," p. 46.
20. Susan V. Lawrence, "Jiang will retain his post as Chinese military head," *The Wall Street Journal*, 28 November 2002.

top job in an arranged succession not a democratic election. In the arranged successions of PRC history, Mao Zedong designated the two successors of Liu Shaoqi and Lin Biao but discarded both; and Deng Xiaoping arranged Hu Yaobang and Zhao Ziyang as his successors but also dumped both.

This type of history could indeed repeat for Hu because Jiang placed his protégés in powerful positions after behind-the-scenes horse-trading with other elders at the 16th Congress. The increase in Politburo Standing Committee members from seven to nine for the first time since 1973 is certainly a result of compromise among key members of the outgoing leadership who shoe-horned in protégés and supporters. While Zhu Rongji's favourite, Wen Jiabao, became number three and Li Peng's protégé, Luo Gan, took number nine position in the top leadership, the other six all have greater or lesser links to Jiang, either through personal friendship or as part of a "Shanghai gang" of natives and former officials from the country's financial centre and surrounding provinces. The most important person is Jiang's closest adviser and henchman, Zeng Qinghong, who was promoted to number four position in the Politburo Standing Committee from an alternate Politburo member, skipping the rank of the Politburo membership. As Jiang's "right-hand man" and the political brains behind Jiang's 13-year rule as Party head, Zeng Qinghong took over the day-to-day running of the Party as head of its Secretariat at the 16th Congress and became president of the Central Party School when Hu stepped down as head of the Party's top think-tank a few days after the Congress. Zeng is widely expected to be China's vice-president at the next National People's Congress scheduled in March 2003. In this case, it is not entirely out of line when Western media speculated that "Zeng would then be in an ideal position to succeed Hu, should Hu falter politically – as many communist heirs have done in the past – or if Jiang and other 'party elders' agree Hu should be replaced."[21]

This possibility exists because, although the institutionalization of the retirement system has delivered an orderly leadership succession in stark contrast to the successions in the earlier years of the PRC, Hu was selected to lead the Party and the country by his predecessors rather than elected by his constituents. Looking underneath the surface, the seemingly smooth transfer of power was all decided in secret without input from the public. As a result, "the transition, however smooth, throws up more questions than it answers. In China, age counts for a lot, and it's worth remembering that during none of its communist, nationalist and imperial periods has this country been noted for leaders who willingly gave up power before their deaths."[22] In this case, although members of the new leadership which emerged at the 16th Congress are younger, the impact of generational change upon China's reform policy may not be immediately clear, and continuity is more likely than reorientation at least

21. "Zeng Qinghong replaces Hu Jintao as president of CPC Party School," AFP, 5 December 2002.
22. Orville Schell, "The China syndrome," *Time*, 18 November 2002.

in the near future. With Jiang remaining a powerful force, it would not be a surprise if Hu deferentially echoes almost all of Jiang's policy positions at least until Jiang's physical condition prevents him from intervening in politics.

A Chance for Political Reform

But this does not mean that the leadership change is meaningless and Hu will not have a chance to come out from Jiang's shadow and make bold policy initiatives. The needs for political survival and power consolidation may force Hu to move beyond Jiang and have fresh start, including pushing forward political reform.

Hu may take note that in the course of previous two successful leadership successions, Deng and Jiang both started from relatively weak positions but ended up as paramount leaders. As Lowell Dittmer observed, "the distribution of power varies cyclically in the course of the succession cycle, typically beginning with a relatively equal distribution of power at the outset but tending over time toward a more hierarchically skewed distribution as the paramount leader eliminates rivals and accumulates hegemony." Lowell substantiated his observation by pointing out the fact that:

Deng began by sharing power with Li Xiannian and Chen Yun but in the course of the 1980s succeeded in monopolizing power to the extent that he was able to coordinate the Tiananmen crackdown quite arbitrarily. Jiang Zemin in the early 1990s was considered a somewhat lackluster member of a third-generation cohort that included Chen Xitong, Qiao Shi, Li Peng, and Zhu, but by the end of the 1990s the second generation had died or been retired and he had reduced his own cohort to three (Jiang, Li, Zhu), among whom relations are said to be complicated.[23]

Coming out from the shadows of Deng, Jiang took every opportunity to diminish his rivals and eventually was able to position himself firmly as the representative of the third generation of CCP leadership. This position was clearly demonstrated at the 16th Party Congress as the amended Party constitution put Jiang's "three represents" together with Mao's Thought and Deng's Theory as CCP guidelines to action, and listed Jiang parallel with Mao and Deng as the representatives of three generations of CCP leadership.[24]

However, Hu may also learn from failed succession arrangements in

23. Lowell Dittmer, "The changing shape of elite power politics," *The China Journal*, No. 45 (January 2001), p. 60.

24. The CCP constitution amended at the 16th Party Congress contains the following passages: "The Communist Party of China takes Marxism-Leninism, Mao Zedong Thought, Deng Xiaoping Theory and the important thought of Three Represents as its guide to action. ... The Chinese Communists, with Comrade Mao Zedong as their chief representative, created Mao Zedong Thought ... After the Third Plenary Session of the Eleventh Party Central Committee, the Chinese Communists, with Comrade Deng Xiaoping as the chief representative, summed up their experience ... thus founding Deng Xiaoping Theory. ... Since the Fourth Plenary Session of the Thirteenth Party Central Committee and in the practice of building socialism with Chinese characteristics, the Chinese Communists, with Comrade Jiang Zemin as their chief representative, have acquired a deeper understanding of what socialism is, how to build it and what kind of party to build and how to build it, accumulated new valuable experience in running the Party and state and formed the important thought of Three Represents. ..."

PRC history. To an extent, Jiang's retirement from the post of Party general secretary while retaining the chairmanship of the CMC leaves him sitting at the second front (*erxian*) to watch Hu Jintao's performance at the first front (*yixian*). This is similar to what happened when Mao let Liu Shaoqi and Deng Xiaoping move to the first front in the early 1960s and Deng Xiaoping let Hu Yaobang and Zhao Ziyang move to the second front in the 1980s. This type of arrangement between the first and second fronts has hardly ever worked out well because conflicts inevitably arose between the semi-retired backseat drivers and the frontline leaders. The results have always been the fall of the vulnerable first front leaders. Mao brought down Liu Shaoqi and Deng Xiaoping during the Cultural Revolution. Deng dumped Hu Yaobang and Zhao Ziyang when he found that they did not follow his policy line in the 1980s. Unless Hu Jintao is happy to be a complete puppet figurehead of the Party and the state, which seems doubtful, he may have to find a way to wrest control from Jiang for his own political survival sooner or later. Pushing forward political reform could be one of the ways out.

Many Western observers have talked about political reform in China only in terms of democratization. However, when Chinese government officials and some Chinese scholars talk about political reform, they are not proposing to democratize the polity but to make the single party rule more efficient and institutional or to provide it with a more solid legal base. This top-down approach falls into broadly defined political reform, which "refers to all aspects of change that are deliberately and explicitly decreed or promulgated by the ruling elite to deviate from the established political system."[25] The direction of top-down political reform in China has progressed steadily in the recent decade largely in the form of institutionalization of the leadership system by normative rules and transformation of the CCP from a revolutionary to a conservative ruling party. Hu may enhance political reform along this direction to help consolidate his power position, because if normative rules of China's leadership politics are preserved institutionally, although Jiang may try to linger on for several more years, his political influence can only diminish after officially retiring from the top Party and government posts. Institutionalization, however, may also mean that Hu will not have the opportunity to become another strongman like Deng or even Jiang with dominating personal authority. If Hu accepts the limits, it will be a positive step in China's political reform.

Institutionalization of China's leadership system started in the 1980s when Deng realized that "the lack of effective institutions and checks on arbitrary authority had helped bring about disasters in the Mao years."[26] A number of significant measures have been introduced, including regular Party and state body meetings according to constitutional schedules; a

25. Suisheng Zhao, "Political reform and changing one-party rule in Deng's China," *Problems of Post-Communism*, Vol. 44, No. 5, p. 13.

26. Frederick C. Teiwes, "Normal politics with Chinese characteristics," *The China Journal*, No. 45 (January 2001), p. 74.

constitutionally mandated two-term limit for the premier and presidency and a retirement age to eliminate life-long tenure for all Party and government posts; and a personnel policy emphasizing youth and education. One of the most important consequences of institutionalization is the enhancement of formal institutional authority and the decline of the informal personal authority of top leaders. By definition, personal authority revolves around individuals and derives from the charismatic nature of strong leaders, which supersedes impersonal organization in eliciting the personal loyalty of followers. In contrast, institutional authority derives from and is constrained by impersonal organizational rules. In an ideal type, such authority rests not on individual charisma but on formal position in an institutional setting. Insofar as a leader can issue commands under institutional authority, it is the function of the office he holds rather than of any personal quality.

For many years in PRC history, personal authority and institutional authority were hierarchically ranked because "the influential elders with strong personal authority are supreme decision-makers, whereas the officeholders with institutional authority serve as the chief lieutenants to the powerful elders."[27] This was particularly true during the 1980s when retired senior leaders of revolutionary generations possessed great personal prestige and influence over newly promoted and younger top office-holders. Although Deng gave up most of his formal titles voluntarily at the peak of his power, except the chairmanship of the CMC that he retained for two more years after stepping down from the Politburo Standing Committee in 1987, he still held personal power to exercise ultimate authority because of his personal stature, connections and breadth of experience. He cashiered two of his chosen successors, organized the crackdown on student demonstrators in Tiananmen Square in 1989 and regularly intervened in policy matters until he became incapacitated in the mid-1990s. Deng's ultimate authority was reflected crucially in the secret resolution of the 13th Party Congress in 1987 to refer all important matters to him for final decision, it was revealed later. As a result, Deng ruled China even when his only formal position was honorary chairman of the Chinese Bridge Players' Society.

Institutional authority has advanced to take a more important position than personal authority since the complete demise of the senior revolutionary veterans in the 1990s. After the death of Deng Xiaoping in 1997, there have not been any retired senior leaders who practised footloose informal power as Deng and his cohorts did. As noticed by Dittmer, "after retirement, Yang Shangkun, Yang Baibing, Wan Li, Qiao Shi, Liu Huaqing and Zhang Zhen seem to have vanished into political oblivion without a trace."[28] Even though Jiang may seek to follow the lead of Deng, it is not at all clear that he will succeed in doing so. Jiang does not

27. Suisheng Zhao, "The structure of authority and decision-making: a theoretical framework," in Carol Lee Hamrin and Suisheng Zhao (eds.), *Decision-making in Deng's China: Perspectives from Insiders* (Armonk: NY: M. E. Sharpe, 1995), p. 236.
28. Dittmer, "The changing shape of elite power politics," p. 59.

have the kind of prestige and stature that Deng had and therefore is not able to exercise the level of informal authority that Deng was able to wield. Jiang's authority depended at first upon the approbation of the elders and, later, on his institutional positions. That is why he has tried to retain the CMC chairmanship and keep his name and photograph appearing ahead of Hu Jintao in the official media after the 16th Congress, while Deng could afford to have his name and photograph behind Zhao Ziyang after the 13th Party Congress in 1987. In addition, there has been surprisingly strong anti-Jiang sentiment among the Party elite since he decided to keep the CMC post. With the advance of institutionalization, Jiang's ability to wield power via personal influence will only decline, unless he can reverse the trend of institutionalization and command obedience based on his informal relationships and stature within and across institutions.

In this case, it is certainly in Hu's interest to advance the process of institutionalization to make sure that at least the new elders, including Zhu Rongji, Li Peng, Li Ruihuan, Li Lanqing and eventually Jiang Zemin, enjoy their retirements as Qiao Shi, Yang Shangkun and others did in the 1990s. Hu may not want to offend Jiang while Jiang still exercises influence. But Hu is certainly aware that, as long as Jiang continues to guide policy without holding the top leadership position, his succession is incomplete. To make it complete, Hu may institutionalize a formal structure of collective leadership with him happy to be the first among equals. In fact, such a collective leadership is emerging with or without his intention. The new leadership team has looked like a ministerial cabinet with Hu as the weak first among equals. It is interesting to note that at the ceremony to introduce the new Party leadership, Hu humoured the lowest-ranked but oldest member of the new Standing Committee, calling Luo Gan "*women de dage*" (our elder brother). Indeed, Hu is one of the younger members of the Politburo Standing Committee and appears to be more among peers than a boss. Although age difference has been traditionally important in China to establish authority, Hu's weaker leadership position is not determined only by his younger age but by his lonely position in the leadership team.

As the new leadership has not had a core, the collective leadership and normative rules in decision-making have been reinforced. At the highly publicized first Politburo meeting after the 16th Party Congress, Hu emphasized the rule of law and the role of the constitution. In addition, Hu has worked out a power-sharing scheme with other top leaders such as premier Wen Jiabao. The Politburo and its Standing Committee meetings have been routinely convened, reported and publicized in official media since the 16th Party Congress. It was reported that at the State Council's first executive meeting presided over by Premier Wen Jiabao on 19 March, two days after he assumed the position, a set of working codes for the cabinet was established which emphasized administration by law and enhancing supervision on government work. Wen called for the new administration to strive to make breakthroughs in the three aspects. First, important decisions should be made collectively on the basis of thorough investigations, feasibility studies and soliciting opinions from all walks of life. Secondly, in making decisions concerning the nation's economic and social development, according to the premier, cross-departmental and cross-subject hearings should be conducted and the government should make better use of experts and research institutes. Thirdly, an accountability system should be put in place. Those who violate the decision-making procedures and cause major losses should be held directly responsible for their mistakes.[29]

Making policy decisions at the top more transparent and by normative rules is certainly conducive to building a collective leadership. This development may be positive from the perspective of intra-Party democracy and eventual political development towards pluralism. After all, the top CCP leaders have tended to have less and less personal authority if the institutionalization of leadership politics continues. Hu Jintao, no matter how capable he is, may have less personal authority than Jiang anyway in the years to come. The lack of a strongman in the leadership would at least make members of the new CCP leadership more willing to follow normative rules in decision-making. This formal structure of collective leadership would in turn further strengthen the process of institutionalization on the one hand and broaden participation on the other hand.

It is certainly not an easy undertaking for Hu to push forward political reform in this direction because it is difficult for a formal structure of collective leadership to function effectively within the current political system. As one observer pointed out:

The national leadership has chosen nine people and instructed them to rule collectively in accordance with detailed rules. This is, or should be, a great step forward for the rule of law. In a country with China's enormous problems and powerful interest groups, it is also a great gamble to believe that the ship can be steered by a committee.[30]

The difficulty is partially a result of the emergence of a paradox between the trend of institutionalization and the erosion of political authority of the Communist Party. Political leaders at the apex of an increasingly institutionalized system have been beset with an enormous range of issues and pressures, particularly an erosion of political authority as those who are supposed to have high authority found it more and more difficult to command the actions of those who ultimately implement state policies and persuade society to follow them.

During Mao's years, political authority at the top was enforced by official ideology, Party discipline and a central planning mechanism. The authority of the CCP began to be eroded when economic reform led to the decline of official ideology, lax Party discipline and disintegration of the central planning system. The devolution of power to the lower levels of

29. Commentary," New leaders spearhead new ideas," http://english.peopledaily.com.cn/200308/05/eng20030805_121723.
30. Overholt, "China's Party Congress: the new vision."

the bureaucracy and to local officials "undercut the efficacy of the coercive instruments and undermined the capacity of the central authorities to enforce compliance from local government."[31] In addition, Deng's efforts to "reassess" Maoism to pave the way for economic reform resulted in the widespread demise of communist ideology and "three faith crises" (*san xin weiji*), that is, a crisis of faith in socialism (*xinxin weiji*), crisis of faith in Marxism (*xinyang weiji*) and crisis of faith in the Party (*xinren weiji*).[32] The erosion of authority became more serious under Jiang's leadership as power flowed downwards to such an extent that the centre has increasingly lost control over the initiatives of local authorities. The Party leadership as a whole has become weaker, reflecting the declining role of ideology as a guide to correct political action and the paralysis of Party organizations at grass-root levels as well as rampant corruption. It is astonishing that after several decades of communist rule, communist ideology has quickly become irrelevant to most Chinese people and a communist utopia is criticized as a false path to suit a particular and parochial political objective. Marxism-Leninism-Mao Zedong Thought as the official ideology no longer provides convincing arguments of the need for the general public to preserve communist one-party rule. Nor does it explain how the socialist market economy that the Party has claimed to be building in China is different from, or superior to, the capitalism it once opposed. In this case, as Lucian Pye indicates, "China has reverted to its great tradition of government by feigned compliance. Imperial China possessed impressive bureaucratic structures for governing, but in practice the emperor never had the total power he pretended to have as the Son of Heaven." This system worked well over the centuries because the traditional Chinese social order was relatively simple and could be held together by the bonding spirit of Confucianism. However, it will not do today because, "with modernization, China's economy and society have become more complex and ever great functional specialization and social differentiation have created an ever richer diversity of interests."[33]

As economic progress produces an increasing division of interests, it will become more and more difficult for the new generation of leadership to maintain CCP authority, however institutional and collective it might be. Jiang's idea of the "three represents" may be an innovative way to improve CCP rule. However, as China is no longer a highly homogeneous society, it can only become harder for the Party to claim that what the CCP leadership views as best for China represents the interests of the whole Chinese people. Now that coastal China has significantly different interests from interior China, that urban interests are not those of the countryside, and that the interests of the haves are in conflict with those

31. Suisheng Zhao, "From coercion to negotiation: the changing central – local economic relations in mainland China," *Issues and Studies*, Vol. 28, No. 10 (October 1992), p. 1.

32. For one study of the impact of reform on the official ideology, see Jie Chen, "The impact of reform on the Party and ideology in China," *The Journal of Contemporary China*, No. 9 (Summer 1995), pp. 22–34.

33. Lucian W. Pye, "Pye, "Jiang Zemin's style of rule," p. 48.

of the have-nots, relations among the top leaders have become more complicated than at any time in PRC history. While Jiang has "muddled through" in his 13 years of leadership, Hu may have to confront the various unintended consequences of economic growth and find ways to defuse the conflicts arising from diverse economic interests and the problems left by Jiang such as social inequality, budget deficits, corruption, the decentralization of power and the advent of the market as an alternative source of political resources.

Although Hu may prefer and try to continue the pace of fine adjustment and balancing within the existing framework of one-party rule to muddle through, a sense of authority crisis may force the new generation of leaders to experiment with policy innovations, which could include finding a new direction of political reform such as opening political competition. The Jiang leadership was a prisoner of the fact that its legitimacy stemmed directly from the suppression following the Tiananmen massacre, and thus, even had Jiang wished to, he was not in a good position to champion significant political reform. The Hu generation of leadership is certainly in a better position to do so. However, the new leaders' bureaucratic and technocrat backgrounds as well as their complicated relations with the third generation of leaders may set limits on their capacity as political reformers. In this case, not only is the generational change incomplete as long as Jiang is still lingering after the 16th Party Congress, the direction of political reform still remains uncertain.

Jiang and After: Technocratic Rule, Generational Replacement and Mentor Politics

Yu-Shan Wu

ABSTRACT Following the pattern of historical communism, the Chinese communist regime has evolved into the stage of technocratic stability. In this context, one finds China's post-16th Congress politics characterized by *technocratic rule*, *generational replacement* and *mentor politics* that might lead to re-emergence of gerontocracy. While the first phenomenon is shared by China and historical communist regimes, the other two are uniquely Chinese. The need for economic modernization ushered in technocratic rule. To achieve dynamic stability through economic reform necessitated generational replacement. Finally the persistence of informal politics and the top leader's desire to cling to power generated mentor politics, and bred the possibility of gerontocracy. Among these three phenomena, technocratic rule and generational replacement point to higher degree of rationality, while mentor politics and gerontocracy are a serious drawback. Here the Vietnamese experience is of considerable referent value to the CCP by pointing to a possible direction of improvement.

The 16th National Congress of the Chinese Communist Party (CCP) held in November 2002 marks the official end of Jiang Zemin's rule, as Hu Jintao took his position as the CCP's general secretary. In terms of real power, however, the 16th Congress signifies much less change as Jiang continues exercising power from behind the scenes. Official or real power transfer aside, the true significance of the 16th Congress can be fully grasped only in combination with the 15th National Congress held in 1997. Together these two congresses revealed three features of the CCP's top-echelon politics: technocratic rule that concentrates on stability, generational replacement as mechanism of regime rejuvenation and mentor politics that may lead to gerontocracy. These features are the political manifestations of a reforming communist party-state in pursuit of stability. Indeed since its inception the Jiang regime has been obsessed with stability, and its relative success in political and economic stabilization set it apart from Deng Xiaoping's regime in the 1980s. This overarching concern with stability, however, led paradoxically to more reform in specific areas, for continued reform was considered vital for high growth and thus for stability.

This article begins with a contrast of the 1980s and 1990s. The first decade witnessed bold breakthroughs from the past, and the establishment of main directions of reform. The second decade witnessed a determined pursuit of stability, sometimes on the basis of reform, sometimes at the expense of it. The article then discusses the regime evolution theory, and points out the similarities and dissimilarities between the Chinese and the Soviet evolutionary paths. Both lead toward the stage of technocratic rule centred on stability. However the Soviets and East Europeans pursued stability through static equilibrium, while the Chinese pursued it through dynamic equilibrium. This significant difference introduces the second feature of the Jiang regime: generational replacement. Generational replacement is a powerful mechanism of regime rejuvenation. However, the fact that the regime is a one-party dictatorship with power concentrated at the top leads to an exception to generational replacement, and here there is mentor politics. Excessive mentor politics may lead to gerontocracy, as the 1980s witnessed. The 16th National Congress embodies all these three features of the Jiang regime.

The 1980s and the 1990s: A Contrast

There is a stark contrast between the 1980s and the 1990s, or between Deng's decade and Jiang's decade. In the 1980s, Deng and his associates were primarily concerned with reforming the command system that Mao erected and periodically revamped. The urge was to put to rest the destructive political campaigns, and to stimulate growth and improve living standards so as to restore the regime's legitimacy. As there were only limited examples that the Chinese reformers could follow (such as the Hungarian market socialism reform), they adopted an experimental "trial and error" approach. This was true with both economic and political reform. Valuable lessons were learned and successful models were promoted, resulting in a much more relaxed political atmosphere and bouts of rapid growth. However, the experimental approach naturally led to inconsistencies and disruptions, although the regime was always swift in containing the damage. The 1980s thus witnessed both economic growth and unprecedented inflation, both political relaxation and brutal suppression. Reform and instability characterized this decade of Deng's rule.

In contrast, the 1990s were much more stable. On the political front, Deng's suggestive talks of democratic reform were replaced by Jiang's neo-conservative "mindful of politics" (*jiang zhengzhi*) and the "three represents" (*san ge daibiao*) that aim at co-opting the emerging technological and capitalist elites into the regime. The lively local elections that once reached the county level in the early 1980s were constrained to the villages. The political society that thrived in the Beijing Spring of 1986–87 and Tiananmen demonstrations of 1989 was effectively silenced. The authorities were so vigilant against any sign of social protest that even the religious cult of *falun gong* was targeted for extinction. The passion to reform the political system so evident among the intellectuals in the 1980s was channelled into a drive towards material betterment in the 1990s. Nationalism ran high and added to the regime's resilience against the incursion of Western political ideas. In all one saw less political freedom in China under Jiang than under Deng. Installed in the aftermath of Tiananmen, the Jiang regime enshrined political stability as its overwhelming goal, and that was achieved.

On the economic front, stability was also accomplished, and not at the expense of growth or structural reform. The economy grew by an average of 9.71 per cent in the 1990s, compared with 9.75 per cent in the 1980s. In terms of per capita growth rate, the 1990s averaged 8.48 per cent, compared with 8.18 per cent of the previous decade. At the same time, the average inflation rate was down from 7.3 per cent in the 1980s to 6.1 per cent in the 1990s. The latter half of the 1990s was even more impressive by registering a 3.2 per cent average inflation rate. If one takes a closer look at the economic performance of the two decades, one finds the regime in the 1990s more capable of managing the economic cycles that were the fundamental cause of instability in the previous decade. Jiang and his associates clearly learned from the inexperience and mistakes in the 1980s and adjusted their counter-cyclical policies accordingly.[1] Structural changes such as the expansion of the non-state sector also helped. The inflation of the early 1990s was quite well managed and the "soft landing" of the mid-1990s shows the regime knew how to fine-tune China's reforming and rapidly expanding economy. If one compares the three "landings" of 1985–86, 1988–89 and 1994–95, one finds for the two "hard landings" of the 1980s, inflation was brought down only with significant loss in growth. In 1985–86 inflation was down by 2.8 per cent but GDP was down by 4.7 per cent. In 1988–89 the retrenchment (*zhili zhengdun*) brought down inflation by a meagre 0.7 per cent and yet growth rate suffered a 7.2 per cent contraction. In comparison, the "soft landing" of 1994–95 reduced inflation by an impressive 6.9 per cent at the expense of only 2.1 per cent growth cut (see Figure 1). Clearly this produced a much greater effect in controlling inflation at much less cost in growth. One has to give credit to the Jiang–Zhu regime for this remarkable achievement.

The track record of the Jiang–Zhu regime is even more impressive when one realizes that the high inflation of the early 1990s was actually touched off by Deng's southern inspection (*nanxun*) that relaunched economic reform but at the expense of price stability. Jiang and Zhu were left to deal with an inflated economy that was really not of their own making. The soft landing in the mid-1990s, however, was clearly the achievement of their regime, as Deng was no longer in a position to dictate economic policies in those last years of his life. Since then, the annual growth rate hovered between 7.1 and 9.6 per cent in 1996–2001 while the inflation rate gradually moved into the negative realm (see Figure 1), touching off a discussion on how to handle deflation. One thus sees growth down just a notch from the Deng period (1980s and early 1990s), while inflation was effectively tamed. In the latter half of the 1990s (and the trend extended into the 2000s) both growth and inflation fluctuated in a range unprecedentedly narrow in the PRC's post-1949 history. Growth was high and price was low. Under both Mao and Deng, wide economic fluctuations resulted from political campaigns and econ-

---

1. For a discussion of the various economic and political cycles in China during the reform era, see Lowell Dittmer and Yu-Shan Wu, "The modernization of factionalism in Chinese Politics," *World Politics*, Vol. 47, No. 4 (July 1995), pp. 467–494.

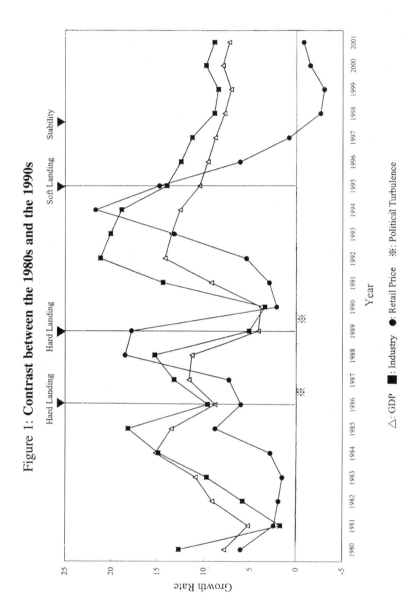

Figure 1: Contrast between the 1980s and the 1990s

omic experiments. When Jiang was at the helm, economic stability was finally achieved.

The success of the soft landing in the mid-1990s was a result of two main factors: a carefully designed contractionary policy that targeted selected sectors, and a structural change that had gradually freed the economy from investment hunger. On the policy side, Zhu Rongji's "macro adjustment" (*hongguan tiaokong*) suppressed over-demand in real estate and in the financial markets. It did not put an abrupt brake on manufacturing, as did all the previous contractionary drives of the 1980s. As a result, the economy gradually cooled down to a reasonable growth level, with inflation effectively checked. On the structural side, *hongguan tiaokong* was implemented in a much more favourable environment than when contractionary policies were attempted in the past. In the 1980s, the thrust of China's economic reform was market socialism, modelled on the Hungarian "new economic mechanism."[2] This mode of reform introduced the market, often in an incomplete manner, while stopping short of de-nationalizing state enterprises. Market socialism tends to bring about soft budget constraint, investment hunger, periodical inflation and up-down cycles. These then became common phenomena in China's state industries, and here lies the fundamental cause of economic instability in the 1980s. However, with the gradual rise of the non-state sector through-out the 1980s and early 1990s, market socialism could no longer sufficiently define China's economy. In the non-state sector, one finds family farming, township and village enterprises, private businesses, foreign-invested firms and many mixed ownership forms. Because soft budget constraint does not apply to them, that is, the state would not automatically bail them out if they go under, their investment activities are ruled by realistic calculations of expected profits. Hence there is built-in constraint on investment in the non-state sector. With the non-state sector growing rapidly to surpass the state sector, the Chinese economy as a whole has become less prone to cycles of investment hunger and inflation. This is the structural cause of the success of the mid-1990s soft landing.

In the 1980s, the economic instability and boom-bust cycles were closely related to political unrest. The two main political upheavals, the Beijing Spring of 1986–87 and the Tiananmen pro-democracy demonstrations, followed the introduction of painful contractionary policies in the wake of high inflation (see Figure 1). Economic instability thus bred political instability. In the 1990s, with economic stability secured against the odds of the post-*nanxun* inflation and the Asian financial crisis, the material base of social disturbances was more or less removed. It is true that many new economic reform measures in the 1990s such as shutting down unprofitable state enterprises did send the unemployed to the streets. However, almost all of the demonstrations were sporadic cases in which citizens registered their anger at specific policies or particular

2. See Yu-Shan Wu, *Comparative Economic Transformations: Mainland China, Hungary, the Soviet Union, and Taiwan* (Stanford: Stanford University Press, 1994), ch. 3.

individual officials, and not against the regime. The sustained high growth acted to relieve social pressure and provided alternative opportunities for employment and upward mobility. Social energy was effectively channelled away from political reform to economic opportunities opened up by continued growth and restructuring (witness *xiahai*). In short, the economic success of the 1990s contributed significantly to political tranquillity that was the overriding objective of Jiang's leadership circle.[3] In all one finds stability the hallmark of Jiang's rule in both a political and an economic sense.

A historical look at China's development trajectories reveals three discernible stages: revolution under Mao, reform under Deng and stability under Jiang. This reminds anyone familiar with the Soviet and East European experiences of the similarities between the European and Asian communist regimes in their historical developments. However, it is necessary to scrutinize the relevant evidence to determine whether the similarities are genuine or more ostensible than real. The following discussion looks into the main features of the CCP politics in comparison with historical European communist regimes. By revealing the similarities and dissimilarities between the two patterns, we can then further grasp the trend of political development in China.

Technocratic Rule: Chinese versus Soviet Style

Historical Communist regimes usually evolved from the stage of high totalitarianism through reform to bureaucratic rule.[4] At the first stage, the totalitarian rulers (such as Stalin and Rakosi) launched political and economic campaigns to transform the society according to a utopian blueprint. The horrendous human costs accompanying the totalitarian transformation traumatized the society and destroyed whatever legitimacy the regime had at the initial stage of its rule. After the death or deposal of the totalitarian despots, the second-generation rulers were usually forced to seek a truce with the society and terminate the rule of terror. A period of reform ensued, characterized by material improvements and political relaxation (the Khrushchevian stage in the Soviet Union).[5] However, the reformers in their zeal to redress the excesses of high totalitarianism often went too far (from the regime's point of view), and created instability. Their tinkering with institutional restructuring risked

3. Lucian W. Pye, "Jiang Zemin's style of rule: go for stability, monopolize power and settle for limited effectiveness," *The China Journal*, No. 45 (January 2001), p. 45.

4. For stage theories of the evolution of Leninist regimes, see Ken Jowitt, "Inclusion and mobilization in European Leninist regimes," *World Politics*, Vol. 28, No. 1(October 1975), pp. 69–96; "Soviet neotraditionalism: the political corruption of a Leninist regime," *Soviet Studies*, Vol. 35, No. 3 (July 1983), pp. 275–297; Richard Löwenthal, "Development versus utopia in communist policy," in Chalmers Johnson (ed.), *Change in Communist Systems* (Stanford: Stanford University Press, 1970); Richard Löwenthal, "The post-revolutionary phase in China and Russia," *Studies in Comparative Communism*, Vol. 16, No. 3 (Autumn 1983), pp. 191–201.

5. One does not necessarily see economic structural reform at this stage, but material betterment surely replaced ideology as the main rationale of the regime's continued rule. The case of the GDR (East Germany) is a good example.

the regime's political control over the society. The cadres' huge vested interest was also threatened by the uncertainties inherent in institutional changes. All this prompted reactions from the technocrats who rose to political prominence after the passing of the revolutionary generation leaders. The result is the third stage of development, that of technocratic stability (the Brezhnevian stage in the Soviet Union).

Just as the reformers naturally acted against the extremities of the revolutionary stage, the technocrats by their nature sought to bring about stability (on both the individual and regime levels) that had been undermined by radical reform policies. Thus institutional experiments were circumvented and political control was tightened. In appearance this seemed like a partial return to totalitarianism, but in essence the emergent technocratic rule was a conservative backlash against both revolution (the first stage) and reform (the second stage). The goal of the regime was no longer to transform the society or redress atrocities in the past, but to consolidate the rule of the party-state.[6] This was what the Brezhnevian era meant in the Soviet Union.[7]

Are we witnessing the same development in China? Mao Zedong was undoubtedly a totalitarian despot, and his rule fits squarely into the profile of the first stage of high totalitarianism. Deng Xiaoping was a reformer *par excellence*. Under him, China was salvaged from Maoist revolutionary fanaticism. In his zeal to redress the extremities of the past, Deng was bold to experiment with economic as well as political institutional reforms. As can be expected of a typical reform stage in communist regime evolution, the Dengist rule was characterized by bold breakthroughs and grave uncertainties. Then came Jiang Zemin, a technocrat by nature, who had every potential to act like a Soviet or East European technocratic leader at the third stage of regime evolution, technocratic stability. The death of Deng and the political ascendancy of Jiang at the 15th Congress in 1997 signified the advent of the technocratic era,[8] even though the trend towards technocratic rule had existed in the regime for a long time, mostly subdued by the ultra-leftists and the radical market reformers.[9] The transfer of power from Jiang and his cohort (the "third echelon leadership") to Hu Jintao and his associates (the "fourth echelon

6. For an excellent discussion of the mechanisms that maintained stability during the Brezhnev era, see Seweryn Bialer, *The Soviet Paradox* (New York: Alfred A. Knopf, 1987).

7. For a juxtaposition of the reform and conservative trends in the Soviet history, see Stephen F. Cohen, *Rethinking the Soviet Experience: Politics and History Since 1917* (New York: Oxford University Press, 1985).

8. Cheng Li and Lynn White, "The Fifteenth Central Committee of the Communist Party: full-fledged technocratic leadership with partial control by Jiang Zemin," *Asian Survey*, Vol. 48, No. 3 (March 1998), pp. 231–264.

9. For a discussion of the conflict of the three main policy groups in the PRC's history, see Yu-Shan Wu, *Yuanli shehuizhuyi: Zhongguo dalu, Sulian he Polan de jingji zhuanxing* (*Away from Socialism: The Economic Transformation of Mainland China, the Soviet Union and Poland*) (Taipei: Cheng-chung, 1996), ch. 3; and Lowell Dittmer, "Patterns of elite strife and succession in Chinese politics," *The China Quarterly*, No. 123 (September 1990), pp. 410–11. For a detailed account of the conflict between the market reformers and the technocrats, see Joseph Fewsmith, *Dilemmas of Reform in China* (Armonk, NY: M.E. Sharpe, 1994).

Figure 2: **Percentage of Members Holding a College Degree**

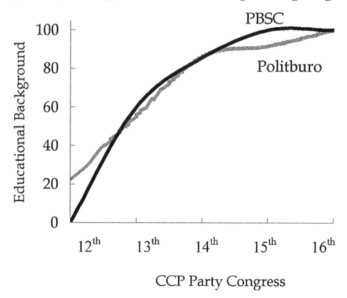

CCP Party Congress

leadership") at the 16th Congress in 2002 consolidated the rule of the technocrats.

Both the third and fourth echelon leaders have more formal and technical education than their predecessors from the revolutionary generation.[10] An amazing 98.6 per cent of the 16th Central Committee members hold college degrees, by far the highest education level ever reached in that body since 1949. Moreover, all the nine members of the Politburo Standing Committee (PBSC) elected at the first session of the 16th Congress were graduates from top universities in mainland China, with four of them from Qinghua (Hu Jintao, Wu Bangguo, Huang Ju and Wu Guanzheng). The general trend towards higher education backgrounds in China's top leadership is shown in Figure 2. There the two curves depicting the percentage of members in the Politburo and the PBSC holding a college degree rise sharply from the 12th Congress to the 16th Congress. The 0 to 100 per cent rise on the PBSC curve is particularly telling. The trend is also shown in the figures in Table 1.

The technocrats are products of an established system and not its creators or builders.[11] Their experience typically concentrates on a non-

10. For example, all the seven members of the 15th PBSC hold college degrees, so do all the nine members of the 16th PBSC. In contrast, in the 14th PBSC it was five out of seven members (71%), in the 13th PBSC it was three out of five (or 60%) and in the 12th PBSC it was one out of 6 (or 17%). For the educational background of the general secretaries since the position was restored in 1982, Hu Yaobang was a primary school graduate and Zhao Ziyang a junior high school graduate, while Jiang Zemin holds a degree from Shanghai's Jiaotong University and Hu Jintao holds a Qinghua University degree.

11. David Bachman, "The limits on leadership in China," *Asian Survey*, Vol. 32, No. 11 (November 1992), p. 1050.

Table 1: **Percentage of College Degree Holders and Average Age in Politburo and PBSC, 1982–2002**

	12th Congress	13th Congress	14th Congress	15th Congress	16th Congress
Percentage of college degree holders (%)					
Politburo	21.42	55.55	86.36	91.66	100
PBSC	0	60.00	85.71	100	100
Age					
Politburo	71.03	64.05	62.22	62.62	60.68
PBSC	73.83	63.60	63.57	65.28	62.00

military functional area. Most of them are engineers by training. This is identical with the background of the leaders of "mature socialism" in the Soviet Union and Eastern Europe in the 1970s and 1980s.[12] The technocrats are intrinsically interested in preserving the status quo and pursuing stability.[13] In this sense, whether it was Hu or any other technocrat who succeeded Jiang is not really important, for the technocratic leaders have common inclinations. They have a realistic understanding of the popular desire for material betterment, they loathe destruction in the name of revolution and the perennial uncertainties brought about by radical reform, they want to absorb Western technology and capital, but they abhor pluralistic ideas and democracy. The post-Deng era has been characterized by a technocratic rule, and stability has been enshrined as the paramount goal.[14] Power struggle takes a purely factional form, in which political leaders clash not over development strategy but over personal power and prestige.[15] Very much like Brezhnev and the "little Brezhnevs" in Eastern Europe, Jiang and Hu are more *primus inter pares* than paramount leader like Mao or Deng, and they lacked the vision of a Mao or Deng.[16] In all, a technical background, the pursuit of stability, a non-ideological mentality, the collective nature of the leadership and a lack of vision are common features of technocratic

12. Frederick C. Teiwes, "The problematic quest for stability: reflections on succession, institutionalization, governability, and legitimacy in post-Deng China," in Hung-mao Tien and Yun-han Chu (eds.), *China under Jiang Zemin* (Boulder, CO: Lynne Rienner, 2000), p. 83.

13. *Ibid.* pp. 71–89.

14. For a similar opinion, see Hong Yung Lee, *From Revolutionary Cadres to Party Bureaucrats in Socialist China* (Berkeley: University of California Press, 1991).

15. In the classical factionalism model, political actors clash over personal interests and turfs, not over different policy preferences. See Andrew Nathan, "A factionalism model for CCP politics," *The China Quarterly*, No. 53 (March 1973), pp. 34–66; for a critical discussion of factional models, see Dittmer and Wu, "The modernization of factionalism in Chinese politics," pp. 467–494.

16. See David Bachman, "Emerging patterns of political conflict in post-Deng China," in Tien and Chu, *China under Jiang Zemin*, p. 69.

rule in China and in the former Soviet Union and Eastern Europe.[17] But here the similarities end.

Although both preoccupied with stability, the Chinese technocrats and the Soviet and East European technocrats pursued this paramount goal quite differently. Because the planned economy was not completely discredited in the former Soviet Union and Eastern Europe when the technocrats took over, their reforms were either in the "perfecting" or "limited market socialism" version.[18] In this context, stability was pursued with static equilibrium under the technocratic rule. This meant secured political career for cadres and job security for managers. The elevation of the education level of the new leaders thus coexisted with personnel petrifaction which gradually became the hallmark of the Soviet and East European top leaderships. This was not the case in China. The bold breakthroughs from the Maoist past were so thorough, primarily because the phase of artificial revolution was extended much longer in China than in "mature socialist" countries in Europe, that when the technocrats took power, they were facing a different environment.[19] Their mission was not to achieve stability in plan, under static equilibrium, but to achieve stability in market, under dynamic equilibrium. The Chinese economy had been growing at such a high speed, the market had been integrated so deeply into the system and the regime had so successfully linked its restored legitimacy to economic performance, that Chinese technocrats could only achieve stability by satisfying the popular expectations of rapid economic growth. Institutional changes and continued reform thus became inevitable if stability *in performance* was to be guaranteed. The Dengist reform had shown to the technocrats that the surest way of securing high growth was by continued marketization and opening up. Thus the Jiang regime sustained the economic reform track for the sake of growth and stability. At the same time, the technocrats were highly conservative regarding political reform, for that was considered destabilizing. Thus under Jiang, one finds static stability in politics and dynamic stability in economics. In order to keep economic dynamism and to adjust swiftly to ever-changing economic situations, the top leadership found it imperative to rejuvenate itself periodically. This

17. The possibility of China moving into a Brezhnevian era is discussed in Constance Squires Meaney, "Is the Soviet present China's future," *World Politics*, Vol. 39, No. 2 (January 1987), pp. 203–230; and in Weng Jieming *et al.* (eds.), *Yu zongshuji tanxin* (*To have an Intimate Talk with the General Secretary*) (Beijing: Zhongguo shehuikexue chubanshe, 1996), ch.2. Both rejected this possibility for it implies stagnation to which mainland is the opposite. However, what is stressed here is not inherent stagnation in China's emergent bureaucratic rule, but its commitment to stability, which was a core feature of the Brezhnevian rule in the Soviet Union. For a view supporting the Brezhnev–Jiang comparison, see Teiwes, "The problematic quest for stability," pp. 71–89.

18. A useful typology of various levels of economic reform in state socialist countries is offered by Janos Kornai. See Janos Kornai, *The Socialist System: The Political Economy of Communism* (Princeton: Princeton University Press, 1992), chs.17, 21; Kornai, *Highways and Byways: Studies on Reform and Post-Communist Transition* (Cambridge, MA: The MIT Press, 1995), pp. 35–56.

19. See Lowell Dittmer, *China's Continuous Revolution: The Post-Liberation Epoch, 1949–1981* (Berkeley: University of California Press, 1987).

leads to the second main feature of Jiang's rule: generational replacement.

Retiring at 70 or 68: Generational Replacement

CCP politics today is obviously not a replica of the Soviet and East European experience 20 years ago, even though they trod similar evolutionary paths. One uniquely Chinese feature in its post-Mao political development is the introduction of the cadre retirement system and a selective application of that system to the top echelon leaders in the Party. This translates to the principle of "generational replacement." It is well known that Deng launched a reform of the leadership system of the party-state (*dang he guojia lingdao zhidu de gaige*) in 1980.[20] His main purpose then was to introduce younger and more professional cadres into the system to invigorate it and to consolidate the reform line.[21] At the end of the 1970s and the beginning of the 1980s, Deng was caught in a dilemma. On the one hand, he needed to rehabilitate old cadres purged during the Cultural Revolution and mobilize them to fight the left forces in the Party.[22] On the other hand, the coming back of the old cadres put a heavy burden on reform, in terms of both their low educational background and their failing health.[23] Thus not long after Deng succeeded in rehabilitating his old comrades, he began busily retiring them and putting in his younger protégés. Age was the main rationale. Since Deng held many top positions in the Party and the state, and wielded undisputable informal authority, he could afford to retire from most of his formal posts in exchange for parallel retirements by his old guard peers. At the same time, Deng was aggressive in promoting like-minded second echelon cadres to the leadership core. Hu Yaobang and Zhao Ziyang were brought to the top positions in this context. In essence, generational change in leadership positions in post-Mao China was initiated by reformers to get rid of senior rivals and to consolidate the reform line.

A system of cadre retirement gradually took shape in the 1980s.[24] Age

20. Chien-wen Kou, "Zhonggong ganbu nianqinghua yu zhengzhi jicheng" ("The 'juvenation' of cadres in the CCP and political succession"), in *Ershiyi shiji Zhongguo, Vol. II: Quanqiuhua yu Zhongguo zhi fazhan (21st Century China, Vol. II: Globalization and China's Development)* (Taipei: Institute of International Relations, 2002), p. 123.

21. See Deng Xiaoping, "Dang he guojia lingdao zhidu de gaige" ("Reform of the leadership system of the Party and the state"), in *Deng Xiaoping wenxuan, 1975–1982 (Selected Works of Deng Xiaoping, 1975–1982)* (Beijing: Renmin chubanshe, 1983), pp. 280–302.

22. Deng's major lieutenant in rehabilitating the old cadres was Hu Yaobang, who headed the organization department of the CCP in 1977. Ruan Ming, *Deng Xiaoping diguo (Deng Xiaoping Empire)* (Taipei: Shibao wenhua, 1993), p. 37.

23. Chien-wen Kou, "Quanli zhuanyi yu 'tidui jieban' jizhi de fazhan" ("Power transfer and the development of the 'echelon shift' mechanism"), in Arthur Shufan Ding (ed.), *Hu Jintao shidai de tiaozhan (The Challenges in Hu Jintao's Era)* (Taipei: Xinxinwen, 2002), p. 55.

24. The age limit on the provincial and ministerial cadres is 60. For department heads in the ministries and in the provincial governments, as well as for cadres on the region level, the age limit is 55. For county leaders, it is 50. See Chien-wen Kou, "The 'juvenation' of cadres," p. 125.

and number of terms were the main criteria.[25] However, it was not directly applied to the very top Party leadership until the 15th Congress in 1997,[26] when Jiang's main rival Qiao Shi was retired for passing the cardinal age line of 70.[27] At that time, ideological or policy strife was no longer a reason to invoke the generation principle but instead sheer power struggle was at the base of the personnel reshuffle. This time at the 16th Congress, the retirement of the whole PBSC with the only exception of Hu Jintao at 59 was justified by the same generation replacement principle; although Li Ruihuan was retired at 68, thus pushing down the retirement age for the top leaders. The nine members of the new PBSC averaged 62 in age. The Politburo and the Central Committee followed the same principle, retiring a third and a half of their members respectively, bringing down their average age. Figure 3 and Table 1 show the general trend towards lower average age in the Politburo and in the PBSC from the 12th to the 16th Congress. Remarkable success has been achieved in lowering the average age of the Politburo and PBSC mem-

Figure 3: **Average Age of Members**

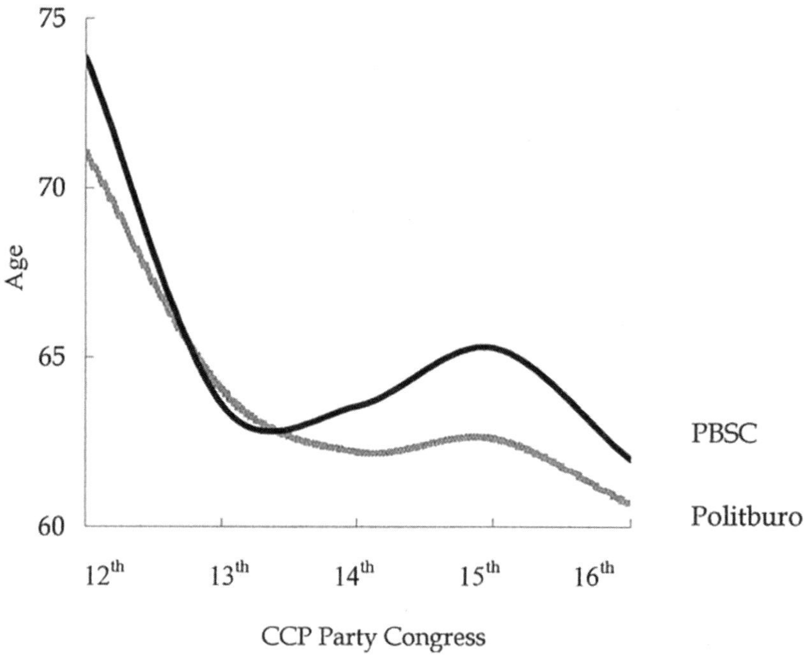

CCP Party Congress

25. For example, the 1982 constitution sets a two-term limit on all the top government positions, including state president and premier.

26. A tacit agreement was reached at a Politburo meeting in 1997 that set 70 as the age limit for all top leaders in the Party and government, including PBSC members, premier and vice-premiers. See Cheng Li, "Shiliu jie zhongweihui renshi goucheng ji qi quanli junheng" ("The composition of the 16th Central Committee and its balance of power"), in Ding, *The Challenges in Hu Jintao's Era*, p. 18.

27. Jiang himself was 71 years old at the time, but retained position in the 15th PBSC.

bers. The same trend can be found in the pre-Congress reshuffle of 31 provincial governors and the same number of Party secretaries.[28] In fact, the age limit imposed on provincial cadres has been enforced more rigidly than the age limit at the central level.[29]

From the early 1980s onwards generational replacement has become the norm in China's politics, from top to bottom. The application of this principle to the top leadership was secured at the 15th and the 16th Congresses during Jiang's reign. This practice breathes fresh air into all levels of leadership, brings young and professional cadres into the system, and sustains economic reform and growth. It also distinguishes the PRC's post-totalitarian, technocratic politics from the Soviet and East European precedents wherein top leaders held life-long tenures. This difference goes a long way towards making the Chinese system more dynamic and more adaptive to changes in the environment (the only other communist regime that can elect a new leadership at regular intervals is in Vietnam).[30] What Deng had in mind as a strategy to retire the opponents to his policies has turned into a built-in safeguard against institutional ageing and inertia.

Mentor Politics: Re-emergence of Gerontocracy?

Generational replacement as a principle of personnel reshuffling is a powerful mechanism in preventing the emergence of gerontocracy. However, a casual look at the PRC's post-Mao politics reveals rampant gerontocracy, particularly in the 1980s. Was it a leftover from past decades? Or was it based on structural forces unleashed by Deng's reform strategy? As both Hu Yaobang and Zhao Ziyang were removed by octogenarians supposedly retired from official positions, one has to look into the informal side of China's politics.[31] A cogent question at this point is whether the 16th Congress has re-created a power structure similar to the one existing in the 1980s that led to rampant gerontocracy. A question mark is put at the end of the sub-title above, however, for whether this phenomenon will appear remains to be seen. Suffice it to say that a gerontocracy-prone structure has been put in place at the 16th Congress, with the implementation of the generational replacement principle and with Jiang still controlling the commanding heights of power.

Deng's strategy of retiring old cadres while promoting his successors

---

28. See Suisheng Zhao's article in this volume.
29. See Chien-wen Kou, "The 'juvenation' of cadres," p. 155.
30. The Vietnamese experience is discussed towards the end of the article.
31. For the concept of informal politics and its significance, see Haruhiro Fukui, "Introduction: on the significance of informal politics," in Lowell Dittmer, Haruhiro Fukui and Peter N.S. Lee (eds.), *Informal Politics in East Asia* (Cambridge: Cambridge University Press, 2000). For an early exploration into China's informal politics, see Lowell Dittmer, "Bases of power in Chinese politics: a theory and an analysis of the fall of the 'gang of four'," *World Politics*, Vol. 31, No. 1 (October 1978), pp. 26–60. For an informal-politics approach to the leadership succession in China, see Peter Nan-shong Lee, "The informal politics of leadership succession in post-Mao China," in Dittmer, Fukui and Lee, *Informal Politics in East Asia*.

was to ensure his reform line would be faithfully implemented. With Chen Yun and all of his major rivals retired and with he himself still chairing the powerful Central Military Commission (CMC), Deng became the only octogenarian who could exercise direct control over the third-generation leaders. This arrangement had its defects, however. As Deng still wielded ultimate control from behind the scenes while his successors acted as the formal leaders of the Party, friction inevitably developed between the mentor and the front-line leaders. This basic power structure easily led to mutual distrust. Major policy differences between the two could and did result in the patriarch's removal of his successors, thus revealing the real power structure. The fate of Hu Yaobang in 1987 and Zhao Ziyang in 1989 vividly exposed the pecking order in the Party. Furthermore, when Deng managed to control the power play from behind the scenes, other octogenarians followed suit, and intervened on behalf of their protégés, or sometimes intervened at the request of Deng who decided to change his successors. The conflicts between front-line leaders and those between the old guards got entangled. The 1980s thus witnessed a group of octogenarian advisors exerting tremendous influence over the front-line leaders whom they had promoted and whom at critical moments they could remove.[32] The octogenarians held real power but no titles, while their protégés had official responsibilities but no real power. Informal politics proved more powerful than formal politics.

The fact that in the 1990s gerontocracy subsided had more to do with contingencies than with institutionalization of CCP politics. In the early 1990s, Deng remained the ultimate ruler of the Party. He single-handedly reversed the retrenchment policy adopted in the autumn of 1988 (*zhili zhengdun*) and re-launched reform in the famous "southern tour" (*nanxun*) of 1992. He brought Zhu Rongji to Beijing and assigned him the job of managing the economy.[33] He inserted Hu Jintao into the 14th PBSC and predesignated him Jiang's successor.[34] He was displeased with Li Peng and Jiang for their conservatism on economic reform and demanded those standing in the way to step down, thus disciplining the post-Tiananmen leadership and bringing them to his line.[35] However, Deng became so weak after the southern tour that he could no longer intervene into Party and state affairs. In general, the old revolutionary guards rapidly faded away in the 1990s and Deng himself died in 1997. One thus sees consolidation of Jiang's power as those senior politicians

32. These octogenarians include Deng Xiaoping (born in 1904), Chen Yun (born 1905), Yang Shangkun (born 1907), Li Xiannian (born 1909), Wang Zheng (born 1908), Bo Yibo (born 1908), Song Renqiong (born 1909), Peng Zhen (born 1902) and Deng Yingchao (born 1904), in descending order of influence.

33. Zhu was promoted to the PBSC at the 14th Congress. He ranked fifth behind Jiang Zemin, Le Peng, Qiao Shi and Li Ruihuan.

34. When Hu Jitao joined the 14th PBSC, he was only 49, the youngest member in a group with an average age of 64. He was promoted from the Central Committee directly to the Standing Committee of the Politburo without first serving as a non-PBSC member of the Politburo.

35. For Deng's dissatisfaction with Jiang, see Lowell Dittmer, "Sizing up China's new leadership," in Tien and Chu, *China under Jiang Zemin*, p. 41.

who could intervene gradually became physically unable to. The decline of gerontocracy in the 1990s was the result of the ticking of biological clocks in the old guards. It was not the result of institutionalization. One cannot but wonder what would happen if another generation of old guards emerges and dominates the front-line leaders.

Very much as the second-generation leaders dominated the third generation, the third generation now overwhelmed the fourth. The retiring PBSC, most in their early and mid-70s, was a group of experienced leaders who presided over a golden decade of China's development, even compared with the reform decade of the 1980s. Sustained high growth and low prices were coupled with political stability. Presumably, the third generation of China's communist leaders deserves to be praised and honoured. By comparison most of their successors, the fourth generation leaders, were faceless technocrats.[36] They were brought to the fore mainly because of the generation replacement principle. As their patrons are only in their early and mid-70s and have all their experience to teach the new leaders, it is likely that these patrons will continue wielding influence from behind the scenes, just like the octogenarians did in the 1980s. This could lead to inherent tension between the old guards and the new front-line leaders.

Specifically, both the old guards (the third generation) and the front-line leaders (the fourth generation) have a *primus inter pares*, or a "core" (*hexin*). The greatest source of friction exists between the old-guard core, now the mentor, and the front-line core, for they naturally compete for the ultimate decision-making power. This is particularly the case when the mentor did not relinquish all formal positions in the party-state and still keeps control of some "commanding heights," such as the CMC. This means the mentor intends to wield ultimate power and deny full authority to his successor. This was the case between Deng and Hu Yaobang, between Deng and Zhao Ziyang, and is the case between Jiang and Hu Jintao. Jiang kept the position of chairman of the CMC at the 16th Congress, a clear sign that he did not intend to relinquish all his powers to Hu Jintao. This is the Dengist model, as Deng for a long time kept control over the powerful CMC while giving up all the other positions in the Party and the government.[37] If Jiang holds the CMC chairmanship for long, his intention to follow Deng in wielding ultimate power from behind the scenes (to be *taishanghuang*) would be even clearer. Jiang has better reason to be dissatisfied with Hu Jintao than Deng had with Hu Yaobang or Zhao Ziyang, for Hu Jintao was imposed by Deng as Jiang's

36. See Richard Baum, "Systemic stresses and political choices: the road ahead," in this issue.

37. This tradition actually dated back to Mao Zedong's strict control over the military through presiding over the CMC from the Zunyi Conference of 1935 to his death in 1976. Hua Guofeng took this position until he was deprived of power by Deng in 1981. Deng presided over the CMC from 1981 to 1989, when he thought it was important for Jiang to hold that position to build his prestige. Jiang then chaired the CMC until now. For the "real" leader to command the military while relinquishing all the other formal (and higher) positions in the Party and in the government says a lot about the lack of institutionalization of the Chinese communist regime, for everyone knows the true leader is the one who commands the guns.

successor, while both Hu Yaobang and Zhao Ziyang were handpicked by Deng himself. The fact that Deng had much greater authority and informal power in the Party than Jiang makes it easier for Hu to challenge Jiang, and for the two to fight. Jiang's forceful retirement of all the old guards in the name of generational replacement except himself, and his stuffing the new PBSC with members from his "Shanghai gang" puts him in a position of advantage to dominate Hu.[38] Natural competition for ultimate power by the two cores, Jiang's continued control over the CMC, Jiang's forced acceptance of Hu as his successor, the relatively weak position of Jiang in the Party and the stuffing of the "Shanghai gang" into the PBSC to monitor Hu all contribute to probable frictions between Jiang and Hu in the future. This situation reminds one of the similar situation in which Deng still held the ultimate power and controlled the CMC after the 13th Congress in 1987, while General Secretary Zhao Ziyang was the nominal leader of the Party. The utterance by Zhao on 16 May 1989 in his conversation with Mikhail Gorbachev on the ultimate power still wielded by Deng since his formal retirement at the 13th Congress was a powerful testimony of the real power distribution in the Party, and of Zhao's titular leadership. That revelation was later used to accuse Zhao of maliciously leaking Party secrets to the outside world and intentionally splitting the Party. [39] One does not know at this stage whether there was agreement at the 16th Congress to give Jiang the same power that the 13th Congress gave Deng 15 years ago, but tension will definitely build in the Jiang–Hu relationship as the Deng–Zhao interaction in 1989 clearly demonstrates. This is the problem of "pre-mortem succession" in a communist regime.[40]

A second source of friction is between the front-line leaders, and that may escalate to entangle the mentor, or entangle several old guards. For one example, the competition between Hu Yaobang and Zhao Ziyang ended in Deng's siding with Zhao and the removal of Hu in 1987. For a second example, the conflict between Zhao Ziyang and Li Peng involved Deng and other old guards, and resulted in Zhao's downfall in 1989. The 16th PBSC is composed of general secretary Hu Jintao and eight other members, most of whom are close allies of Jiang. Naturally Jiang can monitor the working of the PBSC through his protégés therein, particularly through Zeng Qinghong, his most trusted lieutenant.[41] The fact that Hu is the second youngest among the nine members of the PBSC, older

38. The "Shanghai gang" in the PBSC includes Zeng Qinghong, Wu Bangguo and Huang Ju. In the Politburo at large it further includes Zeng Peiyan and Chen Liangyu. It also includes ten 16th Central Committee members, seven alternate members and three members of the Central Commission for Discipline Inspection. See Cheng Li, "The composition of the 16th Central Committee and its balance of power," pp. 34–35.

39. See Zhang Liang, *Zhongguo liusi zhenxiang* (*June Fourth: The True Story*) (Hong Kong: Mingjing, 2001), p. 425.

40. For a discussion of premortem and postmortem succession in a communist regime, see Dittmer, "Patterns of elite strife and succession," p. 427.

41. For a discussion of the respective power bases of Hu Jintao and Zeng Qinghong, and their possible mode of interaction, see Cheng Li, "The composition of the 16th Central Committee and its balance of power," pp. 21–38.

only than Li Changchun by one year, adds to the difficulty with which Hu can build his authority over his colleagues, as seniority is important in deciding authority in any Chinese group. It also adds to the likelihood that other PBSC members will challenge Hu. When conflict arises in the PBSC between Hu and his colleagues (particularly Zeng), it is hard to imagine that Jiang will not intervene. Other old guards may also get involved through their protégés in the PBSC, such as Zhu Rongji intervening on behalf of Wen Jiabao, or Li Peng intervening for Luo Gan. Such a scenario would be a replay of the entanglement of old guards in the conflict between the front-line leaders in the 1980s.[42]

Conclusion

The Chinese communist regime has evolved into the technocratic stability stage, quite like its Soviet and East European predecessors. In the foreseeable future, China's rulers will be pragmatic technocrats who treasure stability more than anything else. The new leaders emerging from the 16th Party Congress vividly demonstrate the technocratic nature of the regime. As far as this broad profile is concerned, China repeats the Soviet and East European experience in the past. However, the Chinese technocrats pursue stability under dynamic equilibrium, unlike their erstwhile comrades in "mature socialist" countries in Europe. The systemic requirement of constant adaptation made petrifaction in top leadership impossible, hence the principle of generational replacement which is a powerful mechanism of institutional rejuvenation. All leaders are forced to retire after reaching the age limits set for different levels in the hierarchy of the party-state. Young and professional cadres are brought into the system through this mechanism, and old guards are retired. The 16th Congress forcefully demonstrates this principle by retiring all members from the 15th PBSC except the 59-year-old Hu Jintao who succeeded Jiang as general secretary of the CCP. This mechanism brings greater dynamism into the Chinese system, and makes it more adaptable to the changing environment.

However, technocratic rule and generational replacement do not capture the full picture of Chinese politics at the 16th Congress. Quite like in the 1980s, the core of the old guards, the mentor, did not retire. Jiang followed Deng's practice in retaining control over the CMC and wields ultimate power from behind the scenes, as mentor of the new leadership. Mentor politics thus became the third main feature of the 16th Congress. One can then identify two possible sources of friction in the leadership: between the mentor and the front-line core, and between the front-line leaders themselves that may entangle the mentor and other old guards. The events in the 1980s of inter-generational power struggle may repeat themselves in the 2000s. By selectively retiring old cadres while saving himself the ultimate power, Jiang is creating a situation that led to

42. In the 1980s, the front-line leaders were named by the octogenarians as their price for retirement. The front-liners were thus beholden to their patrons, such as Yao Yilin to Chen Yun, and Li Peng to Chen Yun and Deng Yingchao. See Dittmer, "Patterns of elite strife and succession," p. 410.

rampant gerontocracy in the 1980s. One thus wonders whether mentor politics will lead to the re-emergence of gerontocracy in China's post-16th Congress politics.

Among the three phenomena, technocratic rule injects a strong dose of stability into the system. The addition of compulsory retirement adds dynamism into it, but selective application of that principle breeds mentor politics and the possibility of gerontocracy. In sum, the Chinese regime has done a great deal to rationalize itself through technocratization and rejuvenation. However, the impossibility of compelling the top leader to succumb to forced retirement opened the back door and may re-invite gerontocracy into the system. It is certainly the case that compelled retirement of top political leaders based on age is rare in the world, and rigid enforcement of such a rule is bound to beget fraud. How to ensure mobility in the top echelon leadership while eschew age-based compulsory retirement is an all-important question that has to be answered by a communist regime.

Here the Vietnamese case is of considerable value. Ever since the death of Ho Chi Minh, the Vietnamese Communist Party has established a firm tradition of collective leadership. From 1980 to the present time, there have been four major leadership changes. The revolutionary "troika" (president–premier–general secretary) of Trung Chinh (1981–86), Pham Van Dong (1955–86) and Le Duan (1960–86) was replaced by Vo Chi Cong (1987–92), Pham Hung (1987–88)/Do Muoi (1988–92) and Nguyen Van Linh (1986–92) at the Sixth Congress in December 1986. There was a turn to *doi moi* (Vietnamese-style "perestroika cum glasnost") as witnessed by the rise of Linh, a staunch reformer based in the south.[43] Five years later, as the Gorbachev line had proved a disaster for the Soviet Union, Vietnam steered back to political authoritarianism, but maintained its economic reform.[44] Reflecting this changed orientation, a new troika was put in place at the Seventh Congress that included President Le Duc Anh (1992–97), Premier Vo Van Kiet (1992–97) and General Secretary Du Muoi (1992–97). A delicate balance was maintained with the general secretary as an economic bureaucrat standing between a commissar-turned-president and a reform-minded premier.[45] At the Tenth National Assembly and the Eighth Congress of the Vietnamese Communist Party in 1997, one saw the emergence of yet another troika that basically kept the balance of 1992. Now President Tran Duc Luong

43. For an analysis of the Sixth Congress of the VCP and the second rise of Nguyen Van Linh, see Lewis M. Stern, *Conflict and Transition in the Vietnamese Economic Reform Program* (Bankok: ISIS, 1988), pp. 66–72.

44. For the mimicking of the Soviet line by the Vietnamese leadership and the ultimate abandonment of the Gorbachev-style reform, see Yu-Shan Wu, *Gongchan shijie de bianqian: si ge gongchan zhengquan de bijiao* (*Communist World in Flux: A Comparison of Four Communist Regimes*) (Taipei: Tung-ta, 1995), ch. 5; and Yu-Shan Wu and Tsai-Wei Sun, "Four faces of Vietnamese communism: small countries' institutional choice under hegemony," *Communist and Post-Communist Studies*, Vol. 31, No. 4 (December 1998), pp. 381–399.

45. See Liang Jinwen, "Yuenan xin 'santoumache' fenxi" ("An analysis of Vietnam's new 'troika'"), *Dongnanya jikan* (*Southeast Asia Quarterly*), Vol. 3, No. 3 (July 1998), p. 22.

(97–present) became the moderate, standing between a commissar-turned-general secretary Le Kha Phieu (1997–2001) and Vo Van Kiet's successor, the reform-minded Phan Van Khai (97–present). The latest change in the troika involves the replacement of Le Kha Phieu by Nong Duc Manh (2001–present) at the Ninth Congress, which signified a further turn to reform as the new general secretary is a moderate bureaucrat.[46] The Vietnamese case shows the ability of the communist regime there to adhere to the principle of collective leadership (there has not been a paramount leader since the death of Ho Chih Minh), to change top leaders regularly following the schedule of the party congress and the National Assembly, to invigorate the leadership by bringing in younger but experienced cadres, to adapt to the ever-changing environment that the party-state faced, and to keep a delicate balance between the north and the south, and among the conservative, moderate and reform forces in the party-state. The Vietnamese relied mainly on term limit, not on age limit. Their institutional mechanism to invigorate periodically the leading organs of the party-state has proved quite effective in dealing with the many problems the country faces. Most importantly, one does not see serious conflict between formal and informal politics in Vietnam, and gerontocracy is not a serious threat.

Whether China would evolve towards the Vietnamese system remains to be seen. As far as the impact of the 16th Congress is concerned, mentor politics continues to undermine formal rules governing power transfer. Undoubtedly as far as political institutionalization is concerned, China is lagging behind Vietnam.[47] The inherent contradictions in the post-16th Congress system would have to be tackled by mentor Jiang, new core

46. At the Eleventh National Assembly held in July 2002, the incumbent President Tran Duc Luong and Premier Phan Van Khai stayed on.

47. If one looks at the change of guards from early 1980s on, one finds all transfers of power in Vietnam conducted in an orderly fashion, following the rules and procedures of collective leadership, even though great policy shifts and personnel reshuffles occurred. The revolutionary old guard Le Duan was replaced by the *doi moi* reformer Nguyen Van Linh in 1986, who was then replaced by a moderate economic bureaucrat Du Muoi five years later. Muoi's replacement by Le Kha Phieu from the military in 1997 was another line change, and so was Phieu's replacement by the moderate Nong Duc Manh. In all these four replacements a lot of factional activities were involved, and the predecessors were voted out of power. Severe line conflict did not hamper the working of the normal procedures. In stark contrast, the CCP's power transfers since the early 1980s were marred by rule bending, irregular or even illegal decision-making, manipulation of procedures and selective application of retirement principles, and gerontocracy. The ousting of Hua Guofeng was a result of power struggle. Both Hu Yaobang and Zhao Ziyang were replaced under highly irregular and extraordinary circumstances, as octogenarians supposedly retired were brought in to vote the general secretary out. Deng Xiaoping was wielding ultimate power during the whole process without holding responsible formal positions. He also engineered the installation and removal of three successors in whatever way he deemed expedient. The 15th Congress was the first time when the general secretary elected in the previous congress was not purged, even though Jiang's main rival Qiao Shi was edged out through selective application of age limit on top leaders. Then at the 16th Congress Jiang took exactly the same strategy as Deng by announcing a formal but not real retirement which in every likelihood would make him the "emperor behind the scenes" (*taishanghuang*). The comparison between political successions in the two Asian communist regimes shows Vietnam is far ahead of China in political institutionalization. For a discussion of the discrepancy between de facto leadership and official status in Chinese high-level politics in the 1980s, see Dittmer, "Patterns of elite strife and succession," pp. 407–410.

Hu, and by all the members of the third and fourth generation leaders. How they solve these potential contradictions will have an enormous impact on the performance of the Chinese communist regime in the next ten years.

The Changing of the Guard: China's New Military Leadership*

David Shambaugh

ABSTRACT In 2003–2004 the "high command" of the People's Liberation Army (PLA) experienced a wholesale turnover of leading personnel. The new cohort of officers will command the military for the next decade. They are generally well-educated (although not particularly well-travelled), possess substantial command experience and are earnest students of modern warfare. They are committed to the comprehensive modernization of the military, with an emphasis on high-technology programmes. In terms of civil–military relations, the new PLA leadership can be expected to stay out of politics and concentrate, personally and institutionally, on modernizing the forces.

The 16th Congress of the Chinese Communist Party (CCP) ushered in a new "high command" in the People's Liberation Army (PLA), who will guide the PLA and its ongoing modernization for much of the next decade. This article identifies this new military leadership, provides data on their backgrounds and priorities, and offers some concluding observations about the implications for future civil–military relations in China.

The sweeping turnover of personnel occurred before, at and after the 16th Congress. This included retiring six and adding three new members of the CCP's Central Military Commission (CMC); replacing the directors of the four general departments (General Staff, Logistics, Political and Armaments) as well as many of deputy directors in these departments; and appointing new commandants of the Academy of Military Sciences (AMS) and National Defence University (NDU). Over the year prior to the Congress, a wholesale rotation of commanders, deputy commanders and political commissars of China's seven military regions also took place. While Jiang Zemin remained as chairman of the CMC at the Congress and Hu Jintao stayed on as vice-chair, there was much more change than continuity in the military leadership as a result of the Congress. All other CMC members over 70 retired.

Taken together, these personnel changes constitute the most thorough shake-up and turnover of leading PLA officers ever. Even in the aftermath of the purges of the Yang brothers (1992) or the Lin Biao clique (1971), such an extensive change did not occur. The fact that a thorough vetting could take place without a purge or crisis is testimony to how regularized and professional personnel procedures have become in the PLA. Unlike in the Party, where the top posts were filled as a result of

* I am very grateful to Chong-pin Lin, Chu Yun-han, John Corbett, James Mulvenon and Ramon Myers for thoughtful comments on an earlier draft. An expanded version of this article appears in Stephen J. Flanagan and Michael Marti (eds.), *China in Transition and the People's Liberation Army* (Washington, DC: National Defense University Press, 2003).

considerable nepotism and after lengthy political jockeying, high-level changes in the military were the result of standardized procedures, meritocratic criteria, a well-defined candidate pool and relative transparency. Although those who would occupy the top jobs were not publicly known until they were appointed, they came from a clearly defined pool of candidates. That is, the new CMC vice-chairmen were chosen from the previous members under the age of 70, the new CMC members were drawn from the ranks of military region commanders (in two cases) and existing deputy directors of the general departments, and some interesting patterns of promotion occurred at the military region level. There were no dark horses or "helicopters" propelled from obscurity to the top ranks. More importantly, as described below, the prior career paths of the new military leadership reveal a number of common features that illustrate how regularized and institutionalized upward mobility in the armed forces has become. Unlike the Party, where one can reach the top through a variety of paths (although provincial service seems to be increasingly *de rigueur*), promotion in the military is increasingly defined, predictable and professional. This is not to say that personal ties and loyalties no longer operate at the top of the PLA – they do, as is evidenced by those promoted officers (Guo Boxiong, Liang Guanglie and Liao Xilong) with ties to retiring Generals Zhang Wannian and Fu Quanyou. But it should not be assumed that these officers were promoted purely because of their career ties to the retiring elders; rather, their career paths intersected with Generals Zhang and Fu, although they had established their own credentials for promotion.

The military leadership in China is essentially comprised of three levels: the CMC and associated organs; the four general departments; and the military region commands. The following section compares the backgrounds of each of the members of the CMC as a means to identify a typology of the new PLA high command. Some interesting patterns emerge which confirm the increasingly professional nature of the military leadership. Unfortunately, there is not yet enough biographical data available on the new crop of general department deputy directors or military region commanders to provide a sufficient profile of the new PLA leadership at these levels – although it is possible to track the channels of promotion.

The New Central Military Commission

The new CMC is somewhat smaller than the outgoing one, with only eight total members (see Table 1). None of the CMC members (other than Hu Jintao) attained a position on the Politburo Standing Committee (PBSC), although Guo Boxiong and Cao Gangchuan became members of the Politburo, replacing Zhang Wannian and Chi Haotian respectively. The failure to appoint a military man to the PBSC is not, in fact, unusual – in fact, over the past 20 years only one uniformed officer (Liu Huaqing) has been elected to the PBSC – nor does it really reveal any lack of PLA "influence" in high Party councils. In addition, interestingly, General Xu

Table 1: **The Central Military Commission**

Member	Age	Previous position	New positions
Jiang Zemin	76	CCP general secretary; PRC president; CMC chairman	CMC chairman
Hu Jintao	59	PBSC member; PRC vice-president; CMC vice-chairman	CCP general secretary; (presumed) president elect; CMC vice-chairman
General Guo Boxiong	60	CMC member	CMC vice-chairman; member of Politburo
General Cao Gangchuan	67	CMC member; director, GAD	CMC vice-chairman; member of Politburo
General Xu Caihou	59	CMC member; executive deputy director, GPD; secretary, PLA Discipline Inspection Commission	CMC member; member of CCP Secretariat
General Liang Guanglie	62	Commander, Nanjing Military Region	CMC member; chief of general staff
General Liao Xilong	62	Commander, Chengdu Military Region	CMC member; director of General Logistics Department
General Li Jinai	60	Political commissar, GAD	CMC member; director, GAD

Caihou was appointed to the Central Committee Secretariat, although he is not a CMC vice-chair; this puts him in a key position of interface between the civilian and military leadership.

More broadly, it is interesting to note that PLA representation on the CCP Central Committee has fallen nearly to its all-time low. At the Eighth Congress in 1956 it was 35 per cent, rose to 45 per cent at the Ninth Congress in 1969, fell to 26 per cent at the Tenth Congress in 1973, rose again to 30 per cent at the 11th Congress in 1977, fell to 22 per cent at the 12th Congress in 1982, fell further to an all-time low of 19 per cent at the 13th Congress in 1987, rose again (in the aftermath of Tiananmen) to 26 per cent at the 14th Congress in 1992, fell to 23 per cent at the 15th Congress in 1997, and fell further to 21 per cent of total Central Committee members (full and alternate combined) at the 16th Congress (see Figure 1).

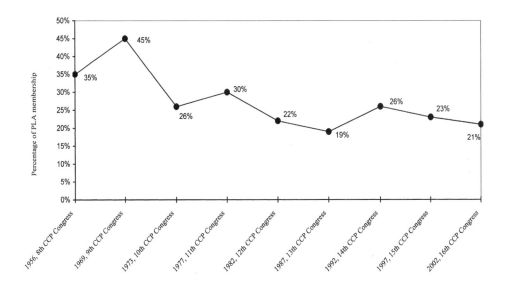

Figure 1: **Percentage of PLA Membership on CCP Central Committee**

Unless they were a new CMC member (when they can remain until 70), most officers near the age of 65 were not re-elected to the Central Committee. Examples include Deputy Chief of General Staff Kui Fulin, Beijing military region Political Commissar Du Tiehuan, Second Artillery Commander Yang Guoliang, and NDU Commandant Xing Shizhong. Fully 60 per cent of the PLA representatives on the Central Committee are new members, with an increasing number from the Lanzhou and Nanjing military regions. Election to the Central Committee appears to have been entirely a function of protocol rank. That is, the commanders and political commissars of all military regions, directors and "executive" (first-ranking) deputy directors of all general departments, commanders and political commissars of all services and the People's Armed Police, and the political commissars of the PLA's three educational institutions (NDU, AMS and National Defence Science and Technology University (NDSTU)), were all elected to the Central Committee. Alternate members included other deputy directors of the general staff department (GSD) and general armaments department (GAD), commandant of the NDSTU, commander of the Xinjiang Military District, commander of the North Sea Fleet, commander of the Macau Garrison, Chief of Staff of the Shenyang and Nanjing military regions, and the commander of the 63rd Group Army. One well-known officer who was not elected to full membership on the Central Committee is the flamboyant and egotistical deputy chief of staff General Xiong Guangkai. Xiong did eek out a position as an alternate, but placed 148th out of 158 elected alternate members. This is interesting not only because Xiong is the best-known PLA officer overseas (insofar as he is in charge of all PLA foreign exchanges and intelligence, and is the principal interlocutor for foreign visitors), but because prior to the Congress he had audaciously bragged to a number of visiting foreign delegations that he would be promoted high up the hierarchy – possibly to become the minister of defence. Xiong's braggadocio resulted in a distinct rebuff at the "polls" – what one Hong Kong newspaper pointedly referred to as a case of "burning down the stove due to overheating."[1]

It was also interesting that the CMC was trimmed from eleven to eight members. This can be attributed to a couple of factors. First, in recent years, the CMC has become increasingly an *ex officio* body, that is, with the directors of the four general departments represented along with two uniformed vice-chairs (with a functional division of labour among them and one simultaneously serving as minister of defence). This is what can be considered to be a streamlined model for the CMC. The previous CMC included three individuals who did not have these portfolios (Wang Ruilin, Guo Boxiong and Xu Caihou). It is also interesting that the position of CMC secretary general was not resurrected or filled. This slot has remained dormant and unfilled (although never formally abolished) since the purge of Yang Baibing in 1992. What this means in practice is that the Director of the General Office of the CMC (currently Lieutenant General Tan Yuexin) administratively directs the CMC on a day-to-day basis, without a CMC member having this authority. Yang Baibing had used (and abused) this position to manipulate meetings, paper flow and personnel assignments during his tenure.

The continuation of Jiang Zemin as CMC chairman is, of course, significant. There had been widespread speculation prior to the Congress that he would step down from this post (including this observer), but it was not to be. There was also speculation that Jiang would stay in the job until the March 2003 Tenth National People's Congress, when he would hand over the chairmanship of both the Party and the state CMC to Hu Jintao.[2] This also was not to be, as Jiang was elected to a new five-year term as chairman of the state CMC.[3] While Jiang's continuation in these twin posts brings continuity to command of the military and civil–military relations, at the same time it creates two procedural anomalies – with someone other than the CCP general secretary heading the

1. N.A., "Military representatives to the CCP Central Committee are 60% new faces – Cao Gangchuan, Guo Boxiong, and Xu Caihou step up to the plate," *Ming bao* (Hong Kong), 15 November 2002, in FBIS-China (hereafter FBIS-CHI), 15 November 2002.

2. See, for example, Andrew Nathan and Bruce Gilley, *China's New Rulers* (New York: New York Review of Books, 2002).

3. "Profile of Central Military Commission chairman Jiang Zemin," Xinhua News Agency, 15 March 2003, in FBIS-CHI, 15 March 2003.

Party CMC and someone other than the state president heading the state CMC. Traditionally the head of the Party (either chairman or general secretary) has served as chairman of the Party CMC, so as to illustrate the principle that the "Party commands the gun." Also, according to National Defence Law of 1997, only the president of the PRC (along with the Standing Committee of the National People's Congress) can mobilize the nation for war or order the military forces into combat. Jiang's continuation as CMC chair while Hu Jintao has become state president violates these principles and law, and clouds the chain of command. Indeed, Jiang's clinging to power has clouded an otherwise smooth succession. Many in China, including in the CCP, recognize this fact and complain about it. Perhaps as a sign of this discontent, the National People's Congress vote to renew Jiang's position as chair of the state was not unanimous. Almost 10 per cent of NPC deputies did not vote in favour of Jiang's reappointment (of 2,951 delegates there were 98 votes against him with 122 abstentions). In addition, the official Xinhua News Agency report that announced his re-election pointedly reported that the 16th CCP Central Committee "let Jiang stay on as chairman of the CMC," while also noting that he had been "relieved of his official duty" as CCP general secretary but "relinquished willingly his state presidency."[4]

The reasons for Jiang's continuation as chairman of the CMC, and the manoeuvring he undertook to accomplish it, have been the source of much speculation both within and outside China.[5] Maintaining the positions will certainly continue to provide an institutional platform for him domestically and internationally. It will also, of course, give him some influence over military affairs. It is true that the military have been comfortable with Jiang as their leader and he has been good to the PLA.[6] In the run-up to the Congress, the PLA media engaged in a sycophantic propaganda campaign – presumably to bolster his position and to signal an institutional desire that he remain as chairman.[7] This followed the apparent decision taken at the summer 2002 leadership retreat at Beidaihe to allow Jiang to stay on in the CMC posts.[8] So Jiang steps down from all other official positions (although it is still unclear if he will relinquish his positions on the foreign affairs, Taiwan, and national security leading

    4. *Ibid.*

    5. For one Hong Kong media account of how Jiang manoeuvred and managed to keep the CMC portfolio, see Lo Ping, "Jiang Zemin maneuvers to hold on as Central Military Commission chairman," *Zhengming* (Hong Kong), 1 December 2002, in FBIS-CHI, 31 December 2002.

    6. For studies of how Jiang has interacted with the PLA see You Ji, "Jiang Zemin's command of the military," *The China Journal*, No. 45 (January 2001), pp. 131–38; Tai Ming Cheung, "Jiang Zemin at the helm: his quest for power and paramount leader status," *China Strategic Review*, Vol. 3, No. 1 (Spring 1996), pp. 167–191; and my "China's commander-in-chief: Jiang Zemin and the PLA," in C. Dennison Lane *et al.* (eds.), *Chinese Military Modernization* (London and Washington, DC: Kegan Paul International and AEI Press, 1996).

    7. For an excellent and careful analysis of this propaganda campaign see James Mulvenon, "The PLA and the 'three represents': Jiang's bodyguards or party-army?" *China Leadership Monitor*, No. 4 (Fall 2002), at www.chinaleadershipmonitor.org.

    8. N.A., "Jiang Zemin to stay on as chairman of Central Military Commission for another five years," *Kaifang* (Hong Kong), 1 February 2003, in FBIS-CHI, 5 February 2003.

small groups), but hangs on to his military portfolio. How long he will do so remains in doubt. There is no statutory term for the Party post but there is a five-year mandate for state position. Whether Jiang remains for the entirety of this tenure, when he would be 81 years old, or hands the positions over to Hu Jintao before then remains to be seen. Jiang seems to fancy himself as a paramount leader *qua* Deng Xiaoping, and is clearly trying to establish himself in such a role as a semi-retired elder. Deng also held on to the CMC chairmanship while giving up his Party and state positions at the 13th Party Congress in 1987, as Jiang is well aware. While Jiang is no Deng, he does possess stature internationally, domestically within the Party and nation, and within the military. Given the far-reaching leadership transition that took place at the 16th Party Congress and Tenth National People's Congress, the military (and perhaps the Party and government too) are somewhat comforted by Jiang's continuation as the CMC chairs. But eventually, he will have to hand over to Hu Jintao, presuming Hu does not encounter difficulties as Party and state leader.

Would the military be comfortable with Hu Jintao as their commander-in-chief? Yes and no. Although Hu has been a vice-chair of the CMC since 1999, and the military has had three years to get used to him (and, more importantly, vice versa), he has no previous military credentials of his own and has not been engaged in military affairs. The only active role Hu has shown concerning the military in recent years was his high-profile involvement in the December 1998 divestiture order, which required PLA units to transfer their financial assets to the State Council. Hu's other involvement came when he was (briefly) Party secretary in Tibet in the late 1980s, and particularly during the crackdown in March 1989. According to a recent Hong Kong press report, Hu was intimately involved in the military planning at the time, particularly with General Liao Xilong, then deputy commander of the Chengdu Military Region.[9] Liao was promoted to the CMC and the position of director of the General Logistics Department at the Congress, and is the only senior officer who evinces ties to Hu Jintao.

Until Hu proves his mettle to the military he is likely to be viewed only with respect for his position as Party and state leader – which does confer authority on him – although he has not established a track record on military affairs. What he needs to do is exactly what Jiang did in the 1990–91 period, after he was catapulted to the CMC chair in November 1989. Jiang very assiduously and carefully went about visiting every military region, all the general departments and a large number of units. These visits, his speeches and personal meetings with key PLA officers all addressed the various institutional and sub-institutional needs of the PLA, thus astutely building an inner-PLA bureaucratic coalition of

---

9. See Lin Jie, "Liao Xilong's accession to the Central Military Commission will help Hu assume the reins of military power," *Xin bao* (Hong Kong), 21 November 2002, in FBIS-CHI, 21 November 2002.

support.[10] Within a short time (by 1993) Jiang's influence with the military had grown and he had won the support of various constituencies in the PLA. Many of the regional commanders he had met on his tours were transferred to Beijing. Hu Jintao needs similarly to cultivate and build his own independent base of support in the military. Jiang's continuation as CMC chair could work both ways: it could help or hinder Hu's ability to build this base.

As a group, the PLA officers of the new CMC display several notable characteristics. First, their average age is 61. Only Cao Gangchuan is 67. This means that all the others will be members for the remainder of this decade. Secondly, their career paths are diverse, but each has worked an entire career in different functional systems in the PLA. This provides a kind of division of labour among them. Three have commanded military regions (Guo Boxiong, Liang Guanglie and Liao Xilong), two come from GPD backgrounds (Xu Caihou and Li Jinai), and one (Cao Gangchuan) is a veteran of the military-industrial establishment. None has "helicoptered" to the top, and all have meticulously climbed the career ladder in their respective service or department. Thirdly, several have commanded particularly important military regions and have overseen particularly sensitive operations, during which they have proved their political loyalty to their military superiors and the Party: Guo Boxiong was commander of the 47th Group Army during the anti-separatist operations in Xinjiang between 1990–92; Liao Xilong commanded the forces that quelled the rebellion in Lhasa, Tibet in 1989; Liang Guanglie reportedly commanded the 54th Group Army to suppress the uprising in Beijing in 1989; and all three (particularly Liang Guanglie) have served as commander or deputy commander of military exercises directed against Taiwan.[11] Fourthly, CMC membership continues to be dominated by the ground forces, although arguably the air, naval and missile forces are now more important in the PLA's orientation and potential missions. Li Jinai does have a background in the strategic and tactical missile forces (second artillery), but it was as a political commissar rather than as a technician or base commander. And finally, these are professional military men, with proven careers and a clear sense of mission. In addition to lengthy experience at the command level, they have all had some advanced professional military education.

The following subsections briefly consider the backgrounds of each uniformed member of the new CMC.[12]

10. This process is detailed in Shambaugh, "China's commander-in-chief."

11. I am indebted to James Mulvenon on this point. See his "The PLA and the 16th Party Congress: Jiang controls the gun?" *China Leadership Monitor*, No. 5 (Winter 2003), at www.chinaleadershipmonitor.org.

12. The biographical data used below are drawn from four principal sources: the official New China News Agency biographies issued on 15 November 2002; Zong Hairen, *Di si dai* (*The Fourth Generation*) (Hong Kong: Mirror Books, 2002); Ling Haijian, *Zhonggong jundui xin zhangxing* (*The Chinese Communist Military's New Characteristics*) (Hong Kong: Mirror Books, 1999); "Zonghe" (pseudonym), "Zhonggong zhongyang junwei de xin fangxiang" ("The new orientation of the Central Military Commission"), *Xin bao* (December 2002), pp. 28–30.

Guo Boxiong. General Guo was first appointed to the CMC in September 1999. It was clear at the time that he and Xu Caihou were to form the core of the "fourth generation" officers on the post-Congress CMC; the only questions were whether Guo would become chief of logistics or chief of staff and whether he would rise to become a vice-chairman or simply remain a member of the CMC. The answers became clear with his elevation to one of the three vice-chair positions. He inherits Zhang Wannian's portfolio, becoming the leading PLA officer with principal authority over doctrine, force structure and training issues. Although it is rumoured that General Guo has suffered serious health problems since 2000 (reportedly stomach cancer), he is clearly the most important uniformed officer in the PLA today.

General Guo, a native of Shaanxi, has spent the majority of his military career in his home province. He joined the PLA in 1961 and did a two-year course at the Military Academy in Nanjing (the forerunner to the NDU) during 1981–83. Guo rose through the ranks of the Lanzhou military region, serving successively as a squad leader, platoon leader, regimental propaganda cadre, headquarters staff officer and eventually military region deputy chief of staff. He spent a total of 24 years (1961–85) in these positions with a single unit, the 55th Division of the 19th Army Corps. From 1985 to 1990 he served as deputy chief of staff of the Lanzhou military region. From 1990 to 1993 he was commander of the 47th Group Army, directly under Fu Quanyou's command. In 1993 he was transferred to the Beijing military region, and served as deputy military region commander until 1997, when he was transferred back to take over the Lanzhou military region command – capping his career in the region. He served in this capacity until 1999, when he was tapped for promotion to the CMC and returned to Beijing. Guo is considered a specialist in ground force operations and training, and was one of the first to experiment with large-scale force-on-force mechanized infantry exercises.

Cao Gangchuan. General Cao is now the second-highest ranking officer in the PLA, with a portfolio covering both equipment and foreign military relations. He likely to be appointed as minister of defence at the National People's Congress in March 2003, succeeding Chi Haotian. Cao is a native of Henan and joined the PLA in 1954.

Two characteristics distinguish Cao Gangchuan's career path: expertise in conventional land armaments and ties to Russia. He began studying artillery in the PLA's new Third Artillery Ordnance Technical School in Zhengzhou, and graduated two years later. He was then sent to Dalian for a year of Russian language training, before being sent to the Soviet Union for six years of study at the Artillery Engineering Academy of the Artillery Corps of the Soviet Armed Forces. He stayed through the Sino-Soviet split and returned to China in 1963. Cao's subsequent career was entirely concerned with ordnance and military equipment in the general logistics department (1963–82). There are some reports that he was sent to the front lines on the Vietnamese border in 1979 to co-ordinate artillery fire, but this has not been confirmed. In 1982 he was assigned to the GSD headquarters, where he worked in the military equipment department until 1989. He then began a two-year stint as director of the military affairs of the general staff. Following his appointment as director of the military trade office of the CMC in 1990 Cao subsequently became the PLA point man for negotiating weapons purchases and military co-operation with Russia. In this capacity he has played a key and instrumental role in the modernization of PLA weaponry and equipment. This lasted for two years until he was promoted to be a deputy chief of general staff from 1992 to 1996 (in charge of weaponry and equipment). In 1996 Cao succeeded Ding Henggao as director of the Commission on Science, Technology and Industry for National Defence (COSTIND), and then presided over its reorganization and move under the administrative control of the State Council in a 1998 shake-up of the military-industrial complex. He had been known previously to express great frustration with COSTIND and its many failings to produce high-quality weaponry. General Cao was therefore the logical choice to be appointed to be the inaugural director of the GAD when it was created in 1998. He became a CMC member at the same time.

With his promotion to become a CMC vice-chair at the 16th Party Congress, he will be even more instrumental in guiding the modernization of PLA's weaponry. As the new defence minister, however, his time will have to be increasingly shared with foreign travel and diplomatic duties. But, given the importance of Russia to the PLA's modernization, there probably could not be a better choice for minister of defence than Cao Gangchuan.

Xu Caihou. General Xu has had a career in PLA political and personnel work. Geographically, he has spent most of his career in the Jilin military district of the Shenyang military region, although at the time of his promotion to the CMC in 1999 he worked in the Jinan military region. In Jilin Xu held a succession of propaganda and general political department (GPD) jobs. In November 1992, he was transferred to Beijing where he became assistant to GPD chief Yu Yongbo, but also worked closely with Wang Ruilin. With this backing, Xu was destined to head the GPD following their retirements. In mid-1993, Xu also assumed co-editorship of the *Liberation Army Daily*. This was a sensitive time following the purge of Yang Baibing, and the need to gain control over the GPD apparatus. Xu performed well and was promoted to deputy director of the GPD in July 1994. From 1996 to 1999 he served as political commissar of the Jinan military region.

Xu is a native of Liaoning and joined the army in 1963. He graduated with BA and MA degrees in electronic engineering from the Harbin Institute of Military Engineering in 1968 and was immediately sent to the countryside for manual labour, where he spent two years. He joined the Party under the worker-peasant-soldier affirmative action programme in 1971. From 1971 to 1992 he worked in various personnel management

management and political work positions in the GPD of the Jilin military district of the Shenyang military region.

Xu will play a critical role in all personnel decisions in the PLA, including all senior-level promotions. In this regard, he will be an indispensable asset to Hu Jintao, if Hu decides to build his own network of loyal officers across military regions. Xu also has the distinction of being the only PLA officer serving on the Central Committee Secretariat, the body charged with running the day-to-day affairs of the Party. This places Xu as a key interface with civilian Party leaders, as well as the key individual for managing Party–army relations and the Party's influence in the military. This responsibility is buttressed not only by Xu's director-ship of the GPD, but also the fact that he is the secretary of the CCP Discipline Inspection Commission in the PLA. If the Party is to continue to command the gun, Xu Caihou will play an important role.

Liang Guanglie. A new CMC member and the new chief of general staff is General Liang Guanglie. General Liang's three years of service as commander of the Nanjing military region has prompted a lot of specu-lation in foreign media that the PLA will cast a more aggressive stance towards Taiwan.[13] It is true that Liang had an instrumental role in planning and executing the exercises that simulated scenarios for attack-ing Taiwan, and that these exercises increased in scope, pace and intensity during his tenure, but he did not initiate this trend (it started post-1996) and it is very likely to continue well into the future.

A native of Sichuan, after joining the PLA in 1958 most of General Liang's early career was in the former Wuhan military region (which was divided between the Guangdong and Chengdu military regions in 1985). From 1958 to 1970 he served in a variety of engineering and infantry units (including a 14-month stint in an infantry academy), and then served in the operations department of the Wuhan military region from 1970 to 1979. From 1979 to 1990 he served in a succession of positions in the 20th Army Corps, based in Kaifeng, Henan, rising to become the commander from 1985 to 1990. During this time Liang was twice sent for mid-career training: for a year (March 1982–January 1983) at the Military Academy in Nanjing, and from August to December 1987 to the NDU in Beijing. He also completed a continuing education correspondence degree in political theory from Henan University from 1984 to 1986. He became commander of the 20th Corps in 1985 and, according to his official biography, served in this position until 1990, when he was then appointed commander of the 54th Group Army, based in Xinxiang, Henan, where he served until 1993. However a Hong Kong source indicates that Liang took command in September 1988 and that the 54th Group Army "enforced martial law in Beijing during June 1989."[14] It is unclear if this unit participated in the 3–4 June massacre or entered the

13. See, for example, "Promotion of Liang Guanglie indicates military pressure on Taiwan," *Ming bao* (Hong Kong), 16 November 2002, in FBIS-CHI, 18 November 2002.
14. Ling Haijin, *The Chinese Communist Military's New Characteristics*, p. 211.

city later in the month, nor is it clear when the unit returned to base in Xinxiang.

Liang continued as commander of the 54th Group Army until 1993, although in 1991 he was once again selected for a four-month specialized course at the NDU in Beijing. After eight years as a group army commander, Liang was tapped for promotion and assignment to the Beijing military region – where he served as chief of staff (1993–95), and deputy military region commander (1995–97). He was then assigned as commander of the Shenyang military region (1997–99), and was shifted to command the Nanjing military region from 1999 to 2002. Thus General Liang brings many years of experience commanding ground force units, including serving at the pinnacle of command in three different military regions. He is a logical and qualified choice to replace Fu Quanyou as PLA chief of staff.

Liao Xilong. General Liao is another example of an officer who has risen methodically through the ranks. Born into a poor farming family in a mountainous village in poverty-stricken Guizhou province, Liao joined the army at the age of 19. Thereafter he has spent his entire career in the south-western Kunming and (after 1987) Chengdu military region. He served in and had commands at the platoon, regiment, division, group army and military region levels. During the border war with Vietnam in 1979, Liao commanded a regiment that captured the border village of Phong To, for which he received a commendation from the CMC.[15] As a result he was also promoted to division commander (31st) and again engaged Vietnamese forces at Lao Shan and Zheying Shan in 1984. The overall commander of PLA forces in this engagement was none other than Fu Quanyou. For his actions Liao is said to have been personally decorated by Deng Xiaoping, and was promoted to deputy army corps commander. Six months later, at the age of 44, Liao became the youngest group army commander in the PLA. Six months after that he was tapped to become deputy military region commander under Fu Quanyou (again the youngest in the country). He served in this position for ten years, although General Fu was transferred to command the Lanzhou military region and eventually was promoted to the CMC. After Fu left, Liao continued to serve as deputy military region commander to Generals Zhang Taiheng, Liu Jiulong and Kui Fulin. As noted above, he played an instrumental role in co-ordinating the 1989 crackdown in Tibet. Thereafter he befriended Hu Jintao, who came to Chengdu because of his altitude sickness in Lhasa. In 1995 Liao was finally rewarded with the appointment of Chendu military region commander, a position in which he served for seven years until he was brought to Beijing in 2002 and appointed director of the general logistics department and member of the CMC. General Liao has very strong military credentials, but he also possesses important ties to a variety of other senior PLA officers with

15. Lin Jie, "Liao Xilong's accession." Liao's regiment was the 91st regiment of the 31st division of the 11th Army Corps.

whom he has served. Being decorated by Deng Xiaoping and being close to Hu Jintao further burnishes his standing. At 62, Liao Xilong and Liang Guanglie will have the predominant impact on shaping PLA force modernization.

Li Jinai. The final member and new appointment to the CMC is General Li Jinai, who succeeds Cao Gangchuan as director of the GAD. Unlike the other newcomers, Li moves up within the same organization, as he has served as GAD political commissar since 1998.

While Li's prior career track has been a mixture of working at a series of missile bases and in the defence industrial and science and technology establishment, in both cases it has been entirely on the political side. Although he has a degree in mechanical engineering from Harbin Institute of Military Engineering, he is not a "techie." His entire career since 1970 has been spent in political and propaganda work in the PLA. After joining the military in 1967 he did serve in an engineering corps construction regiment and as a regimental deputy platoon leader of the 807 launch brigade at Base No. 51 of the Second Artillery (1969–70). From 1970 to 1971 he worked in the propaganda section of the GPD at base no. 52 at Huangshan (Tunxi), Anhui province. From 1971 to 1977 he held a similar position in the 811th launch brigade at Qimen, Jiangxi (part of the no. 52 base complex). From 1977 to 1983 Li was transferred to Beijing to head the youth section of the Second Artillery's organization department. From 1983 to 1985 he was transferred to the Luoyang strategic nuclear weapons base in Henan province (base no. 54), where he was deputy political commissar. In 1985 Li was tapped to return to Beijing as director of the GPD cadres department (one of seven departments), where stayed until 1990. He was then promoted to be one of several deputy directors of the GPD for two years. In 1992 he was transferred to be deputy political commissar of COSTIND, where he served until 1998 when he was appointed as the political commissar of the newly created GAD. In this capacity he worked closely with Cao Gangchuan, and he succeeded General Cao after the 16th Party Congress when Cao was promoted to be CMC vice-chairman.

Thus, while General Li now heads the key organ responsible for co-ordinating all defence industrial production and research and development, his career has not been on the technical side. His background in the strategic rocket forces is an interesting fact, but it is not clear how much technical knowledge he gained during those assignments. His career has rather been on the political side, and he could be in line to succeed Xu Caihou as GPD director should Xu move up.

The Second Echelon

While there are no extensive biographical data on those officers beneath the CMC, it is also important to note that a number of changes in leading PLA personnel took place in the military regions, general departments and services in the year prior to the Congress. While some of these personnel changes were precipitated by the promotion of other military officers or illness (Air Force Commander Liu Shunyao) leaving vacancies, others were the result of regular rotations. In these appointments a relatively consistent pattern of promotion emerges, whereby officers are elevated progressively to the next level of command – from group army commander to military region deputy chief of staff to military region chief of staff to military region deputy commander to military region commander. In a few cases officers leapfrogged two positions up the hierarchy,[16] but, for the most part, the promotion pattern was incremental. This was evident in the appointments of the following:

- Li Wenhua moved from Beijing garrison command political commissar to become Beijing military region deputy political commissar;
- Liu Zhenwu went from deputy commander to commander of the Guangzhou military region;
- Song Wenhan went from Guangzhou military region chief of staff to military region deputy commander;
- Ye Aiqun went from commanding the 42nd group army to replacing Song Wenhan as Guangzhou military region chief of staff;
- Wu Shengli went from deputy commander of the PLA Navy South Sea Fleet to become commander of the East Sea Fleet (he was replaced by Zhang Dingfa in June 2003);
- Gui Quanzhi went from Chengdu military region chief of staff to become military region deputy commander;
- Liu Yahong went from commander of the 14th group army to replace Gui Quanzhi as Chengdu military region chief of staff;
- Qu Fanghuan, went from Lanzhou military region chief of staff to military region deputy commander;
- Chang Wanhan went from commander of the 47th group army to replace Qu as Lanzhou military region chief of staff;
- Zhong Shengqin moved from Jinan military region chief of staff to deputy military region commander.

Thus, in the Beijing, Chengdu, Lanzhou, Guangzhou and Jinan military regions there was a very clear pattern of officers moving directly up into the next billet (or two in the case of Zhu Qi).[17] It is also clear that, more than ever in the past, commands of divisions and group armies are a prerequisite for higher military region assignments. A similar pattern of incremental promotion is seen in the services and general departments (particularly the GAD).

The second echelon military leadership is shown in Tables 2, 3, 4 and 5. One sees similar incremental promotion patterns in these institutions, although in the PLA academies/universities some interesting precedents were set. The new NDU president, Lieutenant-General Pei Hualiang, was

16. Zhu Qi moved up from Beijing military region chief of staff to Beijing military region commander; and Zhu Wenquan did the same in the Nanjing military region.
17. See "PRC makes pre-CCP Congress' military region personnel changes," *Ming bao* (Hong Kong), 9 February 2002, in FBIS-CHI, 9 February 2002.

Table 2: **Military Regions**

Military region	Commander	Political commissar
Beijing	Zhu Qi	Li Wenhua
Chengdu	Wang Jianmin	Yang Deqing
Guangzhou	Liu Zhenwu	Liu Shutian
Jinan	Chen Bingde	Liu Dongdong
Lanzhou	Li Qianyuan	Liu Yongzhi
Nanjing	Zhu Wenquan	Lei Mingqiu
Shenyang	Qian Guoliang	Jiang Futang

Table 3: **The General Departments**

Department	Director	Deputy directors
General staff	Liang Guanglie	Ge Zhenfeng, Wu Quanxu, Qian Shugen, Xiong Guangkai, Zhang Li
General political	Xu Caihou	Tang Tianbiao, Yuan Shoufang, Zhang Shutian
General logistics	Liao Xilong	Zhang Wentai, Sun Zhiqing, Wang Qian
General armaments	Li Jinai	Li Andong, Zhu Fazhong

Table 4: **CMC Affiliated Educational Institutions**

Institution	Commandant
National Defence University	Pei Huailiang
Academy of Military Sciences	Zheng Shenxia
Science and Technology University for National Defence	Wen Xisen

transferred from his post as deputy commander of the Jinan military region. Given the importance of the NDU in training group army commanders, it is appropriate that someone of Pei's service background heads the NDU. Another precedent was set with the appointment of Vice-Admiral Zhang Dingfa as president of the AMS, the PLA's top research organ. This is the first time that someone of a naval background (or non-ground forces) has served in this AMS capacity or any leading PLA institution for that matter, as the ground forces have monopolized senior appointments to date. This still remains the case, despite Admiral Zhang's appointment. In June 2003, following the purge of the senior naval brass in the aftermath of the sinking of a PLA Navy conventional submarine, Admiral Zhang was promoted from the AMS presidency to

Table 5: **Service Commands**

Service	Commander	Commissar
PLA Navy	Shi Yunsheng	Yang Huaiqing (replaced by Zhang Dingfa in June 2003)
PLA Air Force	Qiao Qingchen	Deng Changyou
PLA Second Artillery	Jing Zhiyuan	Jia Wenxian
People's Armed Police	Wu Shuangzhan	Zhang Yuzhong

become commander of the PLA Navy, and was succeeded by Zheng Shenxia. General Zheng previously served as chief of staff of the PLA Air Force (PLAAF), Shenyang military region deputy commander and commandant of the PLAAF Command College.

Implications for Civil–Military Relations

Taken together, the personnel changes in the PLA high command have been sweeping. The Congress triggered some of the changes, but most were mandated by new standards and regulations (*gangyao*) that have been promulgated in recent years. This cohort not only represents the "fourth generation" of PLA leaders, but also the fifth. It is this pool of officers from which the senior military leadership will be drawn in the years ahead.

The new high command continues to be predominated by the ground forces, its members have had substantial field command experience at the group army level and below, possess university-level educations and have attended at least one military educational academy, and have methodically climbed the career ladder. However, they are not is well-travelled abroad, cannot be considered to be very cosmopolitan or global strategic thinkers, and have not had actual combat experience (other than limited action along the Vietnam border). While the failure to promote naval or air force officers to senior levels outside their own services follows traditional patterns, it is also odd considering the increased importance attached to these services for potential peripheral conflicts and "limited wars under high technology conditions."

Collectively, their policy proclivities can be expected to push ahead fully with the comprehensive modernization of the PLA – hardware, software, command and control, force structure, finance, logistics, science and technology, military education, reconnaissance and intelligence, and so on.[18] Above all, they are professional soldiers who are steadily professionalizing the PLA with every passing day. They are not likely to intervene in high-level politics, nor do they wish to be pulled into

18. These and other aspects are all discussed in my *Modernizing China's Military* (Berkeley & London: University of California Press, 2002).

performing internal security functions (which are to be left to the People's Armed Police). They have a singular focused mission of comprehensive military modernization, and the PLA is being given the necessary resources to fulfil that mission. A quarter of a century from now, when the fourth and fifth generation officers retire, the PLA will be a far more modern and capable force for their efforts.

In terms of the evolving nature of civil–military relations, the turnover in the military leadership described above reflects several trends that have been noticeable in recent years. First and most important, we are witnessing the further institutional "bifurcation" of Party and army. This can be seen in a number of ways. The military played no apparent role in the civilian leadership succession before or at the 16th Congress and vice versa, that is, the civilian Party leaders played no apparent role in the selection of the new military leadership (and that includes, in my view, Jiang Zemin). There was no praetorian impulse to intervene in politics and the military was left to make its own succession choices. Furthermore, no senior Party leader has one day of military experience – while none of the new military leaders has any experience in high-level politics. This is a trend that has been noticeable for the past decade, during the "third generation" of leaders, but is a marked departure from the former "interlocking directorate" that symbiotically fused together the civilian and military leaderships. The continuing decline of military representation in the CCP Central Committee is yet further evidence of the bifurcation.

Secondly, this tendency towards bifurcation reinforces the ongoing trend towards corporatism and professionalism in the PLA. This is to say, the PLA as an institution is now exclusively, more than ever before, concerned with purely military affairs. It is not involved in domestic politics, has withdrawn from its former internal security functions in favour of an exclusively externally-oriented mission, has largely divested itself of its commercial assets and role in the civilian economy, does not play a role or have much of a voice in foreign policy, and even its influence on Taiwan policy has become very circumscribed. To put it simply, the military in China today is concerned with military affairs. Just as importantly, the PLA is being permitted to look after its own affairs by the Party – and it is being given the resources to pursue its programme of comprehensive modernization.[19]

Thirdly, and related to the above trends, one sees few signs of politicization in the military. Except for the "three represents" campaign (which in the military is really more about increasing Jiang Zemin's stature than educating the military about recruiting entrepreneurs into the Party), one sees few indications of political indoctrination in the ranks of the PLA. The GPD today is far more concerned with improving the living standards of officers and their dependents than in indoctrinating the rank and file with ideological dogma. This is yet another signal of increased professionalization in the military. Along with the divestiture of

19. The one (important) qualification to this trend is the increased role by the government (State Council) in monitoring and auditing the PLA's financial affairs.

commercial assets and involvement, the military is now exclusively focused on training and other professional activities.

While it must still be considered a party-army, as long as the CCP rules China and the institutional mechanisms of Party penetration of the armed forces exist,[20] the PLA as an institution is clearly carving out its own corporate and professional identity. It is not yet a "national military," but is incrementally moving in that direction.[21] The new PLA leadership promoted around the 16th Party Congress is further evidence of these macro trends in the Chinese military today.

20. These include the GPD, the CCP's Discipline Inspection Commission, Party committees and branches down to the company level within the military, and the fact that all PLA officers above the rank of colonel are Party members.

21. See my "Civil–military relations in China: party-army or national military?" *The Copenhagen Papers in Asian Studies* (Fall 2002).

Social Change and Political Reform in China: Meeting the Challenge of Success

John W. Lewis and Xue Litai

ABSTRACT This article discusses how two decades of economic reforms have intensified popular unrest and redefined the composition, interests and political attitudes of China's ever more complex social strata. It then analyses some of the fundamental domestic and international issues facing Beijing in the course of those reforms and the social problems that have accompanied economic growth. The Communist Party has responded to the challenges generated by these problems and been forced to undertake more active political reforms or face an even greater loss of its authority. The article explains how the Party under the slogan the "three represents" cast its lot with the emerging beneficiaries of its economic reforms in the belief that only continued rapid development can mitigate the most pressing social problems and ensure stability.

The concept of reform connotes a deliberate and managed process of change. For more than a decade, it has been fashionable to contrast the Russian emphasis on immediate and radical political reform with the Chinese concentration on economic development. It has almost become a cliché to assert that the Chinese way created stable growth, while the Russian path was far more chaotic and painful.

While these comparisons warrant careful reconsideration after a reasonably long record, this article begins with a challenge to the idea that any reform can ever be deliberate for very long or managed with any real certainty about the ultimate outcomes. In the Chinese case, major political changes came after the end of Mao Zedong's rule in 1976. His vaunted rural people's communes collapsed, and vast rural areas reverted to more traditional ways. Moreover, the flood of policies to reorganize the Soviet-style ministries and state-owned enterprises (SOEs) began a process of institutional change with profound implications for central control and bureaucratic planning. The near explosion in telecommunications and access to foreign people, knowledge and cultural values dramatically altered political and social discourse.

This article, which is principally based on extensive interviews in China over the past three years, argues that these underlying changes that accompanied dramatic economic growth created serious internal problems, and these problems in turn forced the leadership to undertake more open political reforms or face rising dissent, deepening corruption and an even greater loss of Party authority. It also looks briefly at the beneficiaries of the economic reforms and the dramatic successes that have paralleled the many unmet challenges. In simplified terms, the forces causing instability have been matched by those advancing broad economic growth. The article first discusses the challenges and then, with these in mind, examines Jiang Zemin's formulation of political reform in terms of the "three represents." It seeks to demonstrate how the Chinese Communist Party (CCP) has cast its lot with the beneficiaries in the apparent belief that only development and expanding opportunities can ensure stability and mitigate the problems. It shows that the promotion of the "three represents" slogan itself brought about several distinct phases in the quest for reform prior to the 16th CCP Congress in November 2002.

Understanding the Causes

In the 1980s and 1990s, China faced daunting internal obstacles to orderly economic growth and social stability. In the Party's lexicon, these obstacles are deemed "contradictions" and are considered normal, even inevitable. All developing nations, as they mature, confront such contradictions, but how each copes with them markedly and uniquely shapes its politics and society. These consequential effects are caused by the demands of the newly affluent and advanced intellectuals for empowerment, by the societal and personal costs of accelerating growth, and by the unexpected institutional adjustments needed to build support and control opposition. The fundamental problems which are of concern here are, first, positive economic growth and the rising social costs of that growth; secondly, the mounting pressures for political reform and the stronger opposition to reform from political losers and entrenched conservatives; and thirdly, increasing international power matched by an ever-greater sense of insecurity.

Positive economic growth and the rising social costs of that growth. At the last national count, China's industrial economy was growing at an annual rate of over 7 per cent, with millions making over $20,000 per year.[1] Even though China is principally a continental economy, its export-driven economic policies have yielded huge foreign currency reserves and billions in foreign investment. The rapid but socially disruptive shift from state-owned to private enterprises and an expanding market economy are producing an ever-larger class of entrepreneurs. In hi-tech manufacturing, China is becoming a global leader.

Yet, the costs of this growth are huge: potential financial and banking crises, corruption, massive unemployment, a rising crime rate, uncontrolled urbanization and overpopulation.[2] In common with many nations, economic successes accentuate social inequities and environmental degra-

---

1. According to the China News Agency, 3,000,000 Chinese currently have assets of more than one million *yuan*. Quoted in www.zaobao.com/special/newspapers/003/02//xmrb2003. html (7 February 2003).

2. For a typical document on the official response to these problems, see the State Council and CCP Central Committee, "Opinion on further strengthening the comprehensive management of public order" (5 September 2001), Xinhua, 18 November 2001.

dation. The ugly head of corruption has come to plague China's body politic. Indeed, success can become as demanding as failure though, of course, in different ways. The costs have generated a persistent debate about priorities and resource allocation, but the debate about corruption and the rule of law is the one that is of most concern here. Corruption is pervasive and corrosive, and many senior leaders have been tainted by it. So long as the nouveaux riches and potentially well-connected are denied legitimate access to power, they will use money, special knowledge and personal relationships to achieve it and to influence policies that affect them. This is true everywhere, but a political system heavily burdened by corruption can quickly lose its cohesion and a unifying commitment to the public interest.

The mounting pressures for and stronger opposition to political reform. The "bottom up" momentum of political reform begun in the late 1970s has now extended throughout society. The signs of change in China are everywhere: ever more open competition for village leadership (though often manipulated), worker and farmer demonstrations against loss of jobs and social displacement, young iconoclasts in ministries and academies demanding more democratic and "objective" decision making, and the onslaught of Western culture – technology, dress, films, fast food, literature and, most importantly, ideas. Revolutionary politics are for the future, not just the past.

To deal with this future, Beijing faces three choices that need not be mutually exclusive: suppression, corruption or more open participation. The most intense reaction by the leadership to these developments is directed against those suspected of seeking foreign support, creating opposition or "separatist" plotting. In China, the Party and state typically show little mercy for these alleged crimes "against the state" and labour to strengthen the institutions of control. At first, the ruling elite has the upper hand and can quickly crush overt outbreaks of protest, but in time the diverse and innumerable local elements begin taking charge of their own lives and quietly resist in less detectable ways. In the end, suppression denies the polity its most creative voices and fosters political cynicism and apathy. Some turn to cult religions and underground political movements, while others openly protest.

In time, the choice becomes clear. The Party leaders can embrace the beneficiaries and consequences of change, or they can resist them. The nature of that embrace is crucial: corruption or participation. The pressures to resist greater participation come from threatened power holders and ideologues, and their opposition typically stiffens as the reform progresses. The beneficiaries can form the new cadre of Party activists even as old-guard critics decry the betrayal of the Party's traditional social base and vision. The most appealing aspect of this choice is that it promises to perpetuate the ruling elite's power, though in a somewhat different form. Yet it remains an open question whether the reforms themselves delay or accelerate the end of one-party rule.

Increasing international power and an ever-greater sense of insecurity. The steady growth of China's regional, if not global, influence and military power has become ever more visible and to some more menacing. To date, China has acted to minimize that threat and, with the exception of Taiwan, has succeeded in reducing tensions and avoiding conflict. Peace in Asia, especially Korea, depends more on China than on any other East Asian country, including Japan. Throughout the 1990s, Beijing had sought to initiate negotiations with Taiwan and to solve a number of border disputes. On the economic front, it had worked doggedly to join the World Trade Organization (WTO) and to host a summer Olympics. The guiding principle was: maintain a low posture, solve external conflicts and act on Deng Xiaoping's edict not to be drawn into war for decades to come.[3]

Yet Beijing's international objectives enunciated at the onset of the 1990s did not work out as planned. With unsettling regularity, US–China relations flared to near hostilities as Beijing's Taiwan policy faltered in the wake of rising independence forces on the island. Within the mainland population, increased nationalism weakened the commitment to stability and growth if that meant vitiating the one-China principle. Maintaining the domestic priority may yet prove to be the weak link in Beijing's policy-making.

Chinese views of social instability.[4] Chinese officials acknowledge that the economic reforms over the past two decades have both intensified popular unrest and redefined the composition, interests and political attitudes of the nation's ever more complex social strata. The boundaries between rich and poor have shifted, and the gap between them has grown. The farmers, ordinary workers, demobilized soldiers and other "weakened" groups have lost ground, and their support for the system has waned. In December 2001, *Renmin ribao* (*People's Daily*) reviewed a three-year study published by the Chinese Academy of Social Sciences on the demarcation of ten "social strata" in the nation's rapidly changing society.[5] The study concluded: "The original social strata are disintegrating, and new classes are taking shape and becoming stronger." As a result, the Party has lost its original social base. It now faces a fundamentally uncertain future with five major elements of society: the peasants,

---

3. See, for example, the articles by Wang Yusheng and Zhang Yijun on Deng Xiaoping's "strategy" of "maintaining a low posture" and peacefully resolving disputes in *Renmin ribao* (*People's Daily*) (internet version), 10 August 2001.

4. Unless otherwise cited, most of the information in this section is from the Research Section of the CCP Central Political and Law Commission (ed.), *Weihu shehui wending diaoyan wenji* (*A Collection of Investigation and Research Reports on Maintaining Social Stability*) (Beijing: Law Press, 2001), passim.

5. "CASS demarcates ten social strata in Chinese society," *Renmin ribao* (internet version), 17 December 2001. See also Li Chunling and Chen Guangjin, "A research report on the current social strata in China," in Lü Xin *et al.* (chief eds.), *2002 nian shehui lanpishu: Zhongguo shehui fenxi yu yugu* (*Social Blue Book: 2002 Analysis and Predictions of China's Social Situation*) (Beijing: Social Science Documents Press, 2002), pp. 115–132. See also the excellent study by Yang Jisheng, *Zhongguo shehui ge jieceng fenxi* (*An Analysis of Strata in Chinese Society*) (Hong Kong: Sanlian Bookstore, 2000), passim.

urban workers, minority religious groups, demobilized soldiers and some intellectuals.

The first of these five groups, the nation's farmers, have posed the biggest danger to lasting social stability. When the economic reforms began to take hold in cities in the mid-1980s, the incomes of urban residents surged ahead of those in the interior villages, while many local authorities routinely squeezed the peasants for higher assessments (the so-called "three chaotics": fees, fines and apportionments) and reduced their benefits. In order to attract foreign and private investors, provincial governments reduced the business levies that earlier had provided subsidies for the farmers. While the results varied from place to place, many peasants abandoned their farms for the illusory promise of employment in the towns, and those who remained took their grievances out on local officials. In some instances, these officials even encouraged the villagers to protest against their higher authorities. In parts of southern China, especially Hunan, Jiangxi, Sichuan, Anhui and Guangdong provinces, thousands of peasants repeatedly stormed government buildings, pleading for lower taxes and fees and accusing the officials of corruption.[6] The situation worsened as urban unemployment forced tens of millions of rural immigrants back to their home villages and police repression failed to stem the rising tide of discontent.

Though often viewed as an important step toward democratization, village elections have not eased tensions in the most disaffected rural areas.[7] These "elections" have all too often masked the rule of gang-type groups, especially in the interior provinces. Their power rests on the threat of force and on the reluctance of the armed police to use their weapons to protect the farmers. Rigged voting, protectionism and enforced tax collection under mafia-like "second police departments" in many rural areas make a mockery of "democratic" elections and the rule of law.[8]

While the unrest in the southern rural areas remains largely unchecked, Chinese sources pay equal attention to the growing social crisis in the country's northern cities.[9] Beijing's market-oriented policies have driven thousands of SOEs to close at the cost of millions of jobs. Laid-off workers are offered one-off compensation without pensions or welfare protection. In addition, tens of millions of workers in run-down and antiquated plants across the nation have had their wages cut or

---

6. In more violent cases, which were not uncommon, angry peasants blockaded traffic, held policemen hostage, attacked officials with bricks and clubs, and set police cars ablaze.

7. The actual situation in China's villages varies widely throughout the country. For a scholarly assessment as of early 2000, see the chapters by Kevin J. O'Brien and Lianjiang Li, Robert A. Pastor and Qingshan Tan, and Jean C. Oi and Scott Rozell in Larry Diamond and Ramon H. Myers (eds.), *Elections and Democracy in Greater China* (Oxford: Oxford University Press, 2000).

8. Yang Jisheng, *An Analysis of Strata*, p. 354.

9. In October 2002, Jiang Zemin told the National Conference on Re-Employment to solve five major contradictions involved in the current employment crisis. See "Promote the favorable interaction between economic development and the expansion of employment," *Renmin ribao*, 24 October 2002, p. 1.

"postponed." And the list of grievances grows: redundant workers barely subsisting on a tiny monthly allowance, lost benefits when plants go bankrupt, corrupt plant officers profiteering while their laid-off workers sink deeper into poverty, and unresponsive urban leaders hostile to the workers' plight. Official Chinese sources confirm the rising tide of worker protests. Some demonstrations are peaceful, but others have taken a violent turn: protestors block roads and bridges, attack Party and state offices, and on occasion resort to looting and arson.

While bureaucratic corruption most often ignites conflicts between officials and alienated urban workers, the primary causes of urban unrest are the widening gap between rich and poor and the prospect for worsening employment opportunities. Inequality, official reports admit, has reached the "alarm level," but the response of the local authorities has been tentative and piecemeal. Some city administrations have told their local banks to pay off the demonstrators or have provided make-work jobs, but most have done little or nothing. Many protest organizers are detained and charged with leading "illegal gatherings." The cycle of peaceful rallies, "strike hard" crackdowns and more violent protests goes on, though urban disturbances thus far have proved easier to control than those in the countryside.

The third social grouping threatening the prescribed social order consists of religious and sectarian groups, including the *falun gong*, Muslim Uyghurs, Tibetan Buddhists, and underground Catholics and Protestants. Officials have particularly targeted non-mainstream religions with harassment, extortion and detention, and take lessons from Chinese history to justify their fears. Cultist uprisings had catastrophic effects on Qing society, beginning with the White Lotus rebellion in the late 18th century, and religious movements linked to nationalistic uprisings were the bane of later governments. Beijing has especially damned those religions that allegedly have external ties, but has not yet effectively coped with them. As a result, the feckless suppression of the *falun gong*, for example, has illuminated rather than lessened the pervasive mood of disobedience.[10]

Demobilized soldiers pose the fourth socio-political challenge to Beijing, and the closure of thousands of SOEs that had employed many of these soldiers' spouses has worsened their plight.[11] Although the government has told existing SOEs to hire ex-soldiers with urban backgrounds, the uncertain fate of the SOEs makes these veterans' futures quite bleak.[12] Moreover, countless servicemen who had been drafted from the rural areas are no longer willing to return to farm work, and many from both

10. John Pomfret, "China tightens its grip on Falun Gong," *Washington Post*, 31 October 1999, p. A31.

11. When demobilized, ordinary servicemen and junior and middle-level officers receive a one-off payment; retired senior officers receive a reasonably good pension; and handicapped servicemen and officers receive a small fixed pension. All those demobilized receive some assistance in finding jobs, but that assistance is much greater for those from urban areas.

12. Zhou Ben and Xi Yanfeng, "Yu Yongbo emphasizes at a national meeting on work to resettle military cadres transferred to civilian work," *Jiefangjun bao* (*Liberation Army Daily*), 27 May 2002, p. 1.

the cities and countryside have become activists in anti-government demonstrations. These former soldiers are often more educated and politically experienced than their civilian brothers and sisters and have tended to become protest organizers and activists. Perhaps most troublesome of all, they have knowledge of official documents that can be used to justify their actions. These demobilized soldiers, now numbering some 20 million, have become living examples for those currently in service of what their lives could become upon retirement. To date, the efforts to meet the retirees' demands have faltered, and Beijing's leaders have just begun to worry about how far they can count on the military in domestic crises.

Finally, a special group of university graduates has become an unexpected source of trouble, according to Chinese sources. In recent years, universities have enrolled large numbers of students with questionable qualifications partially in order to meet the demand for expanded educational opportunities and partially to raise money. These students come to the campuses as "expanded enrolled students" (*kuo zhao sheng*), and when they carry this stigma to the job market they cannot compete with "regular" college graduates. Tens of thousands of *kuo zhao sheng* began graduating from universities in 2003, and their number is increasing. Some simply rail against the status quo, but growing numbers have begun to join forces with the rural migrants and urban unemployed and have become their tutors and protest leaders. They too can cite central government documents to justify their grievances and to frustrate actions against them by the government. So, once more in Chinese history a major group of intellectuals has found its social status marginalized and then politicized. Chinese intellectuals became largely irrelevant after the Qing dynasty abolished the elite examination system, for example, and many of them gravitated to the revolutionary movement of Sun Yat-sen. Viewed from Beijing, the combination of radicalized intellectuals, urban workers, farmers and retired army men has explosive potential, and has led to tightened societal controls.

The beneficiaries of reform. It is important to balance the foregoing discussion of societal problems with the recognition of those social forces that have so dramatically energized the economy, caused it to grow and reaped its benefits. The social changes examined in the previous sections have, as stressed above, surfaced in the course of rapid economic and social progress. Given the stunning successes in this regard, it would be wrong to overestimate the negative impact of those byproducts on the nation's stability and direction. To a remarkable degree thus far, the beneficiaries and victims of the just-ending era of economic reform have synergistically formed a system of checks and balances. Weaknesses and opposition have been checked by countervailing strengths and opportunities. On balance, Party leaders appear to believe that increasing the nation's pool of creative and entrepreneurial elements can help ensure effective governance and continued economic construction.

Here it is argued that modern China, like many other developing countries, has always had to balance stability and development. While many difficulties are caused by economic change, it is the increase in the pool of beneficiaries and in their political support that, Party leaders appear to believe, will ensure continued stability and economic growth over the long term. Comprehending this process is the key to understanding the case for the accelerated political reforms mandated by the 16th Party Congress.

It is not necessary to spend much time delineating the meaning of "beneficiaries." Clearly, some elements in the society have seen their status and living standards disproportionately enhanced. The Party of equality and mutual benefit disappeared long ago, and the values of the market economy and globalization have undermined its ideological roots. The leadership would argue, of course, that eventually all will benefit from rapid development and that the ever-widening universe of opportunity provides hope to the present losers, whose ranks will gradually shrink.

Many official policies have actively promoted the expansion of the private sector, with members including entrepreneurs (from large enterprises to small shops), employees in foreign-owned or joint-venture businesses and the self-employed. Both private and semi-private companies have become the engine for China's remarkable economic progress and the source of the growing middle and upper classes. One authoritative source estimates the size of this group in 2000 as over 130 million in 1.5 million private enterprises and 31 million small shops.[13] If one includes family members, this group numbers roughly 20 per cent of the population. Although its fate remains closely linked to Beijing's current economic policies, the nature or range of its members' political attitudes cannot be inferred from such links.

Finally, the educated have prospered. Teachers, advanced researchers and experts, engineers, artists, and other "intellectuals" have helped connect Chinese society to advanced knowledge and to the Western world. Hundreds of thousands have studied abroad, and many are now returning home to seek their fortune.

Most intellectuals, officials and entrepreneurs, and many employees in the private sector comprise the beneficiaries. They give some hope to those in trouble, and their example serves to mute the demands of those who would denounce the system. The support of the beneficiaries is thus magnified by the reticence of many current losers to denounce the system too vigorously when they, too, might eventually find avenues for advancement within it. Their dilemma is matched by the Party's: how to become the vanguard of the rich and smart without losing the mantle of the protector and vanguard of the common citizen?

Not surprisingly, the publicity surrounding these dilemmas has somewhat obscured the fact that a number of those who can be termed beneficiaries were already becoming part of the ruling elite. Many of the newly rich and more prominent managers had long ago joined the Party

13. Yang Jisheng, *An Analysis of Strata*, p. 16.

and its more powerful councils. Yet their rising status and wealth have lacked legal or ideological sanction, and entrenched conservatives could easily find lawful justification for expelling them from the Party, blocking their business activities or confiscating their property. Becoming a beneficiary often added to an individual's anxieties, and many of the rising stars with questionable class backgrounds began to explore ways to transfer their new-found wealth abroad and quietly promoted the emigration of family members to the West. The need for de jure protection of the beneficiaries was becoming an urgent requirement for securing and legitimizing their ongoing contributions.

The Choice

To date, the government has adopted a piecemeal or "firefighting" strategy to cope with the problems and laboured to break up any opposition that could coalesce against it. At the same time, it has enhanced the social position and livelihood of groups deemed essential to rapid development. Moreover, the situation is likely to remain fluid and unpredictable – assuming no conflict over Taiwan – and many potential opponents are far from giving up on the established system. Thus, it has proved reasonable for the leadership to pin its hopes on sustained economic development and its prime movers in order to neutralize or "digest" the downside of their economic reform policies. The established doctrine has not been "development versus stability" but "more rapid development and cautious political change" that can ensure stability and Party rule.

Since early 2000, however, the incremental approach to political reform no longer appeared adequate. Neither the winners nor the losers were satisfied, and Beijing made a basic assessment and a choice in favour of the beneficiaries that should hold unless Taipei takes the unprecedented step of declaring the island's independence. Simply put, no external issue except the future of Taiwan could compare to the threats or the opportunities within the nation, though in extremis the leadership could use an international crisis to generate domestic support.

The logic behind Beijing's strategic calculus mostly remains in place: the perpetuation of Party rule needs domestic political stability, prolonged political stability requires sustained economic development, and that development depends on a peaceful international environment. Underlying the formulation of the political reform policies has been the still-controversial assumption that those policies must be congruent with that bedrock strategic calculus. Consistent with the priority given to the domestic beneficiaries and development, Jiang Zemin's report to the 16th Party Congress for the first time placed "developed countries" ahead of those in the "third world."[14]

14. Jiang Zemin, "Build a well-off society in an all round way and create a new situation in building socialism with Chinese characteristics – report to the 16th Congress of

Reaching a consensus on the "three represents." Dating from the late 1970s, Deng Xiaoping's conclusion had been that the Party must reform in order to neutralize social resentment and restore the nation's unified sense of purpose. From Deng to Jiang, Party leaders called for installing the rule of law, enhancing supervisory functions "over the use of power" at all levels, and implementing a performance-based cadre and personnel system.[15] Yet solving existing problems caused a host of others, including the social inequality and unrest noted earlier. Caught in the web of the basic societal problems and at a turning point in China's development, Beijing's leadership at first reacted with its trademark caution in order to deflect the assault on its political legitimacy. Each corrective step, however, generated the need to manage its unintended consequences, and by the end of the 1990s, the risks of inaction had begun to outweigh those of more radical change. The need was for a bold new political formulation, a call for a changed understanding or "cognition" about the Party's future.

According to most sources, Jiang Zemin first couched his ideas about Party reform in the catchphrase "three represents" (*san ge daibiao*) during an inspection tour in Guangdong province in February 2000. He later said, "to scientifically evaluate the Party's historical status, we proposed the important *thinking* of the 'three represents'."[16] In his vision, the Party of the future would represent the demand for development of "advanced productive forces, China's advanced culture and the fundamental interests of the largest majority of the Chinese people." This was assumed to be just another addition to the endless onslaught of political slogans, and few Chinese in the coming months took Jiang's vision seriously.

Stage one: the dialogue of change. Nevertheless, the campaign to publicize the possibility of high-level political reform gained momentum in the spring of 2000, and that May, a senior Chinese official told us: "You Americans simply have not paid attention to the importance of President Jiang's initiatives for changing the character of the Chinese Communist Party … . You dismiss the 'three represents' as just another Party slogan." Yet throughout that year, many foreign scholars who tried to probe their real significance were met with ritualistic repetition and simplistic explanations.

By the end of the year, however, some senior Chinese officials would try to explain why they had earlier been so vague about the "three

---

footnote continued

Communist Party of China," in *Documents of the 16th National Congress of the Communist Party of China* (Beijing: Foreign Languages Press, 2002), pp. 58–59.

15. See, for example, the CCP Central Documentation Research Section (ed.), *Deng Xiaoping sixiang nianpu 1975–1997 (Chronological Record of Deng Xiaoping's Thought (1975–1997))* (Beijing, 1998), pp. 57, 75–76, 92–93, 101; Jiang Zemin, "Speech at the meeting celebrating the 80th anniversary of the founding of the Communist Party of China," Xinhua, 1 July 2001; and Jiang Zemin, "Build a well-off society," pp. 23, 37–45.

16. Jiang Zemin, "Build a well-off society," pp. 13–14. We have used the original Chinese in translating this sentence.

represents." The difficulty, they said, was fierce political opposition. One commented: "President Jiang advanced reform at great political risk. In fact, he met with strong resistance from the Party conservatives."

The Chinese leader also began to express his doubts about communism, and the most dramatic example of this came at a March 2001 meeting of the Chinese People's Political Consultative Conference. Jiang attended the deliberations of one of its committees, and there he startled the committee members by saying, "What is communism? No one knows. I don't know." "This comment," one participant told us, "spread through the conference like wildfire. Jiang, like most bureaucrats, makes long speeches that say nothing, but this was highly significant: a cryptic speech that implied a lot."

"What Jiang was proposing with the 'three represents'," another official said, "was a total reform of the Party," and this interpretation was made explicit in internal documents to its more than 64 million members at that time. He continued: "What these members were told was that the Party would no longer represent just the working classes. Jiang was challenging the historic 'vanguard' role of the Party and the special place of the proletariat in it."

Many of those interviewed in China in 2001 and 2002 linked the fate of Jiang's proposed political reforms to foreign policy. Several Chinese officials said that Jiang had staked much of his reputation on maintaining stable and positive relations with the United States and that a major cost of the increased tensions in US–China relations was the erosion of Jiang's reputation within the Party and broader population with negative consequences for genuine political reform. In early 2001, one official complained, "the conservatives in our country have won the battle."

Whatever the validity of this assertion, it was clear in visits at that time that the "three represents" were under attack and were being modified. One official said:

President Jiang is very interested in social democracy. However, his concern is not to move too fast toward political reform. You know that China would go the way of Indonesia or the Philippines if there were excessive democracy here. The level of democracy should be consistent with the level of popular education. So, not only do the conservatives oppose moving too fast [toward democracy], but so too do the east China urban educated. They know that the people in the smaller towns and in China's west are potentially very radical.[17]

A truly democratic China, it was noted, might have greater legitimacy, but popular rule might prove more nationalistic and unyielding to outside pressures. This complex controversy apparently also involved differences over globalization and China's entry into the WTO and over any moves toward a major new opening up of China to foreign companies as proposed by Jiang at a forum in May 2001.

At about that time, Jiang's conservative opponents wrote a long

17. See also, for example, Sun Zhi, "An interview with Li Liangdong," *Ta kung pao* (*Dagong bao*) (Hong Kong; internet version), 4 September 2002.

"10,000-word document" (*wan yan shu*) denouncing the "three represents" as "a flag of revisionism," the same leftist slogan used by Mao Zedong to defeat what he considered the more liberal elements in the Party in the 1960s. The "real purpose" of the document, we were told, was to expose the alleged failure of Jiang's pro-American policies and thereby undermine his overall political and economic strategy.

Stage two: Jiang's anniversary speech, the intensification of cadre indoctrination and the intrusion of the Taiwan issue. On 1 July 2001, Jiang Zemin dramatically acted to end speculations about the delay or demise of his reform initiatives. His speech celebrating the 80th anniversary of the Party's founding devoted more than an hour to the "three represents" and made them the centrepiece of his political strategy.[18] He substantially elaborated on their meaning, and the discussions shifted from interpretation of the "three represents" to the plane of propaganda and cadre indoctrination. Jiang also was muting the importance of the earlier dogma – such as the "four cardinal principles" – and calling for solutions based on "emancipating our minds" and fact-based debate.[19]

On the day after the speech, one senior intellectual told us: "Consider it in this light. By making intellectuals, scientists, engineers, managers, and other 'advanced productive elements' the representatives of the working class, Jiang is signalling a sharp right turn. He also had to emphasize his commitment to Marxism-Leninism and his adherence to revolutionary ideals. The slogan in Deng's time in the early 1990s was to 'make a right turn with a left-hand signal'."

The same day, an official responsible for the education of senior cadres explained to us the reasons for the heavy emphasis on cadre indoctrination that was then becoming such a prominent theme in the Chinese press. In subsequent interviews, the point was repeatedly made that Jiang's anniversary speech had been written to forge an alliance of lower- and high-level officials against a minority of mid-level bureaucrats and the "conservative old guard."

In response, Jiang's most severe critics continued to accuse him of "ignoring the plight of millions of jobless workers and migrant farmers" and of seeking to create a "Party for the rich, the noble, and the powerful." Nevertheless, one Party official confirmed that the resistance to this "revolutionary change" was coming principally from within the Party itself, not the "masses." He said: "The traditionalist officials and bureaucrats will come around, or they will leave the Party." In a sense, this would be a classic high–low political coalition against the entrenched

18. The full English-language text of this speech is found in *China Daily*, 2 July 2001, pp. 4–6.

19. In his report to the 16th Party Congress, Jiang does give passing reference to the "four cardinal principles," but these are seldom mentioned elsewhere. These four principles are "adherence to the socialist road, the people's democratic dictatorship, the leadership of the Communist Party, and Marxism-Leninism and Mao Zedong Thought." See his "Build a well-off society," pp. 10, 37. The quote on "emancipating our minds" and the reference to "seeking truth through facts" is on p. 15.

middle, and the result, if successful, would bring the Party closer to the most progressive elements of society and to a political body more like the European social democratic parties. Its targets were bureaucratism, corruption and outmoded thinking.

A senior Party leader at the same time cautioned: "Modernization has led to the decentralization of decision-making and to an empowering of the lower-level officials in much of China. The system's decentralization makes the central level less relevant. It used to be that when the Party centre spoke, the people all listened and obeyed. That day is gone." His point was that Jiang was responding to China's dominant realities, not inventing new ones. Another official said:

The "three represents" policy directly affects the future course of our relations with Taiwan. With this new policy, the two sides of the Taiwan Strait will be converging, and the mainland will be becoming more like the democratic and capitalist systems of other nations. With respect to the 9.11 incident, we face a common threat and have common interests with America, and our two political systems are now not fundamental rivals or, more accurately, that rivalry will steadily lessen. This should make it much easier to stand together.

Yet in August 2002, this same official flagged the dangers of the rapid movement of the government on Taiwan towards independence, its probable effect on US–China relations and its impact on the implementation of the reform policies. He belittled the alleged American belief that because China's modernization depends on the United States, Beijing must "bow and scrape" before it. "The United States should not hold that China will always rely on it. Such thinking is very dangerous. The Chinese will resist if they are forced into a corner. Do not think that it does not matter to China if someone bullies it. An opportunity now exists. The two sides should make joint efforts to develop constructive and co-operative relations. You should understand that this would affect China's political direction."

By the end of the annual meeting of the Party elite at the resort city of Beidaihe in early August, that opportunity seemed more remote as the debate over Taiwan intensified.[20] At the same time, Jiang Zemin's planned visit to the United States in October had assumed added significance, and many reform-related issues had become entwined in the debate on how to deal with the US. Jiang's reform polices would require domestic tranquility, growing prosperity and, most importantly, good relations with America. Behind the scenes, the tug of war between holding the line in the face of external threats and pressing ahead on reform intensified.

20. On 3 August 2002, at a critical time in the Beidaihe deliberations, Taiwan President Chen Shui-bian advanced the idea "one side, one country" (*yibian, yiguo*) and called for a referendum on Taiwan's future status. Central News Agency (Taipei; internet version), 3 August 2002.

Stage three: institutional and personnel changes. Like the overlapping boundaries of other "stages" under discussion here, the process of indoctrination continued and merged into the subsequent period of institutional and personnel changes. During the spring and summer of 2002, two slogans preceded the call for a party-state institutional system built on the principles of the "three represents." They were "Keep up with the times" (*yushi jujin*) and "Build a moderately well-off society" (*jianshe xiaokang shehui*). In the summer of 2002, the PLA, among a host of others, picked up on these slogans. It denounced laggards who "only talk about the advantages of People's War and lack the sense of keeping up with the times" by failing to build military systems based on modern information technology.[21]

Speaking to the Party's senior leadership on 31 May 2002, Jiang stressed that attaining a "moderately well-off society" meant that China must proceed with changes at an accelerated pace or face falling behind.[22] To do this, the Party would have to implement the requirements of the "three represents" which meant "keeping up with the times." He added, the Chinese people "must be able to see the important changes that have taken place in the world's political, economic, cultural, and scientific-technological fields" since the publication of the Communist Manifesto.

During the early part of the summer, Jiang's attention became directed towards the strengthening of the cadre system, and the burden of these efforts was to fall on the then head of the Central Committee's Organization Department, Zeng Qinghong, a man often referred to as the Party's *da guanjia* or "big manager," and now a senior Politburo member and China's vice-president. Zeng's task was to implement the "three represents" within the main political and military strongholds. This would mean a more highly educated elite and a stronger emphasis on the professionalization of the military. The synergy was obvious: the Party must represent the so-called advanced productive forces so that experts, skilled entrepreneurs and intellectuals, and the requisite institutional "political reforms" would thereby more effectively promote the next era of modernization.

It was with this in mind that on 7 May 2002, the State Council had enacted the "2002–2005 National Outline of Building Contingents of Qualified Personnel,"[23] and on 23 July, this outline was followed by the Party's "Regulations on the Selection and Appointment of Leading Party and Government Cadres."[24] A day or so after the release of these regulations, Zeng gathered his Organization Department colleagues to galvanize them into action and told them to enforce the new standards at

21. *Jiefangjun bao* (internet version), 6 August 2002, p. 2.
22. The text of this speech is found in Xinhua, 31 May 2002. On 3 December 2002, *Renmin ribao* (internet version) published a lengthy article by Wang Mengkui entitled "A grand program for building a well-off society."
23. The text of this document can be found in Xinhua, 11 June 2002.
24. The full text of the regulations was published by Xinhua, 23 July 2002. The most authoritative statement on them is the editorial in *Remin ribao* (internet version), 24 July 2002. The editorial speaks of the regulations as setting "sound" standards for "selecting, appointing, supervising and managing cadres."

all Party, state and military levels.[25] In early August, the Personnel Ministry issued a state circular on implementing the new regulations as one more in a sequence of steps to implement the first and second represents throughout the national bureaucracy.[26]

The motivations behind the emphasis on more qualified personnel entering the national bureaucracy were thus becoming clearer. This carefully sculptured form of reform would strengthen the Party and state apparatus and also, perhaps, make it more attractive to educated Chinese, including those trained abroad. Beijing was attempting to marry loyalty, power, expertise and wealth. It would thereby advance state interests in much the same way that leaders in Japan, Korea and Singapore had earlier used state power to create and foster new forms of public-private enterprises and meritocracy.

Stage four: power struggle and the 16th Party Congress. During the years after Jiang first floated the "three represents" in early 2000, the Party's more traditionalist and conservative elements had fought against the projected political reform and had helped block the promotion of Zeng Qinghong, one of its principal promoters, to full membership on the Politburo. Rumours of a power struggle in the Party, always the fare of the Hong Kong, Taiwanese and Japanese sensationalist press, did contain kernels of fact, and those facts became more numerous and credible during the summer of 2002.[27]

The showdown allegedly came at Beidaihe in July and August 2002, and one piece of evidence concerning the intensity of the debate was the decision to postpone the opening of the 16th Party Congress. The public announcement of the retirement of Jiang as Party general secretary in favour of Hu Jintao also appeared to have been temporarily put on hold until the leadership hammered out a consensus on the Party's top-tier leadership.

A modicum of agreement appears to have been reached in Beidaihe and most certainly by the time the 16th Party Congress opened on 7 November. One example of this was the action to legitimate further a modern capitalist market economy. Laws would be put in place to protect private enterprise and attack "crony capitalism." One well-informed Chinese said that this would ease the insecurity of the new capitalists and foreign investors and create "a new ideological framework to justify institutional change and the reform of the command economy."[28]

The other major elements of agreement of relevance here concerned the structure of the Party Politburo and Central Military Commission and

---

25. Xinhua, 25 July 2002.
26. For a review of the circular, see Xinhua, 6 August 2002.
27. See, for example, Tadashi Ito, "PRC elders oppose Jiang Zemin staying on as Party head," *Sankei shimbun* (internet version), 26 August 2002. It quoted an unnamed source as saying the next Party Congress would not be held on schedule "because renegotiations became necessary since not only the leadership reshuffle but also the Congress work report and the proposal to revise the Party constitution did not gain a consensus at Beidaihe."
28. Information from a well-informed scholar, 8 October 2002.

the revision of the CCP constitution to include reference to the "three represents" and the direction of future political reforms. Jiang for the first time highlighted the need for a new "political civilization" and thereby mandated a fundamental ideological framework for long-term political reform.[29] With those agreements in place, Jiang triumphantly handed the job of Party general secretary over to Hu Jintao. Equally important, he engineered the recomposition of the Standing Committee to include Zeng Qinghong and other close associates who had stood beside him throughout the long campaign to organize support for the "three represents."

That campaign, it should be noted, had centred mostly on the first two represents, and one might ask what had happened to the Party's commitment to representing the "broad masses," the third represent. Clearly the problem areas within the population do continue to plague the Party leadership, as witnessed by the visits of Hu Jintao, Zeng Qinghong and other Politburo members to some of the poorest areas of China in early 2003. However, a recent analysis by new Politburo member Li Changchun concerning the failures of the state-run media to attract popular interest suggests a deeper meaning. In Beijing meetings in February 2003, we learned that Li had referred to the broad masses as the "broad market" and turned the meaning of the three represents into an argument whereby the advanced entrepreneurs working within a growing economy, an advancing cultural environment and an ever more sophisticated domestic market would promote overall economic construction and prosperity. In essence the "three represents" constituted the main economic plank and a fundamentally new way of thinking in the Party's long-term policy platform.

What we have learned about the transformations rocking China today and over the past quarter-century can now be summarized in terms of three interlocked and mutually reinforcing changes: modernization, political reform and globalization. Each of these changes has made possible and necessitated the others, and each has advanced to a new stage. At the 16th Party Congress, Jiang called on China to "take the path of new industrialization" based on science and education, sustainable development, and the accelerated deployment of information technology.[30] These priorities reflect the interactions of policy declarations, institutional changes and new incentive structures. Such interactions may well decide whether and how the leadership can fundamentally restructure and revitalize the behaviour of the governing institutions and political participation.

For China, the die has been cast, and all nations will watch as the grand reform experiment is played out. By linking the reform to this new vision of modernization and to those progressive elements or beneficiaries that can pursue it, the post-Congress Party has placed a bet on a new era or type of progress. It has engineered the first peaceful transfer of power in modern Chinese history.

29. Jiang Zemin, "Build a well-off society," part V. Previously, the Party had stressed only the underlying material and spiritual civilizations.
30. *Ibid.*

If the fate of other one-party systems in Asia is any guide, then one-party rule in China is living on borrowed time. In China, the private economic sector has surpassed the state-owned one and is creating a myriad of new private interests that are independent of and in competition with the Party's interests. The pressures are increasing in the direction of factionalized national, regional and local politics. More challenging forms of political competition will sooner or later emerge as divergent interests further fracture Party unity and as the disfranchised and disconnected elements of society seek political justice and coalesce into a viable opposition. The Party has taken a huge gamble, and the problems with which we began this analysis could grow and overwhelm its chosen strategy.

State and Society in Urban China in the Wake of the 16th Party Congress*

Dorothy J. Solinger

ABSTRACT At the time of the convening of the 16th Party Congress in November 2002, the Party leadership confronted an urban society splintered by the blessings and the blows of two decades of ever-deepening marketization. This article explores the composition of urban society at that juncture, and aims to delineate its changing social structural break-down. It also investigates the correlation between Jiang Zemin's "three represents" and the various separate social groups making up the cities at the turn of the century. While arguing that in Jiang's vision the lowest stratum of society may have been intentionally excluded from his "represents," the piece also shows the stance of the state towards several groupings and its means of dealing with each. The piece concludes with a suggestion that new top leaders Hu Jintao and Wen Jiabao appeared, as of the time they took office, to be turning a new leaf.

The Urban Scene in Late 2002

As China's top leadership elite congregated in session to put forward a new Party line for the forthcoming five years and to unveil an altered line-up of the powerful, it confronted an urban society splintered by the blessings and the blows of two decades of ever-deepening marketization. While a growing middle class and a tiny but highly visible wealthy stratum basked in benefits of urban reform, other social elements, also resident in the cities, who were wrestling with the throes of downward mobility, sudden job loss and unaccustomed poverty, threatened to unravel the gains in which their neighbours revelled. This article takes a look at the urban scene as a whole as it presented itself just past the turn of the century. But it gives a bit more emphasis to the situation of a segment of society that is often forgotten or discounted in the more optimistic, congratulatory accounts of the post-1978 period of market reforms.

On the plus side, during the Ninth Five-Year Plan period (1996–2001), per household disposable income increased at an average annual per person rate of 5.7 per cent in real terms, while the urban wage for staff and workers' wages experienced an average per person annual increase of 15.9 per cent. Deducting for price factors, the average real growth in disposable income, wages and urban consumer expenditures saw annual average increases of 6.8, 6.9 and 6.7 per cent respectively. Permanent residents' average disposable income had risen to 6860 *yuan*, an improvement of 18.88-fold over the year when reforms began in 1978.[1] The

* I would like to thank the Smith Richardson Foundation for research support while I was preparing this article.
1. Yang Yiyong and Huang Yanfen, "Zhongguo jumin shouru fenpei xin geju" ("The new pattern in income distribution among Chinese urbanites"), in Ru Xin, Lu Xueyi and Li Peilin

lifestyle of this well-to-do, increasingly cosmopolitan and consumerist upper crust featured private car and home ownership, travel abroad, holidays and every manner of electronic convenience and luxury; urban dwellers held an average of 228,300 *yuan* in total assets, growing at an annual rate of about 25 per cent since 1984, according to a National Bureau of Statistics report. Real estate on average worth 109,400 *yuan* accounted for about 50 per cent of total assets. Moreover, each home in the study possessed 11,500 *yuan* worth of consumer goods.[2]

Accordingly, a recent volume paints an alluring portrait of city folk enjoying leisure activities and consumption patterns that include bowling, purchasing Western wedding garb, sending greeting cards and dining at McDonalds.[3] These are the partakers in a much-acclaimed "consumer revolution" that emerged in the 1990s in China's extra-large and most cosmopolitan metropolises and they are almost certainly contented with their present lives. If this assumption is correct, these people form a part of the contigent of all urbanites who, in a 2002 survey conducted for the project on "East Asia barometer: comparative survey of democratization and value changes," claimed their lives had improved (49 per cent) or even got much better (4.2 per cent) over the previous five years.[4]

This article begins with material in an internal report suggesting that the total of those laid off from state enterprises and the unemployed (both registered and unregistered) combined could have been as high as 60 million as of mid-2001.[5] A similar reckoning offered in a conference paper delivered in Hong Kong at the end of 2001 held that those city residents of working age who were not in full-time formal work numbered not less than 60 million, amounting to an unemployment rate of 12 to 15 per cent.[6]

If these two less public reports have some validity, that would call into serious question an official total of unemployed and laid-off for the year 2000 of a mere 12 million.[7] One scholar has written – in a journal that is

---

footnote continued

(eds.), *2003 nian shehui lanpishu: Zhongguo shehui xingshi fenxi yu yuce* (*Social Blue Book: 2003 Analysis and Predictions of China's Social Situation*) (Beijing: Shehui kexue wenxian chubanshe, 2003), pp. 226–234.

2. Reported in China News Digest, 28 September 2002, from the Agence France Presse.

3. Deborah S. Davis (ed.), *The Consumer Revolution in Urban China* (Berkeley: University of California Press, 2000).

4. Data courtesty of Tianjian Shi. The calculations here are from the unweighted sample (the only version available as of May 2003).

5. Wang Depei, " 'San min' yu 'erci gaige' " (" 'Three people' and 'the second reform' "), *Gaige neican* (*Reform Internal Reference*) (hereafter *GGNC*), No. 7 (2001), p. 25. Economist Hu Angang stated that China had laid off 55 million people from 1995 to mid-2002 (China News Digest, 9 July 2002).

6. Tang Jun, "Dibao zhiduzhong de shehui paichi" ("Social discrimination in the minimum living guarantee system"), paper presented at the Conference on Social Exclusion and Marginality in Chinese Societies, sponsored by the Centre for Social Policy Studies of the Department of Applied Social Sciences, the Hong Kong Polytechnic University and the Social Policy Research Centre, Institute of Sociology, the Chinese Academy of Social Sciences, Hong Kong, 16–17 November 2001, p. 1.

7. Qiao Jian, "Jiaru WTO beijingxia de Zhongguo zhigong zhuangkuang" ("The condition of China's staff and workers against the background of entering WTO"), in Li Peilin,

translated into English – that about 30 million workers had been laid off as of 2001, which he estimated as amounting to about 30 per cent of the state enterprise workers in place in 1995.[8] But if 60 million have actually been dismissed, obviously 30 per cent is far too low. Another study calculated the urban workforce at about 210 million in recent years[9]; if that is accurate, then somewhere between 14 and 29 per cent of the urban workforce could be counted as unemployed. A more modest estimate ranges from 15 to 20 per cent nation-wide, as of spring 2002.[10] And as told in the labour department's own statistics, just 21 million – less than half even of the 46 million whose jobs are gone officially,[11] not to mention millions of others whose firms have crashed that the regime does not tally – registered for the government-sponsored re-employment programme between May 1998 and the end of the year 2000.

In the same survey of residents' opinions on their lives mentioned above, a full 29 per cent of the Chinese population asserted that their family's economic situation was bad or very bad (22.5 per cent and 6.5 per cent respectively), while 20.9 per cent termed their family's economic situation worse than at the time of the 15th Party Congress held five years earlier in September 1997. This is quite a bit more than the 8.5 per cent who had felt that way as they looked backwards five years from the 15th to the 14th Party Congress.[12] And in a probability survey carried out under the auspices of the Chinese Academy of Social Sciences in

---

footnote continued

Huang Ping and Lu Jianhua (eds.), *2001 nian: Zhongguo shehui xingshi fenxi yu yuce* (*Year 2001: Analysis and Forecast of China's Social Situation*). (Beijing: Shehui kexue wenxuan chubanshe, 2001), p. 315 claims that at the end of June 2000 the total was 11.2 million. Laodong he shehui baozhangbu, Guojia tongjiju (Ministry of Labour and Social Security, National Bureau of Statistics), "2000 niandu laodong baozhang shiye fazhan tongji gongbao" ("The year 2000's statistical report of the developments in labour and social security), *LDBZTX*, No. 6 (2001), p. 36 notes 6.57 million laid-off as of the end of 2000, but Wang Dongjin, Deputy Minister of Labour and Social Security, referred in February 2001 to "some 20 million laid-off workers" (Reuters, "China to lay off 6.5 million urban workers a month," *Inside China Today*, 16 February 2001).

8. Zhang Wanli, "Twenty years of research on stratified social structure in contemporary China," *Social Sciences in* China, Vol. 23, No. 1 (Spring 2002), p. 52.

9. As of June 2000, 200.72 million people comprised the urban workforce, according to the National Bureau of Statistics. See n.a., "2000 nian shangbannian laodong he shehui baozhang qingkuang tongji baogao" ("A statistical report on the situation in labour and social security in the first half of 2000"), *ZGLD*, No. 10 (2000), p. 57; by the end of that year, that sector had risen to 212.74 million people (Laodong he shehui baozhangbu, Guojia tongjiju, "2000 niandu laodong baozhang shiye fazhan tongji gongbao" ("The year 2000's statistical report of the developments in labour and social security"), p. 36.

10. Matthew Forney and Neil Gough, "Working man blues," *Time*, Vol. 159, No. 12 (1 April 2002), pp. 26–27, based on the calculations of Beijing University's Xiao Zhuoji.

11. Hu Angang, "China's present economic situation and its macro-economic policies," RAND-China Reform Forum conference, 29–30 November 2001), p. 9. Hu says here that between 1996 and 2000, the number of workers and staff in state firms was reduced by 31.42 million, amounting to 27.9% of the previous workforce there, and that, combined with the 15.17 million cut from collective enterprises, the two together totalled 46.59 million lost jobs, or 32.7% overall. See also Also Hu Angang, "Chuangzhaoxing de cuihui: Zhongguo de jiegou biange (1996–2000 nian)" ("Creative destruction: China's structural evolution (1996–2000)"), Ms, 2001, p. 1.

12. Data courtesy of Tianjian Shi.

mid-2001, targeting 6,000 urbanites in 12 provinces and 72 cities, counties and districts, a similar result was obtained: 23.8 per cent declared their standard of living had changed for the worse (12.6 per cent said somewhat worse, 11.2 said very much worse) compared with 1995.[13]

Similar data come from some individual cities. In a survey done in Wuhan in 2000, for instance, 23 per cent of respondents reported that their income had declined somewhat (13.3 per cent) or a lot (9.6 per cent) since 1995.[14] The same study also found that 42 per cent of the city's population was living in households where the average monthly income per person was US$156 per month or less.[15] Research on 1,000 laid-off workers in Beijing performed in 1999 revealed that their average income fell by 61 per cent, while that of the "especially poverty-stricken" (*tekunhu*) dropped even more.[16]

Linked to findings of this sort is material exposed in an internal report on "social disturbances" published by the Party's Organization Department in 2001. This volume announced ominously if confidentially that the Gini coefficient was approaching a dangerous 0.4 nation-wide as of the year 2001.[17] The statistic included both urban and rural people, and the latter live far worse, on average, than do the former.[18] Gaps are pronounced among regions, too. By one research team's calculations, the urban population accounts for 36.09 per cent of the total population overall, but the proportions vary greatly by geographic area: the statistics are 49.42 per cent in the east, and just 29.45 per cent in central and western China.[19]

The same Organization Department study revealed that the National Bureau of Statistics, in collaboration with the State Council Research Office and other units, had discovered that nation-wide 20 to 30 million urban workers had fallen into poverty in recent years, giving a total, with their family members, of about 40 to 50 million people, or almost 13 per

13. Lu Xueyi, *Dangdai Zhongguo shehui jieceng yanjiu baogao* (*A Research Report on China's Current Social Structure*) (Beijng: shehui kexue wenxian chubanshe, 2002), pp. 3, 39.

14. Benwen ketizu (the research group for this document), "Xin shiqi Wuhan shehui jieceng jiegou yanjiu" ("Research on Wuhan's social structure in the new period"), *Changjiang luntan* (*Yangtze Tribune*), No. 5 (2002), p. 31.

15. *Ibid.* p. 30. The breakdown here was that 28% were living in households where the annual average income per person was 8,000 to 15,000 *yuan*, and 14.4% were living in households where the annual average income per person was under 8,000 *renminbi*. This translates into US$976 per year per person or less in the lowest 14.4% of the population.

16. *Ibid.* p. 15.

17. Zhonggong zhongyang zuzhibu ketizu (Chinese central organization department research group), *2000–2001 Zhongguo diaocha baogao – xin xingshi xia renmin neibu maodun yanjiu* (*2000–2001 Chinese Investigation Report – Research on Internal Contradictions Within the People Under the New Situation*) (Beijing: Zhongyang bianyi chubanshe, 2001), p. 70. According to an email communication from Arthur R. Kroeber, 12 March 2003, recent World Bank data show that the year 2000 Gini coefficient in China was 0.44.

18. Yang Yiyong and Huang Yanfen, "The new pattern in income distribution among Chinese urbanites," p. 227, gives the following progressively increasing urban–rural income differentials for the years 1996 to 2001, expressed as the amount greater the urban average income is as compared to the rural one. 1996: 2.51; 1997: 2.47; 1998: 2.51; 1999: 2.65; 2000: 2.79; 2001: 2.90.

19. Lu Xueyi, *China's Current Social Structure*, pp. 90, 91.

cent of the urban population.[20] A final grim official statistic from March 2002 admits that 30 milion urbanites who could barely subsist were living in slums and unable to afford some of the basic necessities of life. These most destitute among the city dwellers amounted to nearly 7 per cent of the urban population, which stood at 455.94 million as of the time of the 2000 national census, according to the official count.[21]

Meanwhile, untold numbers of migrants from the countryside had entered the cities in search of work over the preceding two decades. Figures for those who have left their rural homes range from 100 to 200 million, and, though many of them do find jobs[22] – often against central orders and to the distress of furloughed urban workers – the conditions in the municipalities for many of them continue to be most unsavoury. A recent study by Human Rights in China has found continued torment and torture of rural workers picked up at whim in the cities up to the present.[23]

Accompanying these figures is a mounting surge in protests and demonstrations in response, as the Organization Department study reveals. Rising "mass incidents" vex the governors, as they erupt not only in the form of petitions but also by blocking roads, railways and bridges, and assaulting Party and government organs and personnel. In the cities, not just retired and laid-off workers but small proprietors, teachers, students and even cadres have remonstrated and rallied, in the name of such grievances as delayed wages and pensions and unfulfilled compensation for the loss of work posts. Researchers worry as numbers rise, the scale expands, and the wronged become more antagonistic.[24] According to the Hong Kong Centre for Human Rights and Democracy, China witnessed as many as 60,000 labour protests in 1998, most involving former state employees; the following year that number allegedly climbed

20. Zhonggong zhongyang zuzhibu ketizu, *2000–2001 Chinese Investigation Report*, pp. 170–71.

21. These figures are not comparable. The 30 million urbanites who were poverty-stricken in 2002 do not include rural migrants, for poverty counts in cities include only the "non-agricultural population," that is, the population holding urban registration. (For one example of many, see Tang Jun *et al.*, *Zhongguo chengshi pinkun yu fanpinkun baogao* (*Report on Poverty and Anti-poverty in Urban China*) (Beijing: Huaxia chubanshe, 2003), table 2–1, p. 46.) The migrants, however, earn only about half the income that urbanites do, according to some surveys (see, for instance, Benwen ketizu, "Research on Wuhan's social structure," which notes on p. 24 that the average urban income in the year 2000 in Wuhan was 610 *yuan* per person per month, while p. 27 says that the average wage income per person among those who have left the village and were working in Wuhan was 340.05 *yuan* per month.). But the offical total for the urban population does include some migrants. In the 2000 census migrants who had left their homes a full six months before the census was administered were included in the urban population total. See Zhou Yixing and Laurence J. C. Ma, "China's urbanization levels: reconstructing a baseline from the fifth population census," *The China Quarterly*, No. 173 (March 2003), p. 187.

22. According to Hu Angang, workers with rural household registration accounted for just 7.8% of new urban jobs in 1979, but this proportion had risen to 29.85% by 1996 (Hu Angang, "Employment and development," p. 7).

23. See Dorothy J. Solinger, *Contesting Citizenship in Urban China: Peasant Migrants, the State and the Logic of the Market* (Berkeley: University of California Press, 1999) and Human Rights in China, "Institutionalized exclusion: the tenuous legal status of internal migrants in China's major cities," Hong Kong, 6 November 2002.

24. Zhonggong zhongyang zuzhibu ketizu, *2000–2001 Chinese Investigation Report*, pp. 67–69.

to 100,000.[25] While material of this sort by no means ensures that China is set to encounter instability on a massive and uncontrollable scale, it does serve to temper the enthusiasm of reform proponents.

The Current Shape of Social Stratification

In whatever light they are viewed, the data in the previous section surely suggest that the shape of the urban social structure in China has undergone a major transformation in the decades since economic reform began in 1978, and that further alterations have taken place just in the five years between the past two Communist Party Congresses, in 1997 and 2002. As of the turn of the century, several efforts at mapping this shift have emerged, and some of their findings are recounted below. The picture that the surveys undertaken to chart the changes uncover is one to which the post-Congress leadership group must respond; its members need to determine the stance they will adopt and the biases, if any, they are prepared to display as they forge their own agenda.

Over the first few years of the new century there was much talk of the concept of the "three represents" coined by outgoing Party general secretary and state president Jiang Zemin in early 2000. This theory, developed by several of Jiang's academic followers, was first articulated in a speech that Jiang delivered, quite appropriately, in Guangdong province; it became a catch-word for his political platform and indeed for correct policy in the two or three years thereafter while he remained at the helm of power.[26]

Whether the stratification of the urban public in the early years of the century is best conceived as a hierarchy of classes or as one of status groups is difficult to pin down precisely. If one resorts to the most common approach, the Marxian one, which distinguishes collectivities in terms of their common economic condition, and, specifically, their relationship to capital and the means of production, one might simply see the "three represents" as corresponding to an upper class (those responsible for and benefiting from their expertise in manipulating the "advanced productive forces"), a middle class (those with the intellectual and educational attributes for contributing to "advanced culture") and a working class (the rest of "the people"). Alternatively, since not all Jiang's labels are economically-oriented, it might work better to view the divisions to which each "represent" refers as status groups, subjectively appraised assemblages separated more by the particular role they

25. Jiang Xueqin, "Fighting to organize," *Far Eastern Economic Review*, 6 September 2001, pp. 72–75.

26. Joseph Fewsmith, *China Since Tiananmen* (New York: Cambridge University Press, 2001), p. 230; Susan V. Lawrence, "Three cheers for the Party," *Far Eastern Economic Review*, 26 October 2000, p. 32; and Andrew J. Nathan and Bruce Gilley, *China's New Rulers: The Secret Files* (New York: New York Review Books, 2002), pp. 116, 167–68. According to Nathan and Gilley, p. 168, the theorists who developed the concept did so out of a recognition of the growing significance of the middle class. Lawrence's article emphasizes Jiang's fears about Party rule collapsing, as happened in other socialist states, and his desire to recast the Party's identity to meet the challenges of the 21st century.

play in society than by their respective income rankings. Certainly those who might be sorted into either of the first two categories are better differentiated by their function and its prestige than by their level of wealth.

For instance, informal ties and hidden corruption could enable some people with specialized technical expertise – who might seem best placed among those responsible for "advanced culture" – to fall into an upper class economically. Conversely, some enterprise managers, engaged primarily in upgrading the work process, may fall financially into the tier of the middle class and not into the echelon of the most successful private entrepreneurs, even though they may, like the entrepreneurs, be labouring to advance the productive forces. Moreover, among "the people," those still employed surely belong to a different status group than do the laid-off staff and workers (*xiagang zhigong*) or, even worse, the fully unemployed.

Recent social surveys tend to break the population down occupationally, as in the recent authoritative study completed by Lu Xueyi and other researchers at the Chinese Social Science Academy mentioned earlier.[27] That project classified the population of China into just four strata: workers, peasants, "middle (or white-collar) stratum" and private entrepreneurs. It appears, from the way these scholars define the latter group, that, if the workers and peasants were combined, these groups more or less fit Jiang's three categories.[28]

To comprehend the nature of the audience the leadership perceived itself to be addressing, it will be helpful to get a rough sense of the proportions of the urban community occupied by each of the category groups among the three targets of the "represents." For the first of these, those adept at handling "the advanced productive forces," Lu Xueyi's team found that in four urban areas typical of China's range of cities – one that constitutes a special economic zone (Shenzhen), one that is a central China provincial capital (Hefei), a central China county-level city near Wuhan (Hanchuan) and a minority area county-level town in western China (Zhenning) – the peak of what this team calls China's pyramidical social structure is quite small. Indeed, a table in the study notes that a mere 0.6 per cent of the populace nation-wide is taken up by private entrepreneurs. Stated differently, about 7.8 million people could be deemed members of an upper class.[29]

Moreover, overall, the authors estimate, 60 to 70 per cent of the population comprises people with an income below the average of that in

27. Lu Xueyi, *China's Current Social Structure*.

28. Despite the fact that private entrepreneurs comprise a separate category, the authors use this title to apply to the wealthiest among them, or what could be said to be the upper class. For in their definition, the "middle class" is composed of those with "white collars," such as private entrepreneurs, those working in foreign firms, office workers, technical workers, high- and middle-level professors, engineers and those with scarce technical skills, the managers of large state firms and in monopoly sectors, and various types of intermediaries, performers and sports stars, along with those who have profited by relying on "black," semi-legal and illegal trades (*ibid.* p. 249).

29. *Ibid.* p. 44.

their city of residence. More striking, in both the wealthiest and the poorest of the four places investigated, Shenzhen and Zhenning, a full 74 per cent have incomes below the average level in their home towns.[30] The authors also report that, as of 1999, according to their statistical analysis, just 18.3 per cent of the entire population could be counted as being a part of the middle class – perhaps equivalent to the second "represent," those skilled in "advanced culture," but that only 15 per cent of the working population belonged there.[31] Besides, it is only in the larger cities, such as Shenzhen and Hefei, the researchers discovered, that the middle class is composed of what they call the "modern middle stratum," that is, specialized technical personnel and office personnel, whereas in Hanchuan and Zhenning the middle stratum is comprised of "traditional" types, the small-time private industrialists and merchants (*geti gong-shanghu*).[32]

The bulk of the population, some 66.6 per cent of it, lies within a lower stratum containing two categories: industrial workers (*chanye gongren*), of which urban-situated peasant workers (*nongmingong*) account for 7.8 per cent[33]; and peasants, with these two categories representing 22.6 and 44 per cent of the total respectively.[34] Startling variation obtains in the percentages of the urban population that belong to the middle class, as evidenced, for instance, in the study's finding that 46 per cent of Shenzhen's population fit there, but just 38 per cent of Hefei's, only 10 per cent of Hanchuan's and a mere 3 per cent of Zhenning county's.[35]

True, as the authors point out, the middle class has emerged and is growing.[36] But, to put this into a larger perspective, so too are those without steady work. According to Sun Liping, a Chinese social scientist at Tsinghua University's Humanities and Social Science Academy, since the late 1980s China went through a transition from a stage of capital diffusion to one of wealth concentration; by the early 1990s, the process of amassing wealth had really taken off.[37] Following this trend, Sun argues that, while some scholars surmise that the entrepreneurs and

30. *Ibid.* p. 25. According to Benwen ketizu, "Research on Wuhan's social structure," p. 33, 81.4% of the population of Wuhan had incomes in the middle middle, the lower middle and the lower strata of society as of the year 2000.

31. Lu Xueyi, *China's Current Social Structure*, pp. 50, 73. This second statement is a bit hard to comprehend since the authors explicitly define the middle class according to occupational group. According to James Kynge, "Borrowing sustains middle classes in China's Long March to prosperity," *Financial Times*, 28 December 2002, "other (unnamed) commentators have reported that only 40 to 100 million people belong to the middle class, because of their income of more than US$3,000 per year, which would amount to over 2,000 *yuan* per month." Such analysts, then, would be arguing for a middle class representing from only 3.5 to 9% of the total population.

32. Lu Xueyi, *Current Social Structure*, p. 50.

33. The authors list those who are part of the working class on p. 127, including manufacturing labour, miners and electrical, coal, water supply, and construction and transport workers, along with their assistants and service workers.

34. *Ibid.* pp. 44, 74.

35. *Ibid.* p. 88.

36. *Ibid.* p. 49.

37. Sun Liping, "90 niandai zhongqi yilai Zhongguo shehui jiegou yanbian di xin qushi" ("New trends in the evolution of Chinese social structure since the mid-1990s"), *Dangdai Zhongguo yanjiu* (*Modern China Studies*), Vol. 9, No. 3 (2002), pp. 7, 9.

white-collar workers of today are evolving into a middle class, he foresees instead a trend moving China towards severe income polarization, as is found in a number of the societies of South America.[38]

According to his reasoning, the enormous wealth of a few among the population contributes to the growing size of the "weak groups," or the poor population.[39] He charges that although such people's livelihood was gradually improving in the 1980s, since the mid-1990s, even as rather rapid economic growth was taking place, the absolute income of some declined, and the numbers of these have increased over the past few years. Sun also estimates that nearly 100 million surplus rural labourers entered the cities after the early 1990s, a segment not explicitly mentioned in the Lu Xueyi study.[40]

He also maintains that entering the World Trade Organization will mean that those in the highest stratum will eventually see their incomes converge with salaries in the international market. As this occurs, Sun predicts, this elite portion of the population will become more and more divorced from other sections of the Chinese population, intensifying polarization within China and solidifying the rejection of the unemployed.[41] This portrayal of the social structure in urban China, for the present and the time ahead, raises a critical political question: where will the newly installed political leadership stand with regard to the handling of this issue, and is their position differerent from that of the politicians recently retired?

Jiang's Views as Expressed in his Political Report to the Congress

With the delivery of outgoing Party chief Jiang Zemin's political report to the 16th Congress, rich in its references to the "three represents," a canonical imprimatur was seemingly implanted upon the official conception of Chinese society, along with this purportedly departing leader's pronouncement of the Party's foundational switch in its own social base. What could once be studied under the broad rubric of "state and society" in China should now, the speech signalled, be recognized as a matter of the state confronting not just one entity but at least three wholly disparate segments of society, certainly for the urban arena. For the now-sanctioned configuration of the social structure translated "society" into a triple formation, in the first orthodox re-ordering of elements in society since the time when Mao's classes and class struggle were jettisoned over 20 years before.

Thus the relationship between "state" and "society" had shifted, publicly and authoritatively, into one that is multi-layered, stratified by three very dissimilar party-state strategies towards three distinct status groups, as categorized by the "three represents." At some points in the speech, it

38. *Ibid.* p. 11.
39. *Ibid.* p. 13.
40. *Ibid.* p. 14.
41. *Ibid.* pp. 18–19.

almost appears as if a fourth, more lowly segment of society may have been relegated outside "the people" for the forseeable future: whether the poverty-stricken, the new urban poor, those who are without steady jobs, are part of the third group, or whether they instead constitute a residual, more or less forgotten fragment of society, remained uncertain.

On the surface, what rapidly became the most celebrated slogan in the nation-wide media has been read by many as having been intended to stretch the Party's relevance to and recruitment of social elements once disparaged, degraded and debarred from membership not just in the Communist Party but in polite political society as well, namely, private businesspeople and the highly educated. But in fact, insofar as the cities went, it would seem that Jiang's version of this slogan was more divisive than integrative. Thus, his recitation of the idiom amounted to a trifurcated splitting up of the citizenry there, with a not-so-subtle preference signalled for the members of its first two target groupings. Accordingly, the posture of the Party in its prior incarnation as the vanguard of the proletariat is to be jettisoned, replaced by a brand new visage, the Party as a conglomeration fit to command and speak for a competitive, modern and sophisticated constituency, prepared to merge into and contend with superior members of the global economy.

The new centrality of the linkage between China's best citizens and the world beyond is evident in Jiang's bias in his address. This bias grows directly out of the country's new place in the global market, and it appears both early in his speech and also in the talk's parting words. In his opening statement, Jiang pays homage to the "new phase of development" in which the nation now finds itself, an era when, in Jiang's phrases: "Science and technology are advancing rapidly. Competition in overall national strength is becoming increasingly fierce. Given this pressing situation, we must move forward or we will fall behind."[42] Similarly, the oration terminated with another evocation of the intimidating, if alluring, universe abroad: "We must be keenly aware of the rigorous challenges brought about by the ever-sharpening international competition as well as risks and difficulties that may arise on our road ahead."[43]

The leadership's unanimous fixation with China's joining the global economic race, and its concomitant need to match or surpass rivals outside, has been in evidence over the past five years, an up-to-date version of long-held dreams for Chinese leaders. It is this view that powered Jiang's perspective of the Party's prime forthcoming tasks. Indeed, that image of the country's relation to the world, surely magnified once China acceded to the World Trade Organization in late 2001, has unquestionably elevated the significance of sectors among the people who can contribute to the nation's victory in this endeavour.[44] At the same

42. "Full text of Jiang Zemin's report at 16th Party Congress," in http://english. peopledaily.com.cn/200211/18/eng20021118_106983.shtml (hereafter, Report).

43. *Ibid.*

44. Lu Xueyi, *Current Social Structure*, pp. 142–43.

time, it has relegated the under-educated and the unskilled to the margins of society.

True, "the people" (those not part of the "advanced" public) are not neglected altogether in the vision of Jiang Zemin. This third group, referred to as the "overwhelming majority of the people" (in the official English-language translation, *guangda renmin* in the original Chinese) – whose "fundamental interests" (*genben liyi*) are to be safeguarded – seems to constitute the same segment of the population with whose "fundamental interests" Jiang claims the major policy decisions taken by the Central Committee at and since the last Party Congress have been in accord. For the identical Chinese words are used in his speech in discussing both these points.

If by this designation Jiang is indeed referring to the same set of people, then he may be implicitly abandoning – or at any rate omitting from his "three represents" – the victims of the "difficulties" of recent years; for surely, as opinion surveys and statistical data on livelihood have demonstrated, what the Party has done since 1997 is not in their interests. Jiang himself is well aware of those left behind, as he explicitly refers to incomes increasing "only slowly," unemployment, people "still badly off," and those suffering because "things have yet to be straightened out in the matter of income distribution."[45]

Another mention of "represent[ing]" the "fundamental interests" of this "overwhelming majority" in the speech is then *followed by* a sentence admonishing that, "*More importantly*, we must pay great attention to less developed areas and the industries and people in straitened circumstances and show concern for them" (emphasis added), as if referring to an altogether separate portion of the people, perhaps, one might conclude, a segment that is *not* a part of the "three represents." And when Jiang enumerates the "main tasks for economic development and reform in the first two decades of this century," the charge "steadily [to] uplift the people's living standards" is number seven out of seven. One more example: in listing eight rather more concrete assignments, Jiang ranks the first one to "take a new road to industrialization and implement the strategy of rejuvenating the country through science and education and sustainable development." But the mission of reforming the system of income distribution and improving the social security system is only sixth, while doing "everything possible to create more jobs and improve the people's lives" comes last of all.

In the section of the speech concerning economic development, when Jiang turns to income distribution, he explicitly favours "efficiency" over "fairness," through "bringing market forces into play and encouraging part of the people to become rich first."[46] In short, China under the rule of Jiang progressively subjected itself to pressures for excellence and international competition, and, certainly for Jiang Zemin himself, this has spelt a contraction of the relevant political community.

45. Report.
46. Report.

Thus, though most of the light that was directed toward the 16th Party Congress was shone on its sanction of the private sector, and while some have likened China's leaders' perceptions and goals to those embodied in Khrushchev's 1961 notion of the "state of the whole people,"[47] I read Jiang's approach not so much as a version of Ken Jowitt's concept of "inclusion,"[48] an expansion of the Party's target groups in the style of what was supposed to have happened four decades ago in the Soviet Union. For, significantly, something like that is well in the past by now. As I argued in a piece I wrote fully 13 years ago, a symbiotic "merger" of the state with urban entrepreneurs was then already well under way, even in the late 1980s.[49] And Deng Xiaoping's 1979 declaration that intellectuals were members of the working class, along with his removal of "class labels" from the old bourgeoisie and others, achieved "inclusion" for the well educated in China as much as 24 years ago. Accordingly, I would argue that what was communicated in Jiang's agenda was more a *restriction of* and a *shrinkage in* the political community, in terms of the absolute numbers of those whose interests were to be served, and those to whom appeals will be proffered.

What then are the implications of this policy stance for the several status groups within urban society? The answer here must be varied in accordance with the weight now given each of them by the state. Those who have done recent, careful investigations of the relationships between private entrepreneurs and officialdom in the late 1990s, whether they have studied individuals or groups, come to a similar conclusion: at the birth of the new century, the symbiotic bond between the two that had already emerged by the late 1980s has only been consolidated further, if in new and slightly altered forms, according to David Wank.[50] And in a recent study of over 500 businesspeople who owned and operated firms with reported annual sales of over a million *renminbi* per annum, Bruce Dickson has demonstrated that organized entrepreneurs remain "still closely embedded in the state, cooperat[ing] with local officials and willing to be coopted by them."[51] At the time of Dickson's research (in 1997 and 1999), already one-third to two-fifths of the entrepreneurs in his

47. Two examples are Tony Saich, *Governance and Politics of China* (Houndmills, Great Britain: Palgrave, 2001), p. 78 and Nathan and Gilley, *China's New Rulers: The Secret Files*, p. 88.

48. On this, see Ken Jowitt, *New World Disorder: The Leninist Extinction* (Berkeley: University of California Press, 1992), ch. 3. On p. 88, Jowitt defines inclusion to be "attempts by the Party elite to expand the internal boundaries of the regime's political, productive, and decision-making systems, to integrate itself with the unofficial (i.e., non-apparatchik) sectors of society rather than insulate itself from them."

49. "Urban entrepreneurs and the state: the merger of state and society," in Arthur Rosenbaum (ed.), *State and Society in China: The Consequences of Reform* (Boulder: Westview Press, 1992), pp. 121–141.

50. David Wank, "Business-state clientelism in China: decline or evolution?" in Thomas Gold, Doug Guthrie and David Wank (eds.), *Social Connections in China* (Cambridge: Cambridge University Press, 2002), pp. 97–115.

51. Bruce Dickson, "Do good businessmen make good citizens? An emerging collective identity among China's private entrepreneurs," in Merle Goldman and Elizabeth J. Perry (eds.), *Changing Meanings of Citizenship in Modern China* (Cambridge, MA: Harvard University Press, 2002), p. 256.

sample had been absorbed into the Communist Party, while some had joined local people's congresses and political consultative congresses.[52]

Accordingly, Dickson concludes that the state's double-barrelled tactic – of building new organs to link the state with the business sector as a whole, while co-opting individual entrepreneurs into the Party – has successfully subverted any moves toward autonomy among these elements.[53] It appears, then, that in its mission of acting as representative of its first constituency – the promoters of the advanced productive forces – the state is efficaciously enfolding its appointed constituency, and there is no indication that this approach should change in the years ahead. Nothing in the political report suggests otherwise.

The state's strategy towards the middle class, whose most prominent members constitute the second "represent," that is, those capable of bearing "advanced culture," is best observed in its treatment of popular associations. In this realm, through repression and surveillance a skilful fine-tuning has rendered tiny and fragmented those groups that are perceived as dangerous to the regime. Meanwhile, a programme of courting and incorporating people seen as significant to it has managed officially to bind sizeable portions of the intellectual elite to the state.

At the same time, there also remains a space of relative looseness occupied in the cities by the non-dissident intelligentsia and the new professional strata, who exist in relationships with the state in some cases marked by mutual wariness and distrust, but in others by ties of mutual nurturance. Gordon White and Jude Howell's research of the early 1990s uncovered these patterns in state behaviour, which, according to a recent article by Tony Saich, continued in place as of the end of the decade, though by then some better endowed associations were finding ways around the state.[54]

But, Saich shows, 1998 regulations issued by the National People's Congress, while encouraging an expansion of societal intermediary organs, at the same time laid down rules on registration and management that would enhance state controls while – by charging huge fees for registration – limiting efforts by the less well educated and the poor to form bodies of their own.[55] This mode of handling social organized activity, or, one might say, of chiefly "representing" the purveyors of modern business techniques and high-tech knowledge, was the hallmark of Jiang Zemin's rule.

52. *Ibid.* pp. 272, 277.

53. *Ibid.* p. 287.

54. See Gordon White, Jude Howell and Shang Xiaoyuan, *In Search of Civil Society: Market Reform and Social Change in Contemporary China* (Oxford: Clarendon Press, 1996) and Tony Saich, "Negotiating the state: the development of social organizations in China," *The China Quarterly*, No. 161 (March 2000), pp. 124–141, which makes most of the same points, but also underlines the possibilities for groups to negotiate with, evade or feign compliance with the state, presumably if they have independent funds and are well enough placed to do so.

55. Saich, "Negotiating the state," pp. 128–132. See also "Bound and gagged: new regulations further curtail freedom of association," *China Rights Forum*, Spring 1999, pp. 28–33.

For the third stratum for which the Party intends to act as deputy, the majority of "the people," Jiang prescribes a course of trying to raise the proportion of people who are part of the middle-income group while increasing the income of the low-income group.[56] But he does not overtly mention, but is surely thinking of, the startling rise in demonstrations and other disturbances that the reforms have occasioned when he underscores the urgency of ensuring stability, the byword in dealing with protests in official addresses for over a decade.[57] Despite the rallies' frequency and escalation in scale and the leaders' keen awareness and deep unease over them, the regime has been vigilant and vigorous in undercutting and intimidating their participants.[58] The contrast between the realities of repression on the ground and the bland assurances of Jiang Zemin in his speech ("we should strengthen employment management in accordance with law, safeguard the legitimate rights and interests of workers ... "[59]) is sobering indeed.

Granted, he does promise efforts to create more jobs and improve people's lives. But he offers no specific new initiatives, and only pronounces on the protracted nature of the problems entailed, as he muses on them at the very close of the section on economic development. Indeed, every type of plan he offers – from giving policy support to firms that increase jobs or re-employ laid-off workers to helping the general public to change its mentality toward employment – has been tabled time and again over the past five years, and not to much notable effect.[60]

The one novel note for an official report delivered at so weighty a convention is the acknowledgment of the inevitability of cityward migration, plus the certainty that urbanization is set to increase massively in the years to come. Especially interesting here is the order to remove "all the institutional and policy barriers to urbanization."[61] Such admissions and instructions would seem to give greater flexibility to peasants moving into the metropolises. And yet, even here, there is the accustomed emphasis on containing such movement by keeping it "rational and

56. Report.
57. See Gong'anbu disi yanjiusuo "quntixing shijian yanjiu" ketizu (Ministry of Public Security Fourth Research Institute's "mass incidents research" group), "Woguo fasheng quntixing shijian de diaocha yu sikao" ("Investigation and reflections on our country's mass incidents"), *Neibu canyue* (*Internal Consultations*) No. 31 (576) (8/10/2001), pp. 18–25 and Zhonggong zhongyang zuzhibu ketizu, *2000–2001 Chinese Investigation Report.*
58. A chilling piece of reporting on how three labour leaders were respectively jailed, bought off and terrified by police in the north-eastern city of Liaoyang, the site of massive protests in the spring of 2002, is Philip P. Pan, "Three Chinese workers: jail, betrayal and fear: government stifles labor movement," *The Washington Post*, 28 December 2002, p. A01.
59. Report.
60. I have already documented these efforts and their results as of the end of the year 2001 in Dorothy J. Solinger, "Labour market reform and the plight of the laid-off proletariat," *The China Quarterly*, No. 170 (June 2002), pp. 304–326.
61. Within two months of the meeting's convening, the State Council passed new regulations giving rural migrants a legal right to work in cities and prohibiting job discrimination against them. For a summary, see Charles Hutzler and Susan V. Lawrence, "China acts to lower obstacles to urban migration," *Wall Street Journal*, 22 January 2003, Eastern edition, p. A12.

orderly ... [and] guided."[62] This display of the inclinations and practices under the reign of the retiring leaders did not lend much optimism for change in policy towards the disadvantaged.

Signs of an Altered Agenda

Several large questions crop up as one speculates on the time ahead. Has the newly appointed leadership endorsed the programme in the political report unanimously and sincerely, and have political considerations bound that team's members to further the objectives of the report – along with its biases – in their coming rule? And how powerful are the ties of loyalty binding the new Politburo Standing Committee members to the person of Jiang Zemin and what he wants? It does seem possible that now that forebears Mao and Deng have both departed, their respective legacies may be legitimating the adoption of two different political stances, one more akin to the preferences of the former and one more aligned with the policies of the latter.

Recent activities and speeches of the new Party general secretary and perhaps others among the just-appointed elite appear to arouse some doubt as to whether, now that Jiang himself has left his Party post, his successors are in full agreement with him as to the rank ordering of the several sectors of the population to be served under the concept of the "three represents." Luckily for them, if indeed they see things rather differently from him, the notion of representing three separate segments among the public does leave space for flexible interpretation, without departing altogether from the idea of a three-fold society in the cities.

The one top-level leader who had the most liberal leanings on the eve of the Congress was the former Standing Committee member, ex-head of the People's Political Consultative Conference, Li Ruihuan. He was also, according to a new book that draws on Party Organization Department investigatory files on the just appointed political figures, the member of this old committee who appeared least positive about the theory of the "three represents."[63] Interestingly, Li was the sole group discussion leader who emphasized the third of the "three represents" when he met the Tianjin delegates to the Party Congress in small group meetings.[64] This man, however, was dropped from the list of current Standing Committee members just weeks ahead of the meeting, presumably because of his open disdain for Jiang Zemin. His example may be serving as a stern warning to those now at the helm to proceed more gingerly and speak less overtly in tones directly opposed to those of Jiang.

Of those who did make it into the inner circle in the end, it appears from this new book that several of the leaders do take specific stands on issues of economic and social policy. But their standpoints are not

---

62. Report.

63. Nathan and Gilley, *China's New Rulers: The Secret Files*, pp. 51, 80. On pp. 175–76, they note that Li was "outspoken" in visits to poor areas in 1999 and 2001.

64. Thanks to Jeremy Paltiel for this fascinating reference. It appears in www.people. com.cn/BG/shizheng/16/20021109/862600.html.

entirely consistent. Wen Jiabao, named the next premier at the March 2003 meeting of the Tenth National People's Congress, supposedly favours privatizing failing state firms and creating a national pension plan for urbanites, as well as doing more to construct a social welfare system (a critical, but, alas, unfulfilled goal of outgoing premier Zhu Rongji's). Wu Bangguo, on the other hand, who rose from the rank of an ordinary worker, and who has demonstrated his dogged sympathy for state enterprise throughout the 1990s, continues to be cautious about further reforming the sector, hoping even to inject more state investment and technology into firms with difficulties.[65] After that March meeting closed, Wen held a lengthy televised press conference at which he presented his vision of a "kinder, gentler government, focusing on unemployment and economic distress," according to a report in the Western press.[66]

As for the new Party head, Hu Jintao, a number of pieces of information suggest that he too is taking a position on the side of the poverty-stricken. In the run-up period to the Congress, Hu visibly journeyed to a range of provincial capitals, all of them in provinces that either were traditionally poor or had been made so by worker lay-offs and enterprise failures over the past five or six years. During that tour, he held forth on the development of China's west and on the topic of poverty alleviation.[67] In a similar vein, in his commencement address to the incoming class of the Central Party School in September 2002, Hu referred to poverty as the main challenge facing the Party.[68]

Once in power, Hu went still further. In a address he delivered on 6 December at Xibaipo, Hebei (the scene of a major meeting on the eve of Communist victory in 1949), entitled, "Adhere to and carry forward the fine style of plain living and hard struggle, and strive to achieve the magnificent goal of comprehensively building a well-off society," Hu repeatedly invoked Mao's name. In addition, he treated the "three represents" only near the end of his talk, at which point he seems to have lifted a leaf from Li Ruihuan's book. For there he alluded to (or even spoke directly about) just those in difficulty, those in poverty-stricken areas,

65. Nathan and Gilley, *China's New Rulers: The Secret Files*, pp. 92, 104, 180, 181.

66. John Pomfret, "China's leader outlines a social agenda," *Washington Post*, 19 March 2003. Pomfret writes that Wen "set a very different tone from that of his predecessor, former premier Zhu Rongji."

67. Susan V. Lawrence, "The new leadership: it ain't over till it's over," *Far Eastern Economic Review*, 8 August 2002, pp. 24–25. Here Lawrence also notes that in the updating of Hu's English-language biography on the web site of *Renmin ribao*, a new bit was added recently, indicating that Hu had "long years of work in remote and poor areas … "

68. *Renmin ribao* internet edition, 2 September 2002, courtesy of Jeremy Paltiel. Under the rule of Jiang and Premier Zhu Rongji, serious efforts were undertaken, especially in the year 2002, drastically to extend the urban minimum living allowance to the truly destitute. See Tang Jun, "Zhongguo chengshi jumin zuidi shenghuo baozhang zhidu de 'tiaoyueshi' fazhan" ("The leap forward style of development of Chinese urban residents' minimum livelihood guarantee"), in Ru, Lu and Li, *Social Blue Book*, pp. 243–251. On pp. 243–44, he notes that from the second half of 2001 until late 2002, the central government's initial investment for 2001 went from 800 million to an additional 1.5 billion by year's end, and then up to 4.6 billion for the following year. As a result, the numbers of recipients nation-wide grew by nearly 15 million in just one year, rising to about 20 million in late 2002.

enterprises with difficulties, and laid-off workers, among other sorry citizen groups.[69]

And, perhaps most significantly of all, on 12 December a special meeting of the Politburo Standing Committee was convened – and then publicized – whose purpose was to hear relevant departments' reports on solving the production and livelihood problems of those in difficulty. The official news story on this session announced its adoption of a series of measures aimed at grappling with the struggles of these people.[70]

These various incidents and speeches could be viewed in several ways. Perhaps Hu and Wen were in each case appearing just as symbols of service to the poor, in order to persuade the Chinese people that supporters of further economic reforms could champion the impoverished too.[71] Perhaps instead their purpose was simply to signal independence from Jiang Zemin.[72] Whether or not these apparent overtures indeed amount to a sign of a new leadership's shift of emphasis in the state's stance towards the third of the represented collectives – or even more radically to an inclusive nod to the relatively forgotten unemployed – can only be known with time.

69. Xinhua Domestic Service, Beijing, 2 January 2003. Courtesy of Alan Romberg.
70. Duowei xinwen (Chinesenewsnet.com), 12 December 2002. Courtesy of Li Qiang.
71. The analysis of Lawrence in "The new leadership" would lend itself to such an interpretation.
72. Willy Wo-Lap Lam, Hong Kong, CNN, 17 December 2002.

Old Problems for New Leaders: Institutional Disjunctions in Rural China*

Jean C. Oi

ABSTRACT Decollectivization and fiscal reforms inadvertently created excessive peasant burdens. This study traces changes in peasant burdens over time and pinpoints inadequacies in the state's responses. A survey of over 100 villages permits comparisons of burdens in villages that never industrialized, those whose initial industrialization became stalled, and those where it was sustained. In all but the most highly industrialized villages and townships, local officials were forced to increase fees and taxes as other sources of revenues declined. The findings suggest the need for a policy like the "tax-for-fee" (*feigaishui*) reform to standardize and rationalize peasant burdens, but it identifies probable future problems that the new Party leadership will face.

The decollectivization of agriculture and the fiscal reforms opened the door to greater rural prosperity with the dramatic take-off of township and village enterprises (TVEs) in the 1980s. Ironically, these reforms also are at the root of the peasant burden problem and the associated discontent and unrest that constitute major challenges to China's new post-16th Party Congress leadership. The household responsibility system eliminated the right of village authorities to income from agricultural production but failed to provide them with a sufficient alternative source of revenue. This institutional disjuncture made village-retained fees (*tiliu*) the only legitimate village income, if there were no profits from village-owned enterprises. When the legally prescribed limit on these fees became too low, villages found ways to increase it; when that was insufficient, other ad hoc charges were added, including "fund raising" (*jizi*). The poorer the village, the greater is the dependence on such exactions.

The fiscal problems created for villages by decollectivization were exacerbated by the hard budget constraints created by the revenue sharing system, where local governments at the township level and above were forced "to eat in separate kitchens." By the late 1990s, in the wake of the downturn in the economic fortunes of the TVEs beginning in the early to mid-1990s, local governments, especially at the township level, found themselves with increasing expenditures and debt. The situation became critical in a wide range of areas, leaving more than a few townships and even counties unable to pay their wages.

The consequence has been increasingly predatory exactions as many

* I would like to thank Kaoru Shimizu for her research assistance and statistical analysis on which a portion of this article is based.

townships and counties fall into ever deeper debt. The ultimate victims have been China's peasants who have seen village *and* township levies increase by leaps and bounds [1] These additional burdens are all the more heavy in the wake of flattening prices for farm goods, increasing costs of production and the general decrease in overall peasant incomes after rises in the early reform period. Most worrying for the leadership, they have resulted in mounting instances of peasant unrest and mass protests. The period leading up to the 16th Party Congress was filled with peasant demonstrations, petitions to the upper levels, "rightful resistance" and even violent actions to seek retribution, often against what are commonly perceived as unjust exactions stemming from cadre corruption. [2] On the eve of the 16th Party Congress, the situation was such that some raised the issue of whether there was a "crisis in China's hinterland." [3] Top leaders, including Jiang Zemin, acknowledged the seriousness of the breakdown in the relationship between the state and the peasants and identified rural instability as a major threat to the regime.

Fortunately for the Chinese Communist Party (CCP), peasant demonstrations have been largely localized and directed at local-level officials. The central state never lost control of the countryside. In fact, a case can be made that the central state successfully used some of these peasant demonstrations to clean up corruption, while enhancing regime legitimacy in the eyes of the peasants. [4] As in other cases of collective action, state response is a key factor in determining whether a serious situation turns into a crisis and whether the regime can maintain its legitimacy. [5]

The party-state over the course of the reforms has tried a variety of solutions to cut peasant burdens and curb rural cadre corruption, including instituting competitive village elections. Most recently, a tax-for-fee reform (*feigaishui*), which effectively cut peasant burdens, was instituted on the eve of the 16th Party Congress, but it remains to be seen whether this will definitively solve the problem in the long term. New efforts have also been made to strengthen Party control in the countryside, in part to prevent further cadre corruption. However, these efforts create tensions with the new law that has strengthened village self-rule and elections. The sections that follow elaborate the problems and their solutions in an attempt to sketch out the challenges that face the post-16th Party Congress leadership.

1. This is richly documented in Thomas Bernstein and Xiaobo Lü, *Taxation without Representation in Contemporary Rural China* (Cambridge: Cambridge University Press, 2003).

2. See, for example, the work of Kevin O'Brien and Li Lianjiang, David Zweig, and Tom Bernstein. The most developed treatment is Bernstein and Lü, *Taxation without Representation.*

3. The Woodrow Wilson Center organized a panel on the Chinese countryside with the title "Crisis in the hinterland?"

4. See Jean Oi, "Realms of freedom in post-Mao China," in William Kirby (ed.), *Realms of Freedom in Modern China* (Stanford: Stanford University Press, 2004), pp. 264–284.

5. For a discussion of this broader issue see Yongshun Cai, "The silence of the dislocated: Chinese laid-off employees in the reform period," PhD dissertation, Department of Political Science, Stanford University, 2001.

Economic Trends on the Eve of the 16th Party Congress

The relationship between state and peasants in China on the eve of the 16th Party Congress was ambivalent at best. The initial reform policies allowed rural industrialization to mushroom, absorbing surplus peasant labour and providing wages that greatly boosted rural incomes in the 1980s.[6] More than 200 million people escaped poverty, and per capita grain availability reached levels comparable to those in developed countries.[7]

Yet, despite rapid and dramatic growth, some old problems were never solved before new ones emerged. The economic boom continued to be unevenly distributed and inconsistent over the reform period. Coastal and southern China enjoyed rapid growth, areas near big urban centres such as Shanghai were transformed, but those in the interior, central and western China remain largely agricultural and often poor. As the World Bank has reported, over 100 million people still earn less than US$1 per day.[8]

In agricultural areas, in spite of a series of excellent harvests in the mid-1990s, trends that had begun much earlier continued or became more acute. After an initial rise, agricultural incomes began to decline and then stagnate. A national survey reveals that there was a substantial rise (19.3 per cent) in village collective income per capita over the ten-year period 1984–95.[9] However, the increases appeared early in the reform process: incomes increased 17.9 per cent from 1984 to 1988, but they slowed by the late 1980s, increasing only 1.2 per cent from 1988 to 1995.[10] One cause of this decline is the flattening prices for agricultural goods while the costs of production continued to increase, creating a scissors problem for peasants.[11] The situation is likely to worsen with competition from agricultural imports coming into China under the World Trade Organization (WTO) concessions.[12]

The decreasing profitability of agriculture has hastened the movement away from farming. Our survey data show that over the course of the ten-year period 1984–95, average industrial product value increased over 500 per cent, yielding a 12 per cent increase in average industrial product per capita. At the same time, the data show a dramatic decrease (82.9 per

6. See, for example, Jean C. Oi, *Rural China Takes Off: Institutional Foundations of Economic Reform* (Berkeley: University of California Press, 1999).

7. Scott Rozelle, Jikun Huang and Linxiu Zhang, "Emerging markets, evolving institutions, and the new opportunities for growth in China's rural economy," *China Economic Review*, Vol. 13 (December 2002), pp. 345–354.

8. Cited in *ibid.*

9. Author survey. This 1996 survey collected data on various aspects of economic development in rural China as well as information on political institutions. It was conducted in 24 provinces and municipalities, 104 counties, 203 townships and 157 villages. We collected information in 1984, 1988 and 1995.

10. Author survey.

11. See Robert Ash, "China's agricultural reforms: a 20-year retrospective," in Chien-min Chao and Bruce J. Dickson (eds.), *Remaking the Chinese State: Strategies, Society, and Security* (London & New York: Routledge, 2001), pp. 76–100.

12. See Xiao Junyan, "Rural economic situation in 2001 and prospect in 2002," *China Development Review*, Vol. 4, No. 2 (April 2002), pp. 22–36.

cent) in agricultural product value, which when adjusted for population change yields an average agricultural product value per capita drop of 42 per cent.[13] A 2002 forecast expects continuing falls in grain prices, as well as in grain output.[14] It is only because of bumper harvests in the previous years that there is little fear of grain shortfalls, although there remains concern that for the coming harvests China may have to import considerable amounts of grain.[15]

The increasing gap between rich and poor regions remains painfully evident in the provision of public goods and services. Education has been a particular concern as this is one of the costliest items on local government budgets. It is this expense that many townships claim eats up the bulk of their limited monies. This became a major problem on the eve of the 16th Party Congress – to the point where teachers were on the verge of striking to force the leadership to assume responsibility for paying their salaries.

In addition, over time, even in the industrialized areas, the initial economic success shows signs of stalling or even being undone. When our sampled villages are arranged along an agricultural dependence continuum, there is a decrease in village income per capita in almost one-half of the tiers on which there are data, with the greatest declines in villages that are semi-industrial.[16] In the most highly industrialized villages, from 1984 to 1995, there is only a 3.7 per cent increase in income. The arrow is going the right way, but this rate of growth is less than might have been predicted. Moreover, the bulk of the increase in village collective income per capita (VCIPC) appears in the 1984 to 1988 period. Between 1988 and 1995 there is a 27 per cent decrease in incomes. During this later period, TVEs began to suffer from inefficiencies and soft budget constraints,[17] in addition to softening markets, increased competition and decreasing profits. As this decline was occurring, there also was an increase in expenditures for the entire 1984 to 1995 period. Total expenditure per capita increased approximately 40 per cent from 1984 to 1995, but almost 50 per cent for the 1988 to 1995 period.[18]

By the end of the decade, more than a few factories had gone bankrupt, leaving villages in debt. The financial toll from such failures was heavy, both for the villages and ultimately for the individual peasant families who had to pay the bills, and for the rural credit co-operatives that lent the money for the factories but were now in debt themselves. In response

13. Author survey.
14. Grain production in 2001 fell back to 1993 levels. See Xiao Junyan, "Rural economic situation."
15. Also Ash, "China's agricultural reforms," provides an excellent and more detailed discussion of the grain and price situation.
16. Villages are sorted and grouped into eight tiers according to their dependence on agriculture. The dependence on agriculture was determined by agricultural production as a percentage of total village production. Villages in the survey were stratified into eight groups by every half of a standard deviation.
17. See, for example, James Kung, "The evolution of property rights in village enterprises," in Jean Oi and Andrew Walder (eds.), *Property Rights and Economic Reform in China* (Stanford: Stanford University Press, 1999), pp. 95–122.
18. Author survey.

to problems with public ownership and heavy debt, many localities engaged in state sponsored privatization, selling village and township enterprises.[19]

Arranging villages along an agricultural dependence continuum reveals that a wide range of villages, including those that had industrialized, faced a situation where debt was going up rapidly while incomes were slowing or decreasing.[20] Although the sources of the debt were different, there are large increases at both ends of the agricultural dependence spectrum, that is, villages that were highly industrialized and those that were most dependent on agriculture. For example, the survey data show that in the most highly industrialized villages from 1988 to 1995 village debt per capita increased by more than 200 per cent. During the same period, in the most agriculturally dependent villages, collective village debt per capita increased more than 700 per cent.

But even in rich areas that have enjoyed growth and still have high incomes, new problems have emerged as consequences of successful industrialization. One is the acceleration of the enclosure movement (*quandi*) in industrializing rural areas, where farming land is requisitioned and peasants do not get adequate compensation. A related problem is rural industry polluting farm land and water supplies. Rural industry in some places has spoiled rivers and ponds so much that the water is no longer suitable even for irrigation let alone drinking.[21]

These problems were aggravated by the fiscal problems of township and county governments. In the wake of the hardening of budget constraints under revenue sharing, the downturn in the market and the decline of TVEs, local government revenues dropped; many have since gone into debt. Not only has the provision of public goods and services suffered, some do not even have funds to pay their own administrative staff. A Chinese government publication admits that from 1998 to the first half of 2001, the number of counties and townships, especially in the central and western regions of the country, that were unable to pay their wages rose from 14 per cent to 37 per cent. In one province, more than 90 per cent of county and township governments were in debt, with an average of nearly 5 million *yuan*.[22]

The solution for many villages and townships is to squeeze what they can from the peasants. As others who have detailed macro changes in the Chinese rural economy have argued, peasant burdens constitute the moral economy problem in China's countryside.[23] It is these problems that have fuelled the mounting peasant protests as the reforms have proceeded. These are the problems the new 16th Congress leadership must address.

19. Hongbin Li and Scott Rozelle, "Privatizing rural China: insider privatization, innovative contracts and the performance of township enterprises," *The China Quarterly* (forthcoming).
20. Author survey.
21. For pollution problems from TVEs see Mara Warwick, "Environmental information collection and enforcement at small-scale enterprises in Shanghai: the role of the bureaucracy, legislatures and citizens," PhD dissertation, Department of Civil Engineering, Stanford University, 2003.
22. See Xiao Junyan, "Rural economic situation."
23. See Ash, "China's agricultural reforms."

Peasant Burdens

To gain some understanding of the types of solutions the fourth generation leaders must seek, it is useful to analyse the sources and the variation in peasant burdens. The political consequences differ significantly depending on whether the burdens are everywhere or are isolated in remote areas of China.

Increasing peasant burdens have been widely reported. Press reports provide heart-wrenching stories of the suffering of China's poor peasants at the hands of local officials. Recent studies have documented numerous examples of dramatically increasing peasant burdens in different villages. My survey data confirm that total peasant burdens have clearly gone up. However, the aggregate increase masks important variations that shed light on state efforts to address the problem and the difficulties the regime is likely to continue to face, even in the wake of the new *feigaishui* policy.[24] Disaggregating peasant burdens into their various components, one finds some significant patterns of change in the various fees and taxes.[25]

The survey findings support some of the trends that are described in earlier studies, but the overall picture that emerges is more complex and somewhat counter-intuitive. Only some types of peasant burdens have been increasing and only in some types of villages but not in others.[26] Most notably the data show that village-retained fees and township unified fees (*tongchou*), the two most often associated with peasant burdens, went down by 1995 from the late 1980s for the nation as a whole. The problem for the peasants is that other peasant burdens continued to increase. Taxes and other fees that were previously nominal went up during this time. The agricultural tax, for example, which was minimal and stagnant during the Mao period, increased. In some areas, land contract fees were another source of the increase. These findings are significant because they indicate an economic as well as a political logic at work in both patterns of policy implementation and compliance. They also shed light on the effectiveness of state regulation in China's country-side after decollectivization.

Overall, the empirical evidence suggests that the determinants of peasant burdens are embedded in the local political economy – its resource endowments and the political pressures that circumscribe the behaviour of local authorities. Peasant burdens are linked to village collective income and expenditures; they are also linked to township

24. For further details and statistical documentation see Jean C. Oi and Kaoru Shimizu, "Political institutions and peasant burdens in China, 1984 to 1995," paper prepared for the conference on "Grassroots Governance in Contemporary China," Shizuoka University, Shizuoka, Japan, 30 August to 1 September 2002.

25. Peasant burdens can be categorized into the standardized taxes levied by the central state and the surcharges levied by local authorities. The obligatory grain sales to the state technically are a "sale" to the state. This is what Bernstein and Lü list as "hidden burdens" in their *Taxation without Representation*. For the purposes of this discussion, local is defined as county, township and village. While peasant burdens include both monetary and labour levies, this discussion will be limited to the monetary levies. It should be noted that labour levies have similarly increased.

26. All monetary values were adjusted for inflation.

assessments on villages. Burdens are borne by villages as a collective and by individual peasant households.[27]

State responses. The central state has long been aware of the source of peasant burdens. The *feigaishui* policy is only the latest in a string of efforts to address this problem. Initially, the state simply issued directives to reduce peasant burdens. The state sent guidelines to the lower levels that explicitly targeted *tiliu* and *tongchou*, the two fees granted to villages and townships after decollectivization and the two fees that are the most visible examples of the surcharges that peasants must pay above and beyond the state set taxes. Directives ordered that these two fees together should not exceed 5 per cent of peasant incomes.[28] But only in the period immediately preceding the 16th Party Congress did the state adopt more decisive action to stem peasant burdens.

Directives to cut peasant burdens. The early state responses to the peasant burden problem failed because they left the enforcement of these policies to the localities. While the 5 per cent limit was clearly stated, the procedures for assessing *tiliu* and *tongchou* remained vague.[29] Township and village cadres were left with a loophole to increase *tiliu* and *tongchou* by manipulating the base on which these fees were to be assessed, that is, peasant income. Townships and villages could collect more fees and still stay within the allowed limit by inflating peasant incomes.[30] Our survey findings point to the mixed results of the state's initial efforts to limit peasant burdens. On the one hand, the decrease in *tiliu* and *tongchou* points to the effectiveness of increasing political pressure by the centre through the repeated and intensified issuance of directives on limiting these two fees. On the other hand, other fees increased.

There is a political explanation of these seemingly contradictory trends. *Tiliu* and *tongchou* went down because of heavy political pressure from Beijing to cut them. No such political pressures or restrictions were placed on agricultural or special products taxes or on land contract fees. Institutional changes made the agricultural tax "a local tax" which was not shared with the centre, and thus created additional incentives to increase its collection. In agricultural as well as industrialized villages, land contract fees became increasingly attractive income sources when other revenue declined.

While the political explanation holds in some cases, the impact was not uniform across villages: *tiliu* and *tongchou* only decreased in some villages, not all. This suggests that while political pressure is important,

27. Further details can be found in Oi and Shimizu, "Political institutions and peasant burdens in China."
28. See, for example, Liu Jichun, *Nongmin fudan 200 wen* (*200 Questions on Peasant Burdens*) (Beijing: Zhongguo shehui chubanshe, 1999), for various directives warning against illegal increases and the need to decrease peasant burdens.
29. *Ibid.*
30. See Yongshun Cai, "Between state and peasant: local cadres and statistical reporting in rural China," *The China Quarterly*, No. 163 (September 2000), pp. 783–805.

its impact is mediated by other factors. Whether the increasing barrage of directives to cut peasant burdens was effective depended also on the economic context in which the political pressure was applied. A village's resource configuration structures the incentives that shape the composition and size of peasant burdens.

Previous case studies based on fieldwork and anecdotal evidence found very rich villages where the collective pays the *tiliu* for the peasants, in addition to providing subsidies and services to its residents.[31] Studies of agricultural regions also posit that it would be the agriculturally dependent areas where one would be most likely to find the most onerous peasant burdens.[32] Thus, one would expect villages that are still highly dependent on agriculture and where there is relatively little rural industry to have high peasant burdens.

At one level, our data suggest that economic need remained the driving force in determining *tiliu*. Villages with different economic resources reacted differently to the increasing directives to cut this fee. Those that fall into the two tiers most dependent on agriculture show an increase in *tiliu* for the ten-year period (1984–95), as the economic argument and earlier studies would predict. Also as the economic argument would predict, those that were the most industrialized and likely to be the wealthiest showed the largest cuts in *tiliu*, even in the 1988 to 1995 period when economic conditions were deteriorating. These highly industrialized, rich villages could afford to comply with the state's directives to cut peasant burdens.

What fails to support the economic argument and suggests that the state's efforts to limit *tiliu* did have an impact, regardless of a village's wealth, is the finding that villages in the majority of the tiers cut *tiliu* in the 1988 to 1995 period, which is when the state stepped up its political efforts to limit *tiliu* but also when economic conditions worsened. This includes those villages most dependent on agriculture, those that earlier studies would expect to have the greatest stake in keeping *tiliu* high or even increasing the levy. Moreover, the data also show that villages in tier 2, just below the most highly industrialized, increased rather than cut *tiliu* in the 1988 to 1995 period.

These somewhat contradictory findings suggest that rather than relying on a purely economic or political rationale, villages had to weigh the two types of pressure to see which was the most urgent. The data suggest that in the end economic constraints were foremost, even though there were concessions at least minimally to try to comply with political pressure from the state when it was too great to ignore.

It should also be noted that peasant burdens are not just the result of village levies. Regardless of whether *tiliu* decreased, villages also had to pay fees and taxes to the township. Villages had no authority to increase the agricultural or special products tax assessments. They would

31. See, for example, Oi, *Rural China Takes Off*.
32. Thomas Bernstein and Xiaobo Lü, for example, speculate that rural taxation is heaviest in the central, grain-producing provinces. "Taxation without representation: peasants, the central and the local states in reform China," *The China Quarterly*, No. 163 (September 2000), pp. 742–763.

have no interest in increasing the agricultural or special products taxes because they were not allowed to keep any increased assessments or collection of either tax. Payments were made to the township. Increases in these two taxes must be attributed to the county and township levels, which similarly needed to find new revenues.

Again, the institutional changes adopted during the early years of reform laid the foundation for increasing peasant burdens. The incentives to increase both the agricultural tax and the special products tax can be traced to the 1980 fiscal reforms, when both were designated local taxes and thus became part of the extra budgetary funds.[33] The initial decrease in the agricultural tax can be explained by the focus on TVEs as a source of revenue during much of the 1980s. Many rural authorities were trying to industrialize, and peasants were moving out of agriculture, which is reflected in the decline in agricultural output value noted above. However, when the bottom started to fall out of the rural enterprises, beginning in the late 1980s and accelerating in the 1990s, counties and townships intensified their collection of the agricultural tax and special products tax as revenue from industry declined. Our data fit that general trend well. Townships, along with villages, had to look elsewhere for revenue. This became a root cause of the need to increase other peasant burdens.[34] Political pressures and the new fiscal institutions determined the mechanisms by which new income could be obtained from the peasants.

The incentive to increase the agricultural tax and special products tax continued after 1994 when both remained designated local taxes, so that localities continued to have an interest in collecting as much as possible.[35] Moreover, the 1994 tax reforms, which divided taxes into central and local, caused localities to rethink their development strategies to consider which sector would yield central or local taxes. The need for careful calculation was further heightened by the decline of the TVEs. Localities began to focus more on those types of development that yielded the most local revenue. This included finding new agricultural-related development projects. In one county, the special products tax increased by more than 40 per cent in one year after the county first Party secretary decided to switch to developing agricultural-based industries.[36]

The largest increases in township fees occurred at either end of the agricultural dependence spectrum. The most agriculturally dependent as well as the most industrialized villages faced the greatest increases in township demands. This may partially explain the finding that villages at both ends of the agricultural dependence spectrum also had the highest debt. This finding underscores the point that extractions by the township

33. Bernstein and Lü, *Taxation without Representation*, trace the increase in the agricultural tax to the 1994 tax reforms. But the agricultural tax was already designated a local tax in 1980. See Oi, *Rural China Takes Off*, ch. 2.

34. Bernstein and Lü, *Taxation without Representation*, come to a similar conclusion in ch. 3.

35. For details of the division of various taxes between centre and localities under the fiscal reforms, see Oi, *Rural China Takes Off*, ch. 2.

36. *Ibid.* ch. 2.

became a major drain on village enterprises.[37] There is a huge percentage increase in the fees paid by the most industrialized villages for the ten-year period as a whole. In the 1988 to 1995 period the increase is more than 500 per cent. This is probably a reaction to the decreased tax revenues during that period when village and township enterprises began to decline. In contrast, township fees decreased during the boom years (1984–88) when TVEs were prospering and were able to contribute large amounts in taxes to the township and county.

Tax-for-fee reform (feigaishui). The tax-for-fee reform policy, which was announced in the spring of 2001 for nation-wide implementation, explicitly acknowledges the arbitrary and increasing burdens that have plagued China's peasantry.[38] This policy marks a major departure by the state in its response to the peasant burden problem. Unlike earlier directives that simply urged local officials to keep fees in check, the tax-for-fee reform directly and explicitly abolished all the previous fees and taxes. In their place, there are only two taxes on peasants: a reformulated agricultural tax and a surcharge on the new agricultural tax.[39] Instead of paying a *tiliu* and *tongchou* to the village and township, instead of paying a land contract fee, and instead of paying various other ad hoc charges, peasant households will only be assessed one tax, either the agricultural or special agricultural products tax, and its associated surcharge. To ensure that cadres cannot manipulate the new system by padding the quotas, in some provinces each household received a letter explaining the new system. Moreover, each peasant must sign an agreement that states how much his or her household must pay in the tax and surcharge. Although it has not been explicitly stated, the working assumption is that these tax amounts will be fixed for some time to come.

Preliminary fieldwork shows that this new policy has substantially reduced past peasant burdens. In one village peasant burdens have been reduced by 38 per cent from the previous year.[40] In another, the new policy has resulted in a 40 per cent drop compared to the previous year.[41] These findings are in line with a 2002 State Administration of Taxation report that indicates a 31 per cent reduction in tax burden per capita on average in Anhui, 30 per cent in Jiangsu and over 25 per cent in the other pilot areas.[42] A State Council research report indicates that after the

37. See, for example, Bernstein and Lü, *Taxation without Representation*, ch. 3.

38. "Guanyu nongcun shuifen gongzuo gei quansheng nongmin qunzhong de gongkaixin" ("Jiangsu informs peasants on tax-for-fee reform"), *Nanjing xinhua ribao*, 10 April 2001, p. A1.

39. For those areas that have special agricultural products, there is a special agricultural products tax and a surcharge on that tax. Peasant households pay either the agricultural or the special agricultural products tax and its associated surcharge but not both.

40. Author's China interviews (hereafter CI) 101202.

41. CI 101302.

42. Cited in Justin Lin, Ran Tao, Mingxing Liu and Qi Zhang, "Rural direct taxation and government regulations in China: economic analysis and policy implications," unpublished ms., August 2002.

expansion of the *feigaishui* policy to 16 provinces in 2002, in the first half of the year the per capita spending on taxes and fees nation-wide decreased by 3.9 per cent from the same period in the previous year.[43]

The difficulty is that *feigaishui* also substantially cuts the revenues of villages and townships. The new agricultural tax goes to the township; the surcharge on the agricultural tax goes to the village. However, neither amount will equal the earlier total of fees that villages or townships collected. The revenue shortfalls created by the policy were so severe (or feared to be so severe) that its implementation had to be stopped in 2001 shortly after it was announced for expansion nation-wide because of opposition from the localities. As indicated earlier, areas were left unable to pay their expenses, including cadre salaries. The problem only magnifies the already large debt, which was caused by the earlier institutional disjuncture, faced by townships.

Despite the hardships that the new tax system will pose for townships and villages, the leadership forged ahead in 2002 with the implementation of the *feigaishui* policy. Preliminary research reveals that where the policy is currently being implemented, the revenue declines are substantial. In one township, the new system resulted in a 2 million *yuan* loss of revenue; this means that six of its 34 villages will be unable to pay their village cadre salaries, and another five or six villages will be able to pay their cadre salaries but will have no money left for any other expenditures.[44]

Localities are expected to make up lost revenue through increased economic development. In some areas where there are relatively abundant development possibilities, the decreased revenues seem manageable. Some have already earned more this year than they lost with the policy change. Some richer villages never depended on *tiliu*; some paid the *tiliu* for the peasants – but those types of villages are in the minority.

The difficulty is in those areas that lack easy development opportunities. Here, one wonders how long it will be before the same syndrome that drove cuts in one levy but increases in another is going to re-emerge. Anticipating such problems, the regime is restricting additional peasant levies to try to ensure that the new *feigaishui* policy will not be undermined. If a village needs more funds for a project than the surcharge returned to the village can cover, it must convene a village meeting. But even if the village as a whole decides to go forward with a project and raise additional funds, the amount levied on each peasant cannot exceed 15 *yuan* per person per year.

In a concession to the localities, the centre has agreed to grant fiscal transfers to facilitate the implementation of *feigaishui*. The central state is providing some fiscal safety nets, as it did when it implemented its 1980s fiscal reforms, to stem political opposition from the localities.[45] These fiscal transfers will compensate the localities for some of the revenue

43. Xiao Junyan, "Rural economic situation in the first half of 2002 and outlook for the whole year," *China Development Review*, Vol. 4, No. 4 (October 2002), pp. 47–60.
44. Author interviews.
45. See Oi, *Rural China Takes Off*, ch. 2.

shortfalls and allow them to meet basic expenditures. The centre allocates funds to provinces that then funnel their funds to counties and eventually to townships, which will then use the money to help their villages and to supplement their own revenues. For example, one county received more than 39 million *yuan* for its 30 townships. Of that amount, approximately half was used to subsidize villages.[46]

Re-asserting control. In addition to more decisive and effective policies to cut existing peasant burdens, the state is also intensifying monitoring of village cadres to prevent further illegal levies and cadre corruption more generally. The result is a system of control over villages that has not been seen since the collective period. These new control mechanisms are occurring at a time when there is much discussion of the fate of the township as a level of government. There is even talk of doing away with the townships. While it is unlikely that this will come about, beginning in the mid to late 1990s, large numbers of townships were merged to cut administrative costs.

This streamlining has presented real problems for those administering the new, larger townships. According to county and township officials who are running newly merged administrative units, the township is now too large to manage effectively. In response, some townships have subdivided the management of villages under their jurisdiction and strengthened their subordinate organizations to carry out much of the detailed work of monitoring.

To ensure greater fiscal oversight and control, some townships have instituted a new practice called double substitute management (*shuang daiguan*). Under this new policy, villages lose their right to control their books *and* money.[47] To ensure that this programme will work, townships have simultaneously beefed up their economic management stations (*jingguan zhan*).[48] These stations are designated to keep village account books and cash. Villages are only allowed to have on hand a bare minimum in circulation funds. All other cash must be deposited with the *jingguan zhan*. For unexpected expenses not covered by the circulation funds, villages must submit a budget and cash withdrawal request to the *jingguan zhan* and obtain various approvals before the money can be granted.

Accountants at these management stations are required throughout each month to check carefully village receipts and expenditures against budgets to prevent fraud by cadres. In addition, each village has an elected "fiscal oversight small group" (*licai xiaozu*) to verify the accuracy of the receipts and expenditures. This small group, which consists of representatives of the villagers as well as the Party, must be present when receipts are submitted, when expenses are reimbursed and when these are

46. CI 101002.
47. Some townships use only the single substitute management system, which means that they only keep the village books, not the money.
48. The formal name is *jingji guanli tongji shenji zhongxin*.

recorded into the village books. The process culminates in a public posting of village accounts, with all expenditures and revenues listed. This follows the open accounting that the centre has demanded of villages in the wake of the peasant protests.

Realizing that the economic management stations have been weak, some townships have added a Party arm, called a Party general branch (*dang zongzhi*), to their administrative sub-offices to make these organizations more effective.[49] As one township official explained, "the addition of a Party secretary allows this office to be able to tell the villages what to do." The Party secretary of the general branch has the power to assess village officials, set village cadre salaries and approve village budgets.

It is worth noting that efforts to control village cash may also serve another purpose. It is an open secret that the rural credit co-operatives (*xinyongshe*) have been on the brink of financial disaster, laden with uncollected loans. Unlike the state banks that have had the luxury of turning in a portion of their bad debt to the state and being re-capitalized, these credit co-operatives have to find their own ways to make up for the red ink. It may not be a coincidence that the village cash that is turned over is kept in the local credit co-operative. Interviews with village officials reveal that when this new double substitute management system began they had to close all the other bank accounts they had with the four state banks. Village funds turned over to the *jingguan zhan* are kept at the local credit co-operative. Consolidating accounts certainly facilitates monitoring by the township and thus increases control, but this policy also has the added benefit of quickly infusing large amounts of new capital into the credit co-operatives.

New Institutional Disjunctures: Corruption Controls and Village Elections

Paradoxically, the new township control of village affairs is occurring at the same time as new laws better guarantee the right of all villages to hold competitive village elections. The law mandating competitive elections for all village committees was only officially passed in 1998. The obvious question is how the two trends can co-exist. How does taking away the right of villages to keep their own books and money square with the supposed autonomy of village committees? Doesn't the new double substitute management system essentially turn village committees into an administrative arm of the township, reminiscent of the *cunguan suo* (village management office) found in Guangdong and Guangxi early in the reform period? To whom do village cadres owe their loyalty: to the township that assesses their performance or to their villagers?

The questions created by the new increased township control over villages redirect attention to the struggle that has been playing out since the Organic Law of Villagers Committees was first implemented in

---

49. It is unclear at this point how many provinces use this system. My research was in Shandong.

draft form in the late 1980s. Who is the core (*hexin*)? Is it the Party or the elected village committee? The answer, at least up until the summer of 2002, was the Party. The advocates of democratic village elections won a victory in summer 2002 with the issuance of Central Document No. 14, which mandates that all who want to be a village Party secretary must first stand for election to the village committee. This decision is a definite step forward in subjecting all village officials to the electoral process. The issue now is whether village officials, whether they are the village committee head or Party secretary, have autonomy to run the village without interference from the newly strengthened townships.

Repairing Peasant–State Relations

Will the new leadership elected at the 16th Party Congress face the same problems in the countryside as its predecessors? For the short term, the answer is probably yes. The 16th Party Congress needs to repair as quickly as possible the state's frayed relationship with the peasants. It is not surprising that shortly after coming to office Hu Jintao showed concern for and travelled extensively to the poor agricultural regions. Finding permanent solutions to the peasant burden problem must be a top priority.

The task of the new leadership may be helped with further stages of economic development. Some economists taking a longer-term perspective have recently begun to be more optimistic about China's economic future. They see evidence that the problems that have plagued China's economy, including low incomes, are transitional. Rozelle, Huang and Zhang, for example, have highlighted a number of developments that all point in a positive direction, from increasing total factor productivity to decreasing transaction costs of shipping.[50] They see the massive migration of the population off the farm as a positive development for the ability of China to transform its economy.[51] Perhaps most importantly, profitability rates and job creation are again going up after the almost complete (90 per cent) transformation of collectively owned enterprises into either private or partially private firms.

What is likely to remain problematic is the funding of village and township administration. The tax-for-fee reform instituted on the eve of the 16th Party Congress may temporarily reduce peasant burdens, but in the longer term problems are likely to resurface. The new beefed up efforts at control over village cadre corruption may curb illegal spending by officials and allow for citizen oversight of accounts. However effective those measures are, they will not solve the underlying problems that have caused peasant discontent: the increasing fees, taxes and levies

50. This view appears in a series of articles, but the results are succinctly summarized in Rozelle, Huang and Zhang, "Emerging markets, evolving institutions, and the new opportunities for growth in China's rural economy."
51. Almost 85% of all rural households have at least one member in the off-farm sector. *Ibid.* p. 4.

discussed above. In fact, they may only undermine other changes, namely competitive village elections that finally seem to be making headway in closing the gap between the power of the elected leader and that of the Party secretary. With the new controls, not even the Party secretary, regardless of whether he or she stands for competitive election or not, will have the autonomy to manage village self-governance effectively.

This study thus points to the need for a policy like *feigaishui* to standardize and rationalize peasant burdens, but the findings also anticipate the problems that the new leadership will encounter with the tax-for-fee reform. The tax-for-fee system will effectively cut peasant burdens, at least in the short term. The new open accounting, supplemented by economic and political controls, will certainly make village cadre corruption more difficult. These measures go a long way in averting a crisis. In the process, the legitimacy of the regime may be enhanced.

But the basic problem has not been solved: how to fund township and village administration and the provision of public goods adequately. How long and how much can the centre provide in fiscal transfers? Will placing a ceiling on the new taxes present problems as expenditures continue to increase? The tax-for-fee reform policy will limit and reduce the burdens that already are in place, but this will surely mean trouble for some villages, especially the poorer ones with little collective income and those that were largely dependent on *tiliu* and various other fees. It will also be likely to cut deeply into township coffers. If local governments are unable to generate legitimate revenue, then they are likely to seek other ways to squeeze what they need from the peasants, just as villages increased rents and townships exacted the agricultural and special products taxes. The pattern of increasing peasant burdens described earlier is likely to re-emerge. Local officials at the township and village levels will find ways, regardless of the new regulations, to squeeze needed revenues from the peasants.

Until the state institutes a viable long-term solution that provides villages and townships with an adequate level of financing, the provision of public goods will suffer and peasant burdens will be likely to re-emerge as a thorn in state–peasant relations in China. With the addition of village elections to the equation, the situation may become even more complex and potentially threatening. The leadership has promoted village elections as a means to repair state–peasant relations and to provide a safety valve for peasant discontent, but this mechanism is also capable of turning not only the peasants but also their leaders, now elected, against the state if the state continues to ignore fundamental institutional deficiencies within the system and to blame local cadres for what is a systemic failing.

The International Strategy of China's New Leaders

Gerrit W. Gong

ABSTRACT China's new leaders defy conventional assumptions that they are insular bureaucrats who rose to the top by staying at home. Members of the current Politburo Standing Committee average 39.1 years of Party membership, represent 53 collective years of Politburo experience and between them made 42 foreign trips involving 107 visits to 63 different countries in the four years prior to the 16th Party Congress. They are focused on developing comprehensive national strength in a competitive world, and see trade, exchange rate management and financial leverage as strategic instruments. How China's new leaders handle questions of history will shape relations with Japan, the Koreas, Taiwan, the United States and many others. Thus, those who control China's past will affect the Asia-Pacific's future. In this regard, China's new leaders will also continue to confront modern digital technologies and the internet which can jarringly juxtapose past and future. Evidence suggests they will pursue Chinese national development and power in ways that manifest both pride and insecurity during an uncertain transition in a turbulent international system.

This article examines the international strategy of China's new leaders following the 16th Party Congress. The first section discusses the international orientation and experiences of China's new leaders, particularly the nine members of the new Politburo Standing Committee. It analyses continuity and change in China's international strategy framework as articulated by the Congress. It deals with issues such as how China's new leaders and succession affect the way Beijing views and engages the world, how the orientation, capability and limitations of China's next leadership generation will be manifest as Beijing aspires to great power status, what world view China's incoming leaders bring to the job, and differences from the way outgoing leaders looked at the world. The second section summarizes China's international objectives and implementation strategies for the first two decades of the 21st century as declared in Jiang Zemin's 16th Party Congress report. It asks how new-generation leaders define and use China's newly acquired economic and military power, how they perceive their country's weakness and vulnerability as China becomes increasingly enmeshed with the international system, the extent to which China seeks a peaceful external environment to pursue domestic economic reform and cope with ongoing challenges of World Trade Organization (WTO) entry, and the national security concerns of China's new leaders. The third section places China's emerging role in the Asia-Pacific region within its international challenges and strategies. It briefly suggests how these challenges and strategies could influence policies towards various geographic regions and countries.

International Orientation and Experience of China's New Leaders

Beijing sought a smooth leadership transition, and took pride in its accomplishment at the November 2002 16th Party Congress. That Congress placed high priority on the domestic and international stability China sees necessary to accomplish its ambitious declared priority of "building of a well-off society in an all-round way." By most measures, China's new leaders represent more of a generational change than a change in international perspective. Yet their international orientation and preparation belies the widespread initial assumption that they are simply an indigenous transitional generation between earlier Soviet-trained and Soviet-oriented leaders and future potentially internationally trained and oriented ones.

China's nine Politburo Standing Committee members joined the Party at an average age of 22.8 years. Their Party experience now spans almost 40 years each. That experience encompasses the evolution of the Party's international perceptions and orientation since the early 1960s. Within the inner leadership group, Zeng Qinghong joined the Party first, in 1959; Huang Ju joined last, in 1966.

Averaging 39.1 years of Party membership and representing 53 collective years of Politburo experience, this is a seasoned group (see Table 1).[1] They are already deeply entrenched in China's decision-making. They understand well and accept the basic international orientation that has guided the PRC over the last 40 years.

Chinese often recount the past century's tumultuous changes in terms of each successive decade's challenges. Thus, the 1900s saw the Boxer Rebellion, the 1910s the fall of the Qing and Sun Yat-sen's revolution, the 1920s warlordism, the 1930s the anti-Japanese war, and so on. The fundamental domestic and international changes which engulfed China during each decade give credibility to generational analyses of the international orientation and experience of China's new leaders.

Generational analysis of China's new leaders. The initial formative international experiences of the incoming Politburo Standing Committee occurred from the mid-1930s (Luo Gan was born in 1935) to the mid-1940s (Li Changchun was born in 1944). During their first ten years, this group experienced the turmoil of war, both anti-Japanese and civil, and the early establishment of the People's Republic. They spent their tenth to 20th years in the 1950s – a decade often characterized as beginning with the hopeful idealism of revolution and ending with the disillusionment of the anti-rightist campaign and Great Leap. On average, their formative adult 20th to 30th years occurred in the 1960s – the decade of the divisive Sino-Soviet split and the even more traumatic Cultural Revolution.

Of course, serious if familiar caveats apply to such generational

---

1. Basic biographical data from which the author created this table appears in "Profiles of top leaders," *Beijing Review*, Vol. 45, No. 48 (28 November 2002), pp. 15–19.

Table 1: **Politburo Standing Committee Members**

Name	Date born	Age*	Date joined Party	Years in Party*	Age at joining Party	Years Politburo experience*
Hu Jintao	Dec 1942	59	Apr 1964	38	21	10
Wu Bangguo	Jul 1941	61	Apr 1964	38	23	10
Wen Jiabao	Sep 1942	60	Apr 1965	37	23	5
Jia Qinglin	Mar 1940	62	Dec 1959	42	19	5
Zeng Qinghong	Jul 1939	63	Apr 1960	42	21	0
Huang Ju	Sep 1938	64	Mar 1966	36	28	8
Wu Guanzheng	Aug 1938	64	Mar 1962	40	24	5
Li Changchun	Feb 1944	58	Sep 1965	37	21	5
Luo Gan	Jul 1935	67	Jun 1960	42	25	5
Average:		**62**		**39.1**	**22.8**	**53 collective years in Politburo**

*All as of November 16th Party Congress

analysis. However important, early experiences do not necessarily determine subsequent orientation or outlook. Memory and perception are neither linear nor absolute in shaping individual personality, proclivities or decision-making. Individuals often derive different conclusions from seemingly shared experience. Thus, whatever their common experiences, China's new leaders will also no doubt exhibit significant individual and inter-generational or intra-generational differences.

Nevertheless, to the extent each decade of tumultuous change in China's modern history in fact demarcates broadly identifiable generational experiences, these different periods may subtly shape the basic orientation of successive Chinese leadership generations, including China's newest leadership cohort. The perceptual and procedural impact of China's self-declared commitment to successive leadership generations should not be underestimated. To establish age and specific experience (including education and professional training) as prerequisites for Party and government service is to create an expectation that specific generational leadership cohorts will reflect identifiable backgrounds.

It is thus not surprising that China has defined its successive leadership groups as much by generational experience as by chronological age. Thus, for example, Mao Zedong and his compatriots form China's first leadership generation, Deng Xiaoping and his compatriots the second generation, and Jiang Zemin and his compatriots the third generation. Now Hu Jintao and his compatriots have been self-consciously defined and selected as a fourth leadership generation.

Chronological age is a self-declared factor in China's new leadership generational clustering. China proudly notes the average age of its new generation of leaders is 62.0 years. This compares with an average age of 70.3 years for the outgoing generation. The important factor in this 8.3 year average shift is the decade difference in the formative and professional international orientation and experiences of the two groups.

For the outgoing leadership group, the initial major international issue was dealing with a bi-polar world in which Soviet power and Moscow's ideological and economic model were primary concerns for China. This group was on average in their 30s during the 1960s and in their 60s during the 1990s. The challenge at the beginning and end of their careers was to see competition supersede co-operation as the dominant element in the Sino-Soviet relationship (in the 1960s) and then to adjust to the collapse of the Soviet Union as a political and economic power and its consequent challenge to Marxism-Leninism's perceived validity (in the 1990s).

In contrast, while acutely aware of the bi-polar world initially defined by Sino-Soviet tensions, for the incoming leadership group the initial (and ongoing) major international issue is dealing with the United States. Broadly speaking, the power of the United States and the Soviet Union and their respective global roles changed during the formative early years of China's outgoing and incoming leadership groups. The outgoing leadership group's initial international orientation featured adjustment to a changing global power balance symbolized by the 1958 Taiwan Strait crisis, 1962 Cuban missile crisis and 1963 public manifestation of the Sino-Soviet split. Indeed, in many ways, the first two events precipitated the last. The incoming leadership group was in their 30s during the early 1970s. Their initial international orientation featured adjustment to a changing global power balance symbolized by China's efforts to normalize relations with the United States.

Thus, some decisive differences exist in the initial international orientations confronted by the outgoing and incoming leadership groups – particularly in China's adjusting relations with the Soviet Union and United States in ideological as well as political, economic, military and cultural dimensions. The perceptions of China's top leadership group were an underlying impetus in China's normalization with the United States in 1972. And the changing role of the United States was also a fundamental factor as China's leaders calculated their international orientation in light of the current strengths and weaknesses apparent in the rise of capitalist economic models within a globalized economy and international system.

In practical terms, most important international issues with an impact on China now involve in a direct way the United States, as exemplified by the American international use of force in the Gulf War, Bosnia, Afghanistan and Iraq using successive generations of capabilities within a revolution in military affairs, and the full range of collateral issues such as Middle East alignment and energy access.

Thus the experience of China's new leaders with their country's past 24 years of opening and reform began a decade earlier in their lives than it did in the lives of the outgoing Politburo Standing Committee. This means the new leaders have spent half their lives, and almost all their formative adult experiences after their mid-30s, in the period of China's ongoing global involvement and integration.

Foreign travel of China's new leaders: surprisingly systematic. A very telling but relatively unknown indicator of the international orientation and experience of China's new leaders is their recent foreign travel. Tables 2 and 3 illustrate three broad conclusions about that travel.

First, over the past four years, the nine members of China's new Politburo Standing Committee have travelled more widely and more systematically than is commonly known, having collectively visited about a third of the total countries in the world. Secondly, they have increased the number of trips and countries visited and the intensity of their foreign travel. This suggests a deliberate crescendo in their travel in preparation for China's selection of new leaders prior to the 16th Party Congress. Thirdly, individual members' travel also demonstrates a strong, anticipatory pattern: Hu Jintao has travelled the most, and is the only member of the incoming leadership group to have visited the United States.

Foreign trips and countries visited by China's new leaders. Conventional thinking assumes China's new leaders are insular and inward-looking bureaucrats who have risen to the top by staying at home. Of

Table 2: **Countries Visited by Standing Committee Members**

Region	Different countries	Visits
Africa	11	15
Asia	12	28
Europe	22	40
Middle East	6	6
North America	2	2
Oceania	2	6
South America	6	8
Sub-continent	2	2
Total	**63**	**107**

Table 3: **Intensity and Timing of Foreign Travel**

Year	Trips	Visits
2002	10	19
2001	13	32
2000	14	41
1999	5	15
Total	**42**	**107**

course short visits to a large number of countries do not make leaders international experts. At the same time, an important anticipatory pattern seems evident. Preparatory foreign travel and exposure reveal a self-conscious recognition that the highest levels of China's new leadership cohort need direct, experiential awareness of the outside world. Indeed, some cosmopolitan exposure and experience may now be a prerequisite for senior leadership. And, even if initially brief, such travel and exposure provide conceptual and practical "hooks" for subsequent deepened interest and understanding of other countries and international issues.

Significantly, over the past four years, China's new leaders have collectively made 42 foreign trips involving 107 visits to 63 different countries (see Table 2).[2] Countries visited are concentrated in Europe

2. For further and supporting details on new leadership international travel experience see Appendix 1. Basic information from which the author created the tables on international travel is courtesy of Radio Press, Tokyo, 30 December 2002, for which the author expresses appreciation. The author also expresses appreciation to his colleague Dr Eric Hyer for helpful comments and suggestions.

(40), Asia (28) and Africa (15) which together account for 83/107 or 78 per cent of total visits. Next come South America (eight), the Middle East (six) and Oceania (six) with 20/107 or 18 per cent. The Indian subcontinent (two) and North America (two) trail with 4/107, only 4 per cent of total visits. In terms of geographical regions visited by each Standing Committee members, Jia Qinglin has visited countries in six geographic regions; Hu Jintao has visited countries in five; Wu Bangguo, Wu Guanzheng, Li Changchun and Luo Gan have each visited countries in four; followed by Zeng Qinghong (three), Huang Ju (two) and Wen Jiabao (one).

Intensity and timing of foreign travel. Foreign travel for new generation leaders jumped from five foreign trips in 1999 to 14 in 2000, with 13 foreign trips in 2001 and 10 in 2002. Travel of what were incoming Standing Committee members jumped from 15 countries in 1999 to 41 in 2000, then 32 in 2001 and 19 in 2002 (see Table 3).

With one exception, each Standing Committee member visited a specific country only once during the past four years. The exception is Zeng Qinghong who visited Japan twice, on 4–7 April 2000 and 25–28 April 2002. Zeng's Japan travel may be *sui generis* because of helping to prepare Jiang Zemin's Japan travel, although Zeng's ongoing international interests and expertise (including regarding Japan and North Korean issues) are still apparent.

Of the 63 separate countries and 107 total country visits, Singapore was visited most frequently over the past four years, by five incoming Standing Committee members. Japan, France and Spain were each visited by four new Standing Committee members. In Asia, three countries (Laos, North Korea, Thailand) were each visited three times; in Europe, two countries (Germany, Italy) were each visited three times; in Oceania, three new leaders visited Australia and New Zealand; in South America, three visited Brazil.

Individual travel patterns among China's new leaders. Of the nine members of the new Standing Committee, Hu Jintao is the most widely travelled. Over the past four years, he visited 23 different countries – almost twice as many as any of his new colleagues – and is the only one to have visited the United States. Huang Ju and Li Changchun are next, having visited 14 countries each during this period. Wen Jiabao is the least travelled among the group. Over the past four years, he made only two foreign trips to three countries (Italy, United Kingdom, Switzerland) in one geographic region (Europe).

As noted earlier, long Party experience at the national level will channel the international orientation of China's leaders. So will strong elements of continuity in China's conceptual orientation to the "international situation and our external work" as articulated by the 16th Party Congress.

Underlying concepts in China's international orientation. As articulated by the new leaders, China's current international orientation reflects an essential continuity of analytical framework and conclusions. These were first promulgated by Deng Xiaoping and subsequently strongly endorsed by Jiang Zemin. Jiang's conscious harkening to Deng theory and practice has both ideological and practical components: ideologically, Jiang has sought to establish himself as a legitimate and orthodox successor to Deng Xiaoping; practically, he has sought to continue the wide popular support for the benefits of Deng's reform and opening to the outside world. Supported by both ideological theory and pragmatic practice, China's new leaders invoke classic articulations to express international orientations and priorities.[3] In traditional Chinese style, China's international orientation and priorities are expressed in 16 Chinese characters in the form of rhymed couplets:

> *yi ge shijie* (one world)
> *liang zhong zhidu* (two systems)
> *jingzheng duoyuan* (economic and political multipolarity)
> *heping gongchu* (peaceful co-existence).

The 16th Party Congress addressed and updated these four basic analytical axes. It did so in ways that define China's international orientation for the next 20 years as building on the foundation established over the past 20.

First, China's new leaders will continue to integrate China into the single, globalized world, including on issues such as the environment. The 16th Party Congress sought to put China on the side of "the historical tide and safeguarding the common interests of mankind."[4]

Secondly, China's new leaders will remain attentive to a world that maintains different ideological systems. Bipolar confrontation between capitalism and communism was earlier evident in Soviet–US competition and a divided Europe, and is still visible on the Korean peninsula. This now gives way to competition between different forms of capitalism, and between capitalism and socialism with Chinese characteristics. The 16th Party Congress underscored China's ideological challenge: to "create a new situation in building socialism with Chinese characteristics."[5] China's new leaders will need to recognize ongoing differences in ideological and value systems while accommodating those differences within overall trends of peace and development.

Thirdly, China's new leaders will continue to foster economic and political multipolarity. The 16th Party Congress noted "growing trends" towards "world multipolarization and economic globalization."[6] In other

---

3. This articulation is credited to Deng Xiaoping through the conceptualization and wording of his influential foreign affairs advisor Huan Xiang.

4. Jiang Zemin, "Build a well-off society in an all-round way and create a new situation in building socialism with Chinese characteristics," 16th Chinese Party Congress, 8 November 2002, Section IX, "The international situation and our external work," p. 1.

5. *Ibid.*, Introduction, p. 1.

6. *Ibid.*, Section IX, "The international situation and our external work," p. 1.

words, as others, Chinese strategists who forecast the decline of the United States were surprised not only by enduring US power but especially by its demonstration in the Gulf and Kosovo wars, and more recently by the American campaigns in Afghanistan and Iraq. Indeed, in Iraq, the United States committed and used significant numbers of ground troops. China's new leaders understand that whatever the early inclinations of the George W. Bush administration, the events of 11 September 2001 confirmed American willingness and ability to dominate, shape and define the international system.

Finally, China's new leaders will address issues of military preparedness and military budget priority in the context where "peace and development remain the themes of the era."[7] As it watched American capabilities in the Gulf and Kosovo wars, China re-assessed its basic modernization model, including its balance between economic and military priorities. In particular the 7 May 1999 accidental bombing of the PRC embassy in Belgrade ignited debate on two strategic questions: whether or not China could expect to develop peacefully in the 21st century; and whether or not China's comprehensive national strength was one of lagging equilibrium or lagging disequilibrium compared to other countries, especially the United States.[8]

Recent Chinese examination of American national strength, including that evident in the revolution in military affairs, argues that Washington made revolutionary advances between Desert Storm and the Kosovo war. Such analysis suggests China's national strength may not be in lagging equilibrium (behind the United States but at a more or less constant distance), but rather in lagging disequilibrium (not only behind, but falling more so). Yet the 16th Party Congress authoritatively addressed war and peace: "a new world war is unlikely in the foreseeable future."[9] Indeed, "it is realistic to bring about a fairly long period of peace in the world and a favourable climate in areas around China."[10] China still faces threats, including from the United States, though not explicitly labelled as such. After all, "hegemonism and power politics" continue, though they have "new manifestations."[11]

New to the 16th Party Congress's international characterization, but unsurprising in light of current events, is China's declared stand "for fighting terrorism of all forms," including the imperative to "strengthen international co-operation in this regard." This anti-terrorist effort must "address both the symptoms and root causes of terrorism" and "prevent

7. *Ibid.*

8. Thomas J. Christensen, "Posing problems without catching up," *International Security*, Vol. 25, No. 4 (Spring 2001) usefully contributes to this debate, noting "China can pose major problems for American security interests, and especially for Taiwan, without the slightest pretense of catching up with the United States by an overall measure of national military power or technology" (p. 7).

9. Jiang Zemin, "Build a well-off society," Section IX, "The international situation and our external work," p. 1.

10. *Ibid.*

11. *Ibid.*

and combat terrorist activities and work hard to eliminate terrorism at root."[12]

The world view of China's new leaders is framed by three other perceptions. One is that the central task of "building a well-off society" is rooted in a deeply competitive view of the world. Engrained in the thinking of China's new leaders is that there is no substitute for comprehensive national strength when operating in an increasingly competitive international system.

In a world of "ever-sharpening competition,"[13] China has made significant progress towards accomplishing its three major historical tasks of modernization, national reunification including safeguarding world peace and promoting common development, and rejuvenating the Chinese nation. Beijing feels both pride and concern in surpassing the United States as the largest receipt of foreign direct investment (FDI): pride for accomplishment; concern not to feed "China threat" fears. Likewise, China reaching $600 billion in global trade reflects continued ascendancy as an international trade force.

But, Beijing's leaders say, continued effort is required. Indeed, they warn that "competition in overall national strength is becoming increasingly fierce" and China "must move forward, or we will fall behind."[14] It is as though China's new leaders feel the larger international environment reflects and contributes to the economic and social Darwinism that pressurizes continued socialist market economic reform at home. In the pursuit of comprehensive national strength, China should hold "high the banners of patriotism and socialism."[15] Nationalism can be a potent, if double-edged, rallying cry.[16]

A second basic perception of China's new leaders is that China must continue both to "bring in" and "go out" as part of active participation in international economic and technological co-operation and competition.[17] China should persevere in reform and opening up because "reform and opening up are ways to make China powerful."[18] It must learn to navigate or be swamped by the waves of economic globalization. Appropriately participating in the information revolution which created global communications, global capital markets, global technology and labour flows is essential for China to be internationally competitive. So is its continued rapid advance in science and technology.

Over the past 13 years, by adhering to "correct foreign policy and related principles," China has made a historic leap to a "period in which China's overall national strength has risen by a big margin."[19] The focus

---

12. *Ibid.*
13. *Ibid.*, Introduction, p. 2.
14. *Ibid.* p. 1.
15. *Ibid.*, Section I, "Work of the past five years and basic experience of 13 years," p. 4.
16. See, for example, Yongnian Zheng, *Discovering Chinese Nationalism in China* (Cambridge: Cambridge University Press), 1999.
17. Jiang Zemin, "Build a well-off society," Section I, "Work of the past five years and basic experience of 13 years," p. 3
18. *Ibid.*
19. *Ibid.* p. 2.

has been not only on national goals but also on individual and ideological ones: the objective is for the people to "live in a better and happier life" with "more tangible benefits than ever before" as "socialism with Chinese characteristics" demonstrates its superiority.[20]

A third basic perception of China's new leaders is that dealing with issues of rule by law and rule of law[21] is vital to successful governance, both at home and abroad. Rights and obligations ensconced in the international rule of law create opportunities for China to use the rules of the international system into which it is being pulled for its own benefit. As its strength grows, so may China's insistence that it help formulate the rules.[22] This would animate Beijing's active participation in myriad international organizations and bodies. Indeed, China's new leaders will increasingly scrutinize rules and China may only then agree to abide by them, whether those in the new multilateral trade round and WTO or, as recently argued in China's Defence White Paper, those governing the potential militarization of outer space.[23]

In short, China's new leaders come with long Party and wide international travel experience. They inherit a fundamental conceptual framework and analysis of China's international situation that builds on a foundation of successful continuity in its international orientation and priorities.

China's International Objectives and Strategies to 2020

This section considers questions such as how China's next-generation leaders will define and use China's newly acquired economic and military power, including how they will perceive their country's weakness and vulnerability as it becomes increasingly enmeshed in the international system. It asks whether China needs a peaceful external environment in order to pursue domestic economic reform and to cope with the ongoing challenges of WTO entry, and what its new leaders' overriding national security concerns will be.

These questions are best addressed within the context of the goals the 16th Party Congress identified for China for the first two decades of the 21st century, a period the Congress defined as one of "important strategic opportunities." These goals include: quadrupling the GDP of the year 2000 by 2020, as "China's overall national strength and international

20. *Ibid.*

21. See "Rule by law vs. the rule of law," in Wang Gungwu and Zheng Yongnian (eds.), *Reform, Legitimacy, and Dilemmas* (Singapore: Singapore University Press), pp. 135–163 for useful history on this topic.

22. This is also a thesis in Avery Goldstein, "The diplomatic face of China's grand strategy: a rising power's emerging choice," *The China Quarterly*, No 168 (December 2001), pp. 835–864: "China's contemporary grand strategy is designed to engineer the country's rise to the status of a true great power that shapes, rather than simply responds to, the international system" (p. 836).

23. China suggested using the conference on disarmament in Geneva to study a working paper on "Possible elements for a future international legal agreement on the prevention of the deployment of weapons in outer space, the threat of use of force against outer space objects." See White Paper on China's National Defence in 2002, 9 December 2002, Section VII, Arms Control and Disarmament, p. 33.

competitiveness markedly increase"; further improving socialist democracy and the legal system so people "live and work in peace and contentment"; notably enhancing ideological and ethical standards, scientific and cultural qualities, and health; and steadily enhancing sustainable development.[24]

The question of how next-generation leaders define and use China's newly acquired economy and military raises significant questions of the extent to which Chinese perceptions of power and its exercise are congruent with, or possibly divergent from, Western ones. Deeply embedded in the cultural tradition of Sun Tzu is the "key and defining" idea of *shi*, often translated "strategic advantage" but encompassing "a level of discourse through which one actively determines and cultivates the leverage and influence of one's particular place."[25] In that tradition, Chinese definitions of power are often characterized in overall relational terms. These differ markedly from definitions of power that focus on mechanical or static balances. Also, a focus on relational measures of power automatically includes the multi-dimensional psychologies of perception and places an emphasis on deception, camouflage and contingencies.

The traditional definition of "great power" status that "great powers" become such by defeating another "great power" in war has not been required in China's case, at least not directly. It is China's clear economic and technological strength, evidenced in its combined arms abilities bringing military assets on air, land, sea and space, combined with its resilient cultural and social claims to "superior civilization" which have motivated general recognition that China is a "great power."

The new leaders will continue to assert "principled positions" with respect to China's international interests.[26] These look to the future while China is in the midst of development. Expansive "principled positions" not only give China national pride and national objectives, but also assert its ambitions as fact before they are substantiated in practice by actual power. By persuading other countries to treat Beijing as it may become rather than what it currently is, China's new leaders will seek to create self-fulfilling cycles of increasing Chinese power. For example, whatever its many domestic reasons for maintaining currency stability after the 1997 Asian financial crisis, China successfully portrayed itself (especially with the United States) as an emerging global financial power able to affect international exchange rate stability.

In addition, this approach by China's new leaders will not require them to reset China's internal compass. China's ongoing acquisition of power

24. Jiang Zemin, "Build a well-off society," Section III, "Objectives of building a well-off society in an all-round way," p. 1.

25. Roger Ames, *Sun-Tzu: The Art of Warfare* (New York: Ballantine Books, 1993), p. 71.

26. Lowell Dittmer describes China's penchant to "'preceptorial diplomacy,' i.e., persuading other countries to parrot certain 'principles'" as a means "to establish a common normative basis for further discussions." See Lowell Dittmer, "Reform and Chinese foreign policy," in Chien-min Chao and Bruce J. Dickson (eds.), *Remaking the Chinese State* (London & New York: Routledge), p. 171.

will not require major doctrinal or cultural adjustments. It can be an extension of the fundamental Chinese self-identity that China and the Chinese people see for themselves. Some forthcoming landmarks of Chinese national self-identity include: China's manned space flight and space programme, the coming of the world to China for the 2008 summer Olympics, and the centenary of the Party.

We have already seen how China sees itself engaging a sharply competitive world. It is interesting to consider whether China's new leaders will pursue a different kind of long-term competition with the United States or with the international system.[27] The Soviet Union was once a military superpower built on economic, demographic and cultural feet of clay – a model China has explicitly rejected. Japan was once a global economic power – but unlike Japan, China's domestic and international objective has never been primarily motivated by a simple desire to "catch up" with the outside world.

It is true that many Chinese fret about China's national weakness, including its periods of historical humiliation. But, perhaps born of being a large continental power with a significant population and long self-conscious historical pride and importance, China seems as much motivated by an internal sense of regaining a self-assumed international place as by an external challenge of "catching up." China wants to be a country that matters. It wants a say in every important international issue. Beijing's objective may thus not be simple parity, that is, becoming one among equals, but the ongoing both proud and insecure drive to regain an assumed former standing. Paradoxically, that assumed former standing may be a moving target. China may not have a built-in equilibrium point for its role and position in the global power system.

The most important country for China's peace and development remains the United States. Now and projected for the first two decades of the coming century, the United States is China's most significant market, a major investor of capital, technology and management skill, and the single most decisive shaper and definer of the international system. With respect to the United States, China's new leaders will pursue a tripartite approach, involving strategic deterrence, regional superiority and local dominance.

Strategic deterrence involves using as little capability as is required (including through space-based assets) to forestall any threat to China's homeland or international freedom of action while minimizing cost and reducing concerns of a "China threat." This includes carefully cultivating the presumption that the United States or other countries have more to lose economically, politically and militarily than they would gain through "intervention" in China's internal or regional affairs. Secondly, regional superiority, especially in China's surrounding areas (primarily North-East

---

27. See Conclusion in Alastair Iain Johnston and Robert S. Ross (eds.), *Engaging China* (London & New York: Routledge), 1999, for a discussion of the mutual dynamic adjustment of China and the international system along maximal–minimal and containment–engagement axes.

and South-East Asia) can be asserted through focused political, economic and military capabilities. Finally, local dominance in immediate areas of vital interest, such as the Taiwan Strait, includes carefully cultivating the presumption that the United States is a distant country with limited interests in an "internal issue" of vital importance to China.

No wonder Jiang Zemin relegated to himself the key personal relationships and management of Sino-American bilateral relations. No wonder he invested so much political capital (including China's not opposing a UN resolution on Iraq) to secure a personal invitation by President George W. Bush to his Crawford, Texas ranch. Knowing Chinese culinary sensibilities, Crawford's attraction was not black-eyed bean salad or barbequed brisket. It was the prestige of joining a select group of world leaders – Britain's Blair, Russia's Putin, Saudi Arabia's Abdullah – invited by the president of the country which most matters to China for some personal time at his ranch.

Jiang broadly got what he wanted in Texas: recognition in China for his role in promoting and stabilizing Sino-US relations; a statement from the incumbent American president that the United States does not support Taiwan independence; and the promise of more high-level exchange including China visits by Vice-President Cheney in spring 2003 and by President George W. Bush at a time to be determined. No doubt Jiang sees himself playing a significant hosting role when George W. Bush next visits China – arrangements which will be carefully watched to see how much actual authority has transferred to Hu Jintao and his various colleagues. It is thus not surprising that the timing of the 16th Party Congress was co-ordinated with Jiang Zemin's October 2002 visit to Crawford and with Hu Jintao's April 2002 visit to the United States.[28]

China's approach to the WTO represents two elements of economic policy continuity.[29] One is that China's growth strategy still depends on its exports and trading system contributing significantly to overall economic reform. The second is that China continues to see its ongoing reforms attracting the necessary foreign technology, capital, management, quality control and, especially, access to global market and distribution channels. This cycle of self-reinforcing improvement seeks to move China's domestic and international systems up the competitive and value-added ladders.[30]

---

28. The latter remains one of the most carefully orchestrated bilateral visits in recent memory. Characterized by one State Department official as the "constant dilemma of the red carpet," a challenge throughout the visit was to show appropriate deference to Jiang Zemin as China's then-top leader by not making the welcoming red carpet for Hu Jintao overly conspicuous, while at the same time recognizing Hu's likely future role by making the welcoming red carpet during his visit appropriately long and wide.

29. An interesting account of China's WTO decision-making politics, including Premier Zhu Rongji's January 1999 signal to Chairman Alan Greenspan that China was "prepared to offer substantial concessions," can be found in Joseph Fewsmith, *China Since Tiananmen* (Cambridge: Cambridge University Press), in the section on "Nationalism, elite politics, and the WTO," pp. 204–217.

30. See Gerrit W. Gong, "Testimony before the US Trade Deficit Review commission, session on issues, impacts, and future of trade with China," 24 February 2000, for an elaboration of these topics.

China's new leaders will continue to use external WTO standards to attract foreign direct investment, secure long-term markets, reduce domestic deficit-widening subsidies (such as in agriculture) and thereby help maintain reasonable growth momentum by reducing dependence on domestic fiscal stimulus while moving towards more efficient patterns of growth and asset management. As core elements in China's strategic approach to comprehensive national strength, Beijing's new leaders will see trade[31] and exchange rate management as a means and measure, and thereby as an instrument, of national influence.

Senior Chinese policy officials knowledgeable about central bank holdings of dollar-denominated reserves are very familiar with the concept that a country could use dollar holdings as an instrument to influence the United States. An example of this approach in practice occurred during Chairman Alan Greenspan's January 1999 China trip. There discussions reportedly touched the American interest that any shift in PRC reserve holdings of euros and dollars occur gradually and that any PRC draw-down of dollar reserves during potentially volatile times include sensitivity to American markets. Beijing's new leaders understand trade and financial leverage as part of strategic national strength.

Similarly, these new leaders understand that current Chinese international strategy discussions regarding cyber-war, financial war and economic war are still largely concepts in search of operational principles. China's leaders could seek influence in regional economies, for example, from holding, directly or indirectly, Taiwan NT dollars or shares in Taiwanese companies or through those who sell Taiwan stock futures in Hong Kong or Singapore. Stabilization agreements for regional currencies, such as Malaysia's *ringgit*, already offer the Bank of China regional influence. All this will increase the perception that China's new leaders can influence regional markets, including through global, regional or local media.

The most significant structural implications of China's WTO-enhanced trade and financial competitiveness may be those improving China's competitive position in Asia and the world. Some American projections suggest China's export competitiveness under WTO may increase significantly vis-à-vis the Association of South-East Asian Nations (ASEAN) countries (especially Thailand, Indonesia, Malaysia and the Philippines). Other studies indicate that increased Chinese exports may not increase China's share of the American market but instead reduce Korea's or Thailand's share within that market. Chinese export competitiveness vis-à-vis its regional neighbours may reduce the link between countries of strategic importance to the United States while making those countries more susceptible to Chinese influence.

Over time, policy makers in the United States or elsewhere in the Asia-Pacific may find it impossible to distinguish between actions Beijing

---

31. See, for example, Nicholas R. Lardy, *Integrating China into the Global Economy* (Washington, DC: Brookings Institution Press, 2002), pp. 5–9 for discussion of the question Lardy frames as "shallow integration and trade dualism?"

takes for economic or commercial reasons and those it takes specifically to influence strategic alignment. Beijing will probably be able to exert significant economic or financial pressure on Tokyo, Seoul, Jakarta, Thailand or Taipei before it can do so on the United States.

China's Emerging Asia-Pacific Role within its Global Strategy

China's new leaders consider the Asia-Pacific region "the most dynamic region economically with the greatest development potential in the world."[32] By geographic and cultural proximity, China seems destined to play an increasingly important role in the Asia-Pacific. This role will reflect how China's new leaders address basic questions regarding history and demography. It will also influence China's international strategy with respect to specific countries and organizations.

History. Asia's future will be dramatically shaped by how China's new leaders handle questions of history. China's quest for national identity will inescapably be tied to its relations with Japan, the Koreas and Taiwan, among others in the region. Those who control China's past will shape the Asia-Pacific's future.[33]

China's new leaders will need to learn how to handle modern technologies, including digital technologies and the internet, which juxtapose images and sounds with surprising intensity, speed, scope and emotional resonance. For example, Hu Jintao found himself embroiled in striking a national public balance between outcry and understanding after the United States accidentally bombed the PRC embassy in Belgrade on 7 May 1999. Similarly, China's new leaders may have a say in the way North and South Korea address responsibility for the past (war, terrorism, nuclear processing).

Generational perceptions of past concerns throughout the Asia-Pacific will shape China's strategic role, presence and alignment – and vice versa. For example, China's new leaders may have to address emotional remedies for slave and prison labour compensation as settlements in Germany, Japan and the United States play off each other.

At some point, China's new leaders will certainly address the role of the past as it relates to future Sino-Japanese relations. Born on average in the 1940s, the incoming leadership group did not experience the 1930s as their predecessors did. Whether this will make China's new leaders more flexible or more neuralgic on issues of Japan's historical approach remains to be seen. This includes related questions of potential Heisei generation nationalism, Tokyo's evolving self-image as a "normal" country and new interpretations of Article IX of Japan's constitution.

---

32. White Paper on China's National Defence in 2002, Section I, The security situation. It is telling that the 2002 Defence White Paper initial description of China's security situation begins with an extended discussion of economic opportunities in Asia.
33. These themes are elaborated in See Gerrit W. Gong (ed.), *Memory and History in East and Southeast Asia* (Washington, DC: CSIS Press, 2001).

Demography. China's new leaders understand they are leading not only a young Chinese nation but a young Chinese nation set in the midst of a young Asian-Pacific demographic structure. With the exception of Japan (41) and Russia (36), the median age for most of Asia is less than 35 years old.[34] The median age in Indonesia, Malaysia, Vietnam and Mongolia is under 25 years. Half of Asia's citizens are still in their formative years. Formative experiences for these Asian generations over the coming 20 years will shape their perceptions and approaches towards China for the next 40 years. China's new leaders understand winning Asian hearts and minds now will pay dividends for years to come.

The general approaches of China's new leaders will also be manifest in relations with specific countries and international organizations, a few of which are briefly overviewed as follows.

Japan. China's new leaders may continue Beijing's strategy of "containment by guilt" and "concessions by guilt" in their relations with Japan. In fact, as China's leadership succession brings to power next-generation leaders with little personal experience in the anti-Japanese war, those new leaders may be bound to take harder-line stances toward Japan on issues of history than even their predecessors. Tensions could increase if Japan's Heisei generation decides not to be "bullied" by China on historical issues.

China's new leaders will continue to seek gradual ways to draw Japan out of the United States' orbit and to limit Tokyo's strategic co-operation with the United States. At the same time, these new leaders will see and understand the short-term benefits to regional stability if American forces continue to operate from Japan. But China clearly wants its growing power to make Japan increasingly cautious about acting in ways counter to China's expressed interests. China may seek to limit Japanese nationalism, including in the younger generations, and to channel that which occurs towards creating a non-aligned Japan.

North and South Korea. China's new leaders have visited North Korea three times in the past four years. Yet it is unlikely that these new Chinese leaders feel anything of the "lips and teeth" co-operative ties with Pyongyang that their predecessor generation maintained.

At the same time, it is likely that China's new leaders will be unwilling to risk having a nationalistic, unified Korea on its border. So they will continue cleverly to play North and South Korea against themselves, thereby continuing to foster a dependence of each on China. This relational approach to power gives Beijing economic leverage over ROK investment and trade in China, and increases Beijing's economic influence with the DPRK, which may prove unable to maintain itself economically.

China's new leaders will continue a shared interest with Washington in a non-nuclear Korean peninsula, though Beijing is occasionally willing to

34. See Appendix 2.

turn a blind eye to North Korea's missile development and proliferation. Indeed, Beijing may surreptitiously provide some missile telemetry technology or other military assistance to maintain a finger on the pulse of North Korean military developments.

European Union. China's new leaders will continue to court the EU and the constituent countries of the EU (note 40 visits to 22 different European countries over the past four years). Europe provides China's new leaders two interesting international opportunities: to balance the particular interests (including commercial ones) individual European countries pursue in China; and to encourage European countries as a whole to create a major international pole consistent with China's international strategy of encouraging multipolarization.[35]

Thus China's new leaders will encourage United Europe to see and establish itself as a global political, economic, security and cultural power centre. This helps fulfil China's international strategy of fostering major international counterweights to the United States or any single country that tends toward accruing disproportionate international influence. China's stated desire for more formal ties to NATO illustrates Beijing's comprehensive approach to Europe, including in the security area. China will also continue to seek influence among the various countries of Europe (such as Germany, France, the United Kingdom) by seeking to adjudicate their continued pursuit of independent competitive interests, including commercial ones in China and Asia.

Russia. Over the lifetime of China's new leaders, Russia may come to regret its shortsighted willingness to supply advanced military technology to China. Efforts to create an anti-US Sino-Russian entente benefited Beijing more than Moscow, one reason Moscow so quickly joined the anti-terrorism effort and has sought closer alignment with Washington ever since the May 2002 Russian–US summit. Since capability has always mattered as much as intent, Beijing's ability to acquire post-Soviet arms production facilities, technologies and co-operation may ultimately rebound to Moscow's detriment.

China will remain interested in potential overland supplies of energy from Russia and the post-Soviet countries of Central Asia. China's new leaders will also seek to assure that they drive wedges into any potential Russian–Japanese economic or security co-operation.

India and Pakistan. Interestingly, neither of China's new leaders who visited India visited Pakistan and vice versa. This means there is no single Chinese leader with direct experience with both New Delhi and Islamabad. China's continued willingness to help secure Pakistan against India, including through indirect provision of nuclear and missile technology assistance, may remain a point of contention in Sino-US relations.

---

35. See Kay Möller, "Diplomatic relations and mutual strategic perceptions: China and the European Union," *The China Quarterly*, No. 169 (March 2002), pp. 10–32.

Washington will continue to work with China's new leaders to see a nuclear or missile race on the Sub-continent as not in their interest. But the attitudes of the incoming leadership group on India–Pakistan bilateral and multilateral relations remains to be seen. China's new leaders will want to see some semblance of stable balance maintained between India and Pakistan. Depending how the global war on terrorism unfolds, China may also seek to limit American inroads into Afghanistan and other parts of the Islamic world through its ties to Pakistan.

At the same time, Sino-Indian relations will remain basically stable. Both Beijing and New Delhi have more to lose in mutual confrontation than in their uneasy current truce. Their economic relations are limited, with New Delhi jealous of Beijing's continuing ability to acquire high multiples of foreign direct investment compared to India each year.

Middle East. China's new leaders visited six Middle Eastern countries during the past four years. This reflects their continuing interest in oil, and opportunities to play Arab countries and Israel against each other and against the United States in ways advantageous to China, to sell military hardware and other equipment, and to leverage intelligence and military exchanges that give it a place in a perpetual world hotspot.

Israel and China will continue to use their mutual relations, including intelligence and technology exchange, to create respective leverage with Washington. Indeed, excepting energy, the Middle East represents secondary interests for China's new leaders. Their strategic interest is to engage the United States in an area where Beijing can trade its secondary interests in areas the United States considers vital. This asymmetry of interests frequently gives China the opportunity to acquire and use power on favourable terms.

Central Asian countries. China's new leaders will build relations with the Central Asian countries to pursue energy options, to minimize threats of cross-border insurgencies in its north-west and to create leverage on Russia.

International organizations. As part of their strategy of fostering multipolarity, China's new leaders will continue to participate in, and interact with, regional organizations such as ASEAN, Asia-Pacific Economic Co-operation (APEC) and Shanghai Co-operation Organization (SCO). As suggested by China's proposed South-East Asia free trade area, China's new leaders will want to assert their co-operative intent to the ASEAN countries, even while (as this article argues earlier) increasing economic competition with them for global market shares. In general, China's new leaders will seek to shape international rules in favourable ways, to limit the ability of collective regional bodies to take unfavourable positions and to guarantee Taiwan remains diplomatically isolated.

China's new leaders will see value in their UN Security Council permanent membership. They will seek to increase its value by using the UN organization and framework to address international issues in which

China can maximize its presence through multilateral means while being prepared, as recently demonstrated on the UN resolution process regarding Iraq, to demonstrate hard-negotiated flexibility.

In contrast, as in South China Sea territorial disputes, China's new leaders will naturally engage potential competitors bilaterally (such as the Philippines) rather than through regional organizations. This will reduce the potential for common positions by regional organizations (such as ASEAN) different from Beijing.

Conclusion

This article has argued that China's new leaders come grounded in the essential continuities of international orientation that significant Party and recent international experience represent. Yet, unlike initially for their predecessors, the primary challenge of China's new leaders is to deal with the global strength of the United States and the competitive realities of economic globalization. The new leaders will warily manage intensifying domestic and international competition they see as unavoidable in the process of building comprehensive national strength. In this competition, China's accumulating international accomplishments, such as surpassing the United States in attracted foreign direct investment, are counterbalanced by continuing challenges. Only time will tell whether China's new leaders are overly sensitive to their international challenges, so as nationalistically to behave both insecurely and proudly in China's international pursuit of regional power and global influence.

Appendix 1: **Trips Abroad by each Politburo Standing Committee Member**

Hu Jintao

	Trips	*Countries*	
2002	1	3	Malaysia, Singapore, USA
2001	3	11	Iran, Syria, Jordan, Cyprus, Uganda; Vietnam; Russia, UK, France, Spain, Germany
2000	1	5	Myanmar, Thailand, Indonesia, Belarus, Kazakhstan
1999	1	4	Madagascar, Ghana, Ivory Coast, South Africa
Total	**6**	**23**	

Wu Bangguo

	Trips	*Countries*	
2002	1	1	Pakistan
2001	1	3	Spain, Germany, France

2000	2	6	UK, Belgium, Switzerland; Sudan, Egypt, Kuwait
1999	0	0	
Total	**4**	**10**	

Wen Jiabao

	Trips	*Countries*	
2002	1	1	Italy
2001	0	0	
2000	1	2	UK, Switzerland
1999	0	0	
Total	**2**	**3**	

Jia Qinglin

	Trips	*Countries*	
2002	1	1	North Korea
2001	2	4	Brazil, Argentina, New Zealand; Russia
2000	2	4	Egypt; South Africa, Uganda, Austria
1999	1	3	Canada, Australia, Singapore
Total	**6**	**12**	

Zeng Qinghong

	Trips	*Countries*	
2002	3	3	Japan; Switzerland; Austria
2001	3	3	North Korea; Singapore; North Korea
2000	3	7	Australia, New Zealand; South Korea, Japan; Laos, Cambodia, Brunei
1999	0	0	
Total	**9**	**13**	

Huang Ju

	Trips	*Countries*	
2002	1	3	Slovenia, Croatia, Hungary
2001	1	3	Spain, Portugal, Malta
2000	1	4	Vietnam, Laos, Japan, South Korea
1999	1	4	Norway, Finland, Iceland, Denmark
Total	**4**	**14**	

Wu Guanzheng

	Trips	Countries	
2002	1	3	Australia, New Zealand, Singapore
2001	1	3	Tunisia, Nigeria, Morocco
2000	1	3	Uruguay, Brazil, Venezuela
1999	1	1	Japan
Total	**4**	**10**	

Li Changchun

	Trips	Countries	
2002	1	4	Germany, France, Poland, Russia
2001	1	4	Thailand, Malaysia, Singapore, India
2000	1	3	Sweden, Italy, Spain
1999	1	3	Brazil, Chile, Peru
Total	**4**	**14**	

Luo Gan

	Trips	Countries	
2002	0	0	
2001	1	1	Laos
2000	2	7	France, Portugal, Italy, Namibia, Morocco, Qatar; Thailand
1999	0	0	
Total	**3**	**8**	
Overall Total	**42**	**107**	

Detail of Visits by Continent and Country

	Visits	Countries
Africa	**15**	**11**
Egypt	2	
Ghana	1	
Ivory Coast	1	
Madagascar	1	
Morocco	2	
Namibia	1	
Nigeria	1	
South Africa	2	
Sudan	1	
Tunisia	1	
Uganda	2	

Asia	**28**	**12**
Brunei	1	
Cambodia	1	
Indonesia	1	
Japan	4	
Laos	3	
Malaysia	2	
Myanmar	1	
North Korea	3	
Singapore	5	
South Korea	2	
Thailand	3	
Vietnam	2	
Europe	**40**	**22**
Austria	2	
Belarus	1	
Belgium	1	
Croatia	1	
Denmark	1	
Finland	1	
France	4	
Germany	3	
Hungary	1	
Iceland	1	
Italy	3	
Kazakhstan	1	
Malta	1	
Norway	1	
Poland	1	
Portugal	2	
Russia	3	
Slovenia	1	
Spain	4	
Sweden	1	
Switzerland	3	
United Kingdom	3	
Middle East	**6**	**6**
Cyprus	1	
Iran	1	
Jordan	1	
Kuwait	1	
Qatar	1	
Syria	1	
North America	**2**	**2**
Canada	1	
USA	1	
Oceania	**6**	**2**
Australia	3	
New Zealand	3	

South America	**8**	**6**
Argentina	1	
Brazil	3	
Chile	1	
Peru	1	
Uruguay	1	
Venezuela	1	
Sub-continent	**2**	**2**
India	1	
Pakistan	1	
Total	**107**	**63**

Appendix 2: **Median Age by Country**

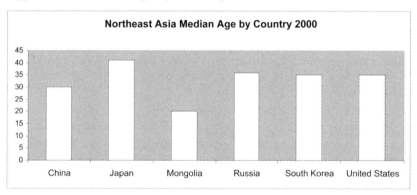

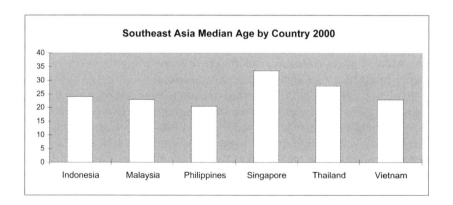

US–China Relations in the Wake of the 16th Party Congress and Tenth National People's Congress

Kenneth Lieberthal

ABSTRACT US–China relations are in more solid shape that any would have anticipated at President Bush's inauguration in January 2001 and, despite the leadership succession in Beijing, both sides want to maintain the strategic co-operation that has developed. The succession itself poses no clear threat to continued development of US–China relations, although if crises should occur the new alloca-tion of power in Beijing could complicate China's handling of the situation. There are, in addition, serious underlying problems – domestic politics in both countries, cross-Strait relations and the evolution of the war on terrorism – that could produce major change for the worse. Unravelling in any one of these three spheres, moreover, makes unravelling in the other two considerably more likely. It will therefore take mutual sensitivity and a serious commitment to the value of the US–China relation-ship itself to sustain the level of common interest and effort that is so evident at the start of 2003.

The Succession and US–China Relations

At the time of writing, there is serious debate as to the extent to which the 16th Party Congress and Tenth National People's Congress (NPC) have ushered in a full leadership transition. Jiang Zemin's success in placing protégés on the new Politburo Standing Committee, in having his name and the "three represents" entered into the revised CCP rules, in being voted anew as the head of the Military Commissions of the CCP and of the state, and having protégés assume key State Council positions has received wide comment and raised legitimate questions as to the ongoing influence that Jiang will seek to exercise.[1]

Nowhere is the extent of leadership transition less clear than in China's foreign affairs system. Jiang Zemin has long regarded his own expertise and experience as especially valuable in China's management of its foreign policy, especially policy towards the United States and Taiwan. By retaining control of the Military Affairs Commission of the CCP Jiang has assured himself an ongoing role in foreign affairs.

Former foreign minister Tang Jiaxuan has replaced Qian Qichen as the vice-premier level official with responsibility for foreign affairs, and Li Zhaoxing, one of the Foreign Ministry's premier America experts, has moved up from vice-minister to take over as minister of foreign affairs. Former head of the international liaison department Dai Bingguo has become executive vice-minister of foreign affairs.

1. Erik Eckholm, "Chinese leader gives up a job but not power," *The New York Times*, 16 November 2002.

It is too early to know how foreign policy decision-making will operate with this new array of incumbents. The leadership overall lacks foreign policy experience. While this can always be said of incoming leaders as compared with those exiting top positions, it is especially true of the new Politburo Standing Committee membership. None of them has extensive personal knowledge of either foreign heads of state or influential personages in the major foreign countries. Few have had much experience in foreign travel at all. Only Hu Jintao has more than marginal exposure to military affairs, and even Hu's experience in this arena is recently acquired.[2]

In addition, the organization of foreign policy decision-making is still uncertain. Leadership small groups are not statutory bodies – their tasking, composition and functions can change according to the decisions of the Politburo Standing Committee leadership.[3] Liu Huaqiu's institutional base and influence, for example, evolved considerably during 1997–2002,[4] and it is not clear whether the new leadership will seek to construct a similar vehicle for foreign policy input for the coming years. Jiang Zemin utilized an informal group of retired ambassadors as a key foreign policy sounding board at various times, but the new leadership may eschew this group or any similar body. Almost certainly, the relative roles and influence of various think tanks will shift as the new leadership settles in.[5]

As far as we are aware, none of the new leaders harbours views towards US–China relations that differ greatly from those of the outgoing Politburo Standing Committee.[6] And the influence of Jiang Zemin and his protégés in the new leadership line-up argues in any case for basic Chinese policy continuity, at least for the near future.

But inevitably leadership change does make a difference. At a minimum, it means that the fairly thick set of personal relationships that have underpinned US–China relations in recent years will be attenuated. This refers not only to ties among top leaders on both sides but also to the significant role that influential business, academic and former government officials play in maintaining lines of communication and informally fleshing out various ideas and concepts. It takes time to build the type of thick fabric that can be very important to making a relationship manageable and effective. The lack of such a fabric was evident in the rocky

2. Hu was appointed a vice-chairman of the CCP's Military Commission in September 1999.
3. Kenneth Lieberthal, *Governing China* (New York: W.W. Norton, 2004).
4. Liu headed the State Council Foreign Affairs Office and then shifted to heading the CCP's Foreign Affairs Office of the Central Committee.
5. The recent roles of think tanks relevant to foreign policy decision-making are analysed in the respective articles by David Shambaugh, "China's international relations think tanks: evolving structure and process," Bonnie Glaser and Phillip Saunders "Chinese foreign policy research institutes: evolving roles and increasing influence," and Bates Gill and James Mulvenon "Chinese military-related think tanks and research institutions" in *The China Quarterly*, No. 171 (September 2002), pp. 575–624.
6. Andrew Nathan and Bruce Gilley, *China's New Rulers* (New York: New York Review Books, 2002), ch. 8.

initial management of the EP-3 reconnaissance plane incident in April 2001.[7]

It is, in sum, not possible to specify clearly the impact of the 16th Congress and Tenth NPC on the future of US–China relations. Too much is unknown, and there may be no consequential disagreement in any case among the new leaders over how to deal with the United States. But the new set-up does reduce the pool of experience among the top echelon leaders in dealing with the United States and therefore potentially makes crisis management more difficult. The fact that Jiang Zemin will continue to head the military for a matter of years while not serving on the Politburo Standing Committee may further complicate crisis decision making. This also introduces the possibility of increased rancour among the top leaders. The potential significance of these three changes can be appreciated only in the context of the recent development of US–China relations and the issues coming up on the US–China agenda.

Recent Development of US–China Relations

There has been a puzzle at the heart of the US–China relationship since the Bush administration took office in January 2001: this American administration has done a great deal that in different times would have caused a very sharp, negative reaction from Beijing, but China instead has steadfastly pursued solid, co-operative relations with the United States. As a consequence, as of early 2003 the US–China relationship can ironically fairly be described by using the term so derided by conservative Republicans when it was used during the late 1990s: the United States and China appear to be building a constructive strategic partnership for the 21st century. Why should this be so?

The bill of particulars. Had Beijing wanted cause for complaint about the new administration, it would not have had far to look. As a candidate, George W. Bush termed China a "strategic competitor."[8] Once in office he appointed people[9] to leadership roles in the Department of Defense who were on record as regarding China as the major long-term strategic threat to the United States. The new national security advisor had no record of support for co-operative US–China relations. Overall, the people appointed to manage policy towards Asia felt that the United States had paid too much attention to China and too little to American

7. Bruce Gilley and David Murphy, "Power play in Hainan," *Far Eastern Economic Review*, 19 April 2001.

8. Alison Mitchell, "The China trade wrangle: the Bush speech," *The New York Times*, 18 May 2000.

9. Donald Rumsfeld, Douglas Feith, Paul Wolfowitz and Andrew Marshal, among others.

allies, especially Japan and South Korea.[10] They voiced determination to redress this imbalance.[11]

The early months of the administration saw additional difficulties. On 25 April, the president stated in a television interview with CNN that the United States would "do whatever it takes" to defend Taiwan should China attack.[12] Despite immediate White House efforts to retract this comment, the Chinese took it seriously (and, a year later, senior Pentagon officials recited it as official US doctrine[13]). On 1 April, a Chinese plane harassing an American EP-3 reconnaissance aircraft in international waters collided with the US plane, prompting a serious crisis.

In the wake of 11 September, America responded with actions and doctrinal statements that could have set off alarms in Beijing. A short summary of the pertinent actions would include the following[14]:

- Establishing a military presence and force projection capability in Central Asia, including actual forces, supplies and facilities in Uzbekistan, Tadzikistan and Afghanistan.
- Establishing a strong security relationship with Pakistan, China's closest strategic partner in the region.
- Increasing military ties with India, especially in naval matters, including making arms sales and holding joint exercises.
- Enhancing the role and presence of the American military in various parts of South-East Asia, including the Philippines and Thailand. Also, renewing some ties with the Indonesian military.
- Successfully encouraging Japan to adopt more expansive rules governing the deployment and use of the Japan defence forces.[15]
- Developing a broad strategic relationship with Russia.[16]
- Changing the role of NATO so that it began to focus on moving towards an ability to commit high quality, mobile forces to conflicts outside the European theatre.[17]

In addition, the Bush administration terminated the ABM treaty and undertook a determined effort to develop and deploy multilayered missile

10. These include: Torkel Patterson as senior director for Asia on the National Security Council; Richard Armitage as deputy secretary and James Kelly as assistant secretary for East Asia and the Pacific at the Department of State; and Paul Wolfowitz, among others, at the Department of Defense.

11. "The United States and Japan: advancing toward a mature partnership," special report to the Institute for National Strategic Studies, 11 October 2000.

12. David E. Sanger, "US would defend Taiwan, Bush says," *The New York Times*, 26 April 2001.

13. Andrea Shalal-Esa, "US vows to do what it takes to aid Taiwan defense," *Reuters*, 9 April 2002.

14. Bates Gill, "11 September and Northeast Asia," *Brookings Review*, Vol. 20, No. 3 (Summer 2002).

15. Most of these are reviewed in Kenneth Lieberthal, "The United States and Asia in 2001," *Asian Survey* (January/February 2002), pp. 1–13.

16. Russia's agreement to accept America's termination of the ABM treaty without major friction marked a major turning point in — and reflection of — the strategic bonds developing between Washington and Moscow.

17. Elisabeth Bumiller, "Bush seeks new NATO at summit meeting," *The New York Times*, 19 November 2002.

defences. It also made quantitative and qualitative changes in arms sale policy towards Taiwan and in the military ties between the United States and Taiwan,[18] While America was upgrading its military ties with Taiwan, moreover, Secretary Rumsfeld utilized his "case-by-case" review of military contacts with the PRC to deny virtually all such activities until November 2002 and allow only minimal contacts after that.[19]

Doctrinally, the Department of Defense's "Quadrennial defense review" of 30 September 2001 and the "National security policy of the United States of America"[20] of September 2002 articulated a set of precepts likely to be anathema to China's strategic thinkers. Most prominently, these documents announced that it is the policy of the United States to maintain total military superiority against every potential threat capability to the extent that no other country will even try to match American military capabilities, and that the United States will feel justified in pre-emptive use of military force to remove a future threat that it sees developing.

There were also more positive developments. But on balance, the array of security measures noted above is so far reaching in its potential consequences for the PRC that Beijing's decision to accommodate it in order to put US–China relations on a solid footing requires explanation. Few China specialists, if given the above bill of particulars in 2000, would have anticipated that Beijing would react as it actually has in the ensuing two years.

Explaining Beijing's America Policy Since January 2001

Four factors dovetail to explain Beijing's America policy since January 2001. Ironically, the first is the unusually daunting array of domestic issues the country faces and the desire by China's leaders not to add to their problems with new foreign policy challenges, while the second is Beijing's newfound confidence that – despite these problems – China has finally become a major player in the international arena and thus need no longer utilize the strategies of weakness that had so much characterized the country's foreign policy under successive regimes over the previous century. The third factor involves managing military policy so as to reduce potential opposition from the PLA. And the fourth is the strong incentives created by the Bush administration's own approach to foreign policy.

Domestic issues and foreign policy. It is difficult objectively to measure the extent to which national leaders feel pressed by the domestic problems they confront. The domestic platter is always very full. In a

18. Jim Wolf, "Top Taiwan defense official visits Pentagon," *Reuters*, 11 September 2002.

19. Michael R. Gordon, "Rumsfeld limiting military contacts with the Chinese," *The New York Times*, 4 June 2001.

20. US Department of Defense, "Quadrennial defense review report," 30 September 2001, pp. 1–25. "The national security strategy of the United States of America": http://www.whitehouse.gov/nsc/nss.html.

country undergoing the type of systemic change that China is experiencing, moreover, domestic strains and crises are usually especially daunting.

Leadership sentiment does, nevertheless, play a very important role in shaping the relationship between domestic issues and foreign policy. In the initial years of the 21st century, the PRC is facing a particularly challenging array of issues, most of which are a direct consequence of the systemic reforms it has been implementing and some of which represent having the bills come due for expenses that were essentially postponed as Beijing focused on maintaining rapid growth during and after the 1997–98 Asian financial crisis.

Discussions with Chinese leaders and the actions those leaders have taken make clear that they see their domestic plate as so full that they made a fundamental decision in 2000 to work hard to establish good relations with the incoming administration in Washington as their top strategic foreign policy priority.[21] They also regard the coming years as critical to setting China on a course that will lead to vastly increased wealth and power in the decades ahead.

The Tenth NPC declared that China will quadruple its GDP by the year 2020. The period from 2003 to then is considered crucial for making the changes necessary to turn China into a relatively well off society and put it on a solid footing for the long-term future. But this goal is unreachable if China's relations with the United States deteriorate markedly. The PRC depends on America to absorb more than 30 per cent of its exports and to be an ongoing source of foreign direct investment. More fundamentally, American hostility could both disrupt China's broader access to the international economy and force the diversion of funds into military expenditures. In short, China's economic growth strategy, which depends on reaping the benefits of increasing global economic interdependence, creates enormous systemic pressures to maintain solid US–China relations.

With China's ambitious economic goals in mind, what is notable about the early 2000s is that Beijing faces a series of extraordinary expenses that come in addition to the normal demands on government coffers. These make it all the more important that the underlying capacity for economic growth remains strong. The most consequential of these expenses include the following:

- Making China's state-owned banks whole. The banking system is awash in non-performing loans (NPLs) to the point where the big four commercial banks are probably technically insolvent. They are able to keep functioning because for most Chinese there is no other place to put their funds. This system must change, as World Trade Organization (WTO) obligations require China within five years to permit foreign banks and financial services access to the RMB economy in China. That change will require both more truculent reforms of the state-

---

21. Chinese officials clearly signalled this foreign policy decision to their Clinton administration counterparts in the early autumn of 2000.

owned enterprises and expensive measures to remove the NPLs from the banks' books and infuse new funds to make the big four banks whole. The bill may exceed the better part of US$600 billion to make these changes.[22]

- Funding an urban pension system and developing a social safety net. China's reforms have made it impossible to deliver social services to the majority of urban residents through the former work unit (*danwei*) system. Beijing is thus trying to develop systems to provide urban residents with unemployment compensation, health care coverage, welfare payments and pensions. These are very expensive undertakings, likely to require commitments of public funds in the hundreds of billions of dollars.[23]

- Making financially whole county and township level governments. The vast majority of local governments – reportedly more than 70 per cent of county governments and 85 per cent of township governments – are now indebted to such an extent that current regulations do not provide an avenue for them to meet their debt burdens. Higher levels are going to have to find funds to put local governments on a sounder financial footing.[24]

- Tackling the north China water shortage, among other environmental expenditures. The north China water shortage is extremely severe. Major infrastructure projects are required in addition to conservation measures. The bill for the project to move water from central China to north China alone will total at least $20 billion and may run to $40 billion or more.[25]

In addition, the succession itself has imposed a sense of caution on the leaders, as they have not wished to complicate internal discussions over the allocation and configuration of posts with disagreements over foreign policy. Thus, for example, Beijing reacted very mildly when during the summer 2002 Beidaihe conference Chen Shui-bian made public remarks about the existence of "one country on each side" (*yi bian yi guo*) of the Taiwan Strait.[26]

Finally, China is now implementing its wide-ranging WTO accession requirements. Its new leaders are, as noted above, experienced overwhelmingly in domestic affairs, and they recognize that major additional economic, social and administrative reforms are required for the country to meet its goals. They have accordingly given their foreign affairs

22. Elisabeth Rosenthal, "Bank of China's mounting problems," *The New York Times*, 1 February 2002; Mark O'Neill, "PBOC challenged on conflict in supervisory role," *South China Morning Post*, 1 April 2002. On the pertinent WTO obligations, see Nick Lardy, *Integrating China in the Global Economy* (Washington, DC: Brookings, 2001).

23. Sarah Cook, *After the Iron Rice Bowl: Extending the Social Safety Net in China* (Brighton: Institute of Development Studies, 2000).

24. *Caijing* (*Finance*), 5 August 2002 article by Hu Yifan.

25. Erik Eckholm, "Chinese will move waters to quench the thirst of cities," *The New York Times*, 27 August 2002.

26. Craig S. Smith, "A distracted China issues censure of Taiwan chief's remarks," *The New York Times*, 6 August 2002.

officials direct orders to avoid international complications and distractions wherever possible.[27]

Against this background, conversations in 2000 with Chinese officials made clear that China's leaders fully recognize a longstanding pattern in American policy towards the PRC: every campaign for the presidency sees the opposition candidate lambaste the incumbent for following too soft a policy towards China, but then over time a new president moves from initial hostility to willingness to find ways to co-operate with Beijing. China's leaders sought to shorten this transition with the new administration in 2001 through persistent signals of a desire to improve relations and through concrete initiatives.

In March, Beijing dispatched Vice-Premier Qian Qichen to Washington to convey China's desire for good relations and establish personal contacts with the new American foreign policy leadership team.[28] Late in the spring, China's Ministry of Foreign Affairs used the annual strategic talks, with policy planning head Richard Haass, to assure Washington that China does not seek to drive America out of Asia.[29] When 11 September occurred, Jiang Zemin was one of the first foreign leaders to call President Bush to offer both his empathy and China's co-operation in the fight.[30] And China has skilfully and usefully acted so as to remain on the American side of that fight ever since.

A flood of informal messages via visiting scholars and officials that highlighted China's desire to establish good relations buttressed the above formal initiatives. This included Track II discussions and numerous other contacts. All in all, Beijing has conveyed since before January 2001 that it seeks to put its relations with the US on a solid footing, largely so that it could pursue vital domestic objectives.

International gravitas. Ironically given its domestic constraints, since 2001 Beijing appears to have concluded that China has at long last achieved sufficient international weight and respect as a major power that it can now act as an accepted member of the group of leading countries. The PRC's accession to the WTO probably played a role in this assessment, as it completed the effort to have the PRC become a member of every major multilateral organization for which it is eligible.[31] This is producing a steadier, less emotional overall approach to foreign policy, one decidedly less prone to moralistic petulance than has been the case in previous PRC policy.[32]

27. Private communication in Beijing.

28. Greg Torode, "Qian to take Bush's pulse," *The South China Morning Post*, 15 March 2001.

29. Private communication to the author.

30. Erik Eckholm, "After the attacks: in Beijing," *The New York Times*, 16 September 2001.

31. The Missile Technology Control Regime is the only possibly significant exception to this statement.

32. Ma Licheng, "New thoughts for China–Japan relations – worrisome problems among Chinese and Japanese people," *Zhanlüe yu guanli* (*Strategy and Management*), 1 December 2002, pp. 41–47 provides a good sense of the thinking behind this new approach.

This approach to foreign policy reflects the completion of the evolution of the CCP from a revolutionary party to a governing party, one that is concerned with managing the ongoing economic development process in an increasingly complex and sophisticated society. In this situation the governing party is determined to make foreign policy serve domestic development needs, and it is proving quite capable of avoiding tantrums in favour of pragmatically seeking marginal advantages where they can be had to reduce international costs and maximize China's economic interests.

In these new terms, Beijing has seen the 11 September tragedy as providing an opportunity to achieve strategic breathing space in relations with the United States.[33] The Chinese seized this opportunity, demonstrating the potential strategic value of good US–China relations and co-operating as the United States shifted its focus from a potential China threat to an actual terrorist threat.

Managing the Army. Potentially the most severe internal critic of China's close ties with the United States is the People's Liberation Army. But Beijing has apparently kept this problem under control by strongly supporting PLA development. Announced military budgets continued to increase in double digits in real terms through 2002, the PLA is purchasing advanced weapons systems and platforms from Russia, and training is improving its capacity to use force against Taiwan.[34] The close strategic ties with the United States, in short, have not come at the cost of activities and initiatives cherished by the military.

Responding to US incentives. In the wake of 11 September, President Bush has made it very clear that he regards all who join in the fight against terrorism as friends and that he will not forget those who fail to join in that fight.[35] The administration has not hesitated since 11 September to join with oppressive regimes such as Uzbekistan where they can assist that fight or to castigate even democracies such as Germany when they voice serious opposition to pertinent Bush initiatives. The very intensity with which the administration has structured US policy around counter-terrorism has made incentives for short-term co-operation especially strong, and this undoubtedly has been taken into account in Beijing.

Results. The results of the above facts have been clear. Beijing has bent over backwards to nurture strong US–China relations. Specifically, China has co-operated extensively in the counter-terrorism effort in encouraging

33. David Lampton, "Bush's chance to engage a new China," *South China Morning Post*, 6 October 2002.

34. David Lague, "Buying some major muscle," *Far Eastern Economic Review*, 24 January 2002; John Pomfret, "China raises defense budget again," *Washington Post*, 5 March 2002.

35. Address on terrorism before a Joint Meeting of Congress, 20 September 2001; reprinted in *The New York Times*, 21 September 2001.

Pakistan to work with the United States, facilitating both a counter-terrorism resolution shortly after 11 September at the UN and then later a resolution against Iraq, sharing intelligence, and in other ways.[36] Beyond the counter-terrorism fight, China has also taken steps to strengthen its non-proliferation regime (adopting dual-use missile technology lists and regulations, tightening up on biological weapons),[37] allowed the Dalai Lama's brother to travel to Tibet accompanied by Lodi Gyari, the Dalai Lama's representative in Washington,[38] virtually going silent on Beijing's objections to the development of a multi-layered missile defence, and so forth. In short, China has made wide-ranging efforts to secure good relations with the United States.

The Bush administration has appreciated both the feasibility and value of strategic co-operation with China. As of early 2003 it is making clear that it does not welcome any developments that would impede such co-operation, including new initiatives from Taipei that might raise cross-Strait tensions.[39]

In sum, in early 2003 US–China relations are in very solid shape, and the leaderships in both Beijing and Washington want to keep things on track for continued effective co-operation.[40] This is the framework that the succession leadership in Beijing is inheriting as it picks up the mantle of China's foreign policy decision-making.

Potential Sources of Change

Even barring a serious unforeseen development, such as the May 1999 embassy bombing in Belgrade or the April 2001 EP-3 incident, there are three underlying issues that could seriously and adversely affect US–China relations in the coming years. These are: domestic politics in both countries; cross-Strait relations; and the evolution of the war on terrorism. If relations begin seriously to unravel in any one of these three areas, moreover, they are more likely to unravel in the other two.

Domestic politics. The succession's impact on US–China relations can, at this point, only be dealt with in a structural fashion. That is, there are no differences that are clear to the outside world among the incoming leaders concerning how to deal with the United States. In addition, as noted above, it is still not clear exactly who among the successors will

36. Lieberthal, "The United States and Asia in 2001."

37. Elisabeth Rosenthal, "China issues rules on export of missile gear," *The New York Times*, 26 August 2002; John Pomfret, "China embraces more moderate foreign policy," *Washington Post*, 24 October 2002.

38. Ben Dolven, "Hope springs eternal," *Far Eastern Economic Review*, 26 September 2002.

39. Indeed, as early as summer 2002 Washington made this point clear to Taipei in the wake of Chen Shui-bian's "one country on each side of the Taiwan Strait" comment noted above.

40. James Dao, "US and China resume high-level military talks after 20 months," *The New York Times*, 10 December 2002); "US warship docks in China in sign of strong ties," *Reuters*, 24 November 2002.

have major control over China's future foreign policy decision-making. The argument here must, therefore, focus not on individual or group perspectives but rather on the dynamics of politics at the top of the Chinese system and whether those dynamics in and of themselves hold risks for US–China relations.

It appears that Jiang Zemin aims to continue for some time to exercise power directly over security affairs, and from behind the scenes over all elite decisions through his protégés on the Politburo Standing Committee. Jiang, however, does not have the kind of power that Deng Xiaoping enjoyed after Deng stepped down from the Politburo in 1987. It is not likely, for example, that all members of the current Politburo Standing Committee would take as given that Jiang's future choices in matters of serious disagreement on the Politburo Standing Committee are decisive and must be accepted as final.

At the Politburo Standing Committee level, moreover, the 16th Congress did not produce an outcome that maximizes the chances for good co-operation among the members. Jiang will continue to try to affect policy, while General Secretary Hu and Premier Wen Jiabao lack their own supporters on the Standing Committee. Zeng Qinghong may wield very substantial power, and it remains to be seen how he manages future co-operation with both Jiang and Hu. Speculatively, there could be considerable jockeying for power and prestige, especially given Jiang's ongoing active engagement.

In this context of potential elite infighting and of Jiang Zemin's potentially trying to exercise influence without actually holding the top executive positions, several problems could arise that can affect US–China relations:

- China's crisis management may be less effective. With some greater potential for elite division and less clear allocation of power and responsibility, there is increased likelihood of missteps in the initial hours when a crisis erupts. That can have entirely unintentional but nevertheless severe effects on US–China relations. As long as Jiang Zemin leads the Military Commission of the CCP but does not serve on the Politburo, moreover, the need for a well-articulated system of crisis management is all the more important.
- The potential for substantive domestic issues to become caught up in leadership infighting will increase, in that how various leaders approach key issues can become influenced by their strategies for political contention at the top of the system. In addition, a divided collective leadership creates greater opportunities for those outside the Politburo to influence key decisions on implementation of WTO obligations that will adversely affect major domestic interests. Should this occur, the politics of WTO implementation, which involves significant changes in regional and bureaucratic interests, can become sharper and more difficult to manage. Lack of unity and focus at the top can easily produce WTO results that will engender trade frustration in the United States and might also turn sentiment in China against the US as

politicians blame American pressures and actions for China's internal discontents.

• If elite disunity should directly focus on how to deal with the United States or on how to manage cross-Strait relations, then the implications for US–China relations can be serious.

In sum, the apparent partial rather than full succession in China during 2002–2003 has raised somewhat the chances of elite infighting over the coming few years that can, in turn, reduce the chances of maintaining smooth US–China strategic co-operation. In addition, there remain many in China's strategic community who are concerned about America's long-term intentions and the extent to which China should stand up to American initiatives.[41] Should elite politics offer an opening for advocating a less co-operative approach to US–China relations, there are many in China who stand ready to take advantage of that opportunity to promote a tougher set of Chinese policies.

American domestic politics are also pertinent to this discussion. President Bush has enjoyed unusual freedom from domestic pressures in pursuing a more co-operative strategic approach to the PRC in the wake of 11 September. The Republican Right in the congress, normally a source of deep scepticism about Chinese trajectories and intentions and of strong support for the aspirations of Taiwan, has been unwilling to challenge the president on this issue, given how supportive he has been and promises to remain on other issues dear to them. They do not want to use China policy to weaken the clout of a president so much to their overall liking.[42] The Democratic Left is normally also deeply sceptical of co-operation with China and is also supportive of Taiwan.[43] For the Left, the key issues against the PRC are human rights and fair trade. But since 11 September human rights activists have found it difficult to identify ways in which to promote their concerns, given the overwhelming centrality of the human rights abuses committed by the terrorists themselves. Human rights criticism of China policy has thus become more muted and politically inconsequential. On the trade side, China joined the WTO in November 2001, and the focus during 2002 was on finding whether Beijing is making a serious effort to implement the required changes in regulations. The actual impact on trade is more likely to become significant – in numbers and politically – during 2003.

Should US–China relations begin to unravel because of other issues, there are many in the US congress who will be prepared to become active

41. See, for example, Lin Limin, "New trend of international pattern in this year," *Beijing Liaowang,* No. 45 (11 November 2002), pp 62–64; and Yang Yunzhong, "Some strategic reflections on the main threats to China's security in the early 21st century," *Beijing dangdai yatai*, No. 10 (15 October 2002), pp. 3–12.

42. Republicans in the congress have already, however, promoted various forms of increased security co-operation with Taiwan, typically against the will of the White House. The last congress, for example, tried to require the Department of Defense to hold joint military exercises with Taiwan's military (*Foreign Relations Authorization Act, Fiscal Year 2003*).

43. The Democratic Left is supportive of Taiwan primarily on human rights and democracy grounds, rather than on security grounds.

on Chinese policy and to seek sanctions against the PRC and new forms of assistance for Taiwan. This could quickly place China policy back into the treacherous cross currents of American domestic politics and could accordingly complicate decision-making in the White House.[44] Beijing itself, viewing these developments, might also again begin to worry about whether the Chinese are being handled via a co-ordinated congressional/ White House "tough cop/soft cop" strategy.[45]

Domestic politics thus present one potential source of difficulty in future US–China co-operation in both China and the United States. Critics have thus far been restrained by the desire of both leaderships to co-operate and the opportunities for co-operation afforded by the focus since 11 September on counter-terrorism. But this strategic co-operation has not sunk deep roots in either political system.

Cross-Strait relations. There is probably no issue that has greater potential to turn US–China amity into enmity than cross-Strait relations. Because the stakes are so high, the odds favour this complex issue being handled in a way that stops short of inviting tragedy for all concerned. But there is sufficient disagreement, distrust, emotion and uncertainty concerning cross-Strait policy that the issue warrants serious consideration in any analysis of potential sources for a breakdown in US–China strategic co-operation.

The United States' view of cross-Strait relations in the Bush White House has changed since the president took office. He has made clear that he does not want new problems to arise in cross-Strait relations, and he therefore has communicated to both Taipei and Beijing the importance of not behaving in a fashion that could seriously raise cross-Strait tensions. At the same time, President Bush, as his predecessors, is very much committed to preserving Taiwan's democratic system, market economy, political freedom and opportunity to sustain prosperity in the event of coercion from across the Strait. In this, President Bush has effectively adopted two of the three longstanding pillars of US policy: "one China" and peaceful resolution.[46]

There is reason to question whether the US Department of Defense has fully adopted the White House view on cross-Strait issues. Specifically, it appears to be prepared to increase US military co-operation with Taiwan in a way that may be at cross purposes with the president's desire

44. Ramon Myers, Michel C. Oksenberg and David Shambaugh (eds.), *Making China Policy: Lessons From the Bush and Clinton Administrations* (Lanham: Rowman and Littlefield, 2001), provides a good overview of the domestic politics of China policy in the United States in recent years.

45. Beijing has often in the past seen a level of White House–congressional conspiracy on China policy that has not been warranted by the facts.

46. The third pillar is cross-Strait dialogue. While there are indications that the White House would like to see cross-Strait dialogue resume, the Bush administration has not seemed to make resumption of this dialogue an affirmative part of US policy towards cross-Strait relations.

to prevent an escalation in tensions across the Strait.[47] In addition, as noted above, there is substantial support in the congress for more American assistance to Taiwan than the White House feels is compatible with overall US policy towards this sensitive issue.

Beijing appears increasingly confident that long-term developments favour a satisfactory resolution of the cross-Strait issue. China's own internal evolution is making it more, rather than less, attractive to many in Taiwan. Already, hundreds of thousands of Taiwan business people reside in the mainland, and recently students from Taiwan have begun choosing to attend mainland universities. The standard of living in Shanghai has become high enough to make it attractive to those who have grown up in Taipei.[48] The PRC's internal evolution is also causing it to play a greater role in the region, arguably decreasing the chances that others would support Taiwan in a radical departure from current policy.

Beijing probably also sees cross-Strait military developments as favouring its own position. Its ongoing deployment of missiles capable of hitting Taiwan, acquisition of weapons and platforms that will increase its ability to project power across the Strait, and increasing sophistication of training of its own forces all argue in favour of a growing superiority over Taiwan's own military forces.[49] These developments are making the US factor even more central to Taiwan's long-term ability to fend off the mainland militarily, and the strategic literature in Beijing has made clear that China is seeking specific capabilities that would significantly increase the potential military cost to the US of intervening in a cross-Strait conflict.[50] It is very likely, in any case, that if Beijing ultimately decides to use military force against Taiwan, this would take the form of a short, shocking application of force followed by an immediate political opening, rather than a prolonged effort to invade and occupy Taiwan. But the unknowns in any such action – and the potential for uncontrollable escalation – would inevitably remain very substantial.[51] And in the aftermath of a US–China armed conflict over Taiwan, the security situation and politics in the East Asia region would be changed for many years to come.

Importantly, Beijing appears to be willing to settle for a face-saving resolution of the cross-Strait issue that would give Beijing its coveted "one China" but would not provide it with operational control over any aspect of Taiwan's internal governance. This broad approach, which has already produced a notable array of PRC offers even before concrete

47. See: "US–Taiwanese military relations: strategic ambiguity," *Jane's Defense Weekly*, 11 December 2002. Also, Yang Yunzhong, "Some strategic reflections," provides a detailed enumeration of recent military activities between the US and Taiwan.

48. David Murphy and Maureen Pao, "A place to call home," *Far Eastern Economic Review*, 5 July 2002.

49. David Isenberg, "Taiwan's air superiority under the gun," *Asia Times*, 5 September 2002.

50. Annual report on the military power of the People's Republic of China (Department of Defense Report to Congress, 2002).

51. Michael Swaine and James C. Mulvenon, *Taiwan's Foreign and Defense Policies* (RAND 2001).

negotiations begin,[52] nevertheless leaves much still to be clarified. Until Beijing is convinced that it need not fear a unilateral declaration of independence by Taiwan, moreover, it is insisting on its right to use force to block or respond to such a declaration. Beijing has indicated that it would be willing to reduce the threat of force as it sees reassuring developments on the Taiwan side, but this remains a very unspecific posture at this point.

Beijing sees US policy as actually giving Taipei the confidence *not* to talk to Beijing and, potentially, to take moves towards independence that could trigger disastrous consequences. Its perspective thus differs 180 degrees from that of the White House, which views security support for Taiwan as giving Taipei the confidence necessary *to* talk to Beijing and potentially reach a settlement.

Taipei finds all of this a difficult situation to manage well. The Democratic Progressive Party (DPP) is internally divided, with a hard core of 20 per cent or so of its supporters ardently pro-independence while the rest are more willing to accept the status quo.[53] The TSU is using its leverage in the Legislative Yuan to pull Chen Shui-bian toward more pro-independence stances, and Lee Teng-hui has called for Taiwan to declare independence in 2008, when hosting the summer Olympics would presumably constrain Beijing's response.[54] Economic integration across the Strait is both providing attractive options for Taiwan's businesses and raising questions about Taiwan's role in the regional economy and about the possibility of a progressive hollowing out of Taiwan's own economy (with understandable fears among the DPP's labour supporters).[55]

Taipei also recognizes that it must maintain close ties with Washington as part of its cross-Strait strategy, but the DPP leadership contains few if any individuals who have a subtle understanding of the complex cross currents of Washington politics on the cross-Strait issue. Taipei must thus navigate to maximize American support while trying to avoid getting tripped up and antagonizing the White House.

Chen Shui-bian is very intelligent, but he has not been known for astute and disciplined management of complex political issues.[56] While Chen himself seems primarily concerned with domestic political reform – specifically, fully breaking the Kuomintang's former one-party mon-

52. These include, *inter alia*: no mainland officials will be sent to Taiwan; no taxes will be collected from Taiwan; Taiwan can maintain its own political, economic, and social systems; Taiwan can retain its own military; the status of Taiwan is undetermined (i.e. Beijing will not necessarily seek to make it a province or special administrative region); the name and flag of the PRC can be changed when a sovereign entity is created that encompasses both the mainland and Taiwan; and Taiwan will be treated as an equal at the negotiating table.
53. Shelley Rigger, "The Democratic Progressive Party in 2000: obstacles and opportunities," *The China Quarterly*, No. 168 (December 2001), pp. 950–54.
54. "Lee Tenghui predicts new state in 2008," *Taiwan News*, 25 July 2002.
55. Ralph N. Clough, *Co-operation or Conflict in the Taiwan Strait* (Lanham: Rowman and Littlefield 1999); Yushan Wu, "Taiwan in 2001: stalemated on all fronts," *Asian Survey* (January/February 2002).
56. Chien-min Chao, "Introduction: the DPP in power," *Journal of Contemporary China*, No. 33 (November 2002), pp. 605–612.

opoly on political power – and getting re-elected in Taiwan, he has not moved effectively to pocket the concessions that Beijing has put on the table, and the prospects for cross-Strait talks remain unclear.

There is, in sum, ongoing danger of miscalculation leading to tragedy across the Taiwan Strait. Beijing distrusts Taipei and thinks Washington is, at best, naive about the effects of its increasing support for Taiwan's military. Washington reads Beijing's refusal to abjure the use of force and its ongoing build-up of military capability as inherently threatening and requiring American counter-measures. America's concern with Taiwan extends both to the importance of not abandoning a democratic government and, given well-known history, the damage to American credibility overall that would accompany any seeming American acquiescence to PRC coercive diplomacy against Taiwan. And Taiwan's current government is determined to build a stronger sense of Taiwanese identity[57] while balancing cross-Strait relations and Taipei's ties with Washington – a set of complex undertakings that may prove too taxing to manage well.

While the White House does not want to see tensions rise across the Strait, there is no indication that the Bush administration has thought through a suitably nuanced strategy to make support for Taiwan compatible with reduction of cross-Strait tensions. Rather, it seems to be relying on a combination of solidifying its counter-terrorism co-operation with Beijing while making clear that it would "do whatever it takes" to counter a mainland move against Taiwan.

There is thus reason to worry about longer-term trends in cross-Strait relations. Optimists can find much evidence to support the idea that the three sides will find ways to keep the situation from escalating, but pessimists can look to domestic politics on all three sides, an escalating cross-Strait arms race[58] and deep ongoing mistrust to draw more worrying conclusions about the future.

The history of the past three decades provides evidence, moreover, that when US–China relations are going relatively well, cross-Strait relations also go more smoothly. Therefore, various factors that could unravel US–China relations also potentially increase the danger to cross-Strait relations.

Evolution of the counter-terrorism war. China shares America's overall concern with terrorism and genuinely seeks ongoing co-operation. China faces its own problems with Muslim terrorists trained in Pakistan or Afghanistan and worries about broader political developments in Central Asia. The Shanghai Co-operation Organization, for example, turned its attention to the need for counter-terrorism co-operation long before 11 September.[59]

---

57. David Lague, "Goodbye to the mainland," *Far Eastern Economic Review*, 7 February 2002.

58. David Lague and Susan V. Lawrence, "China–Taiwan arms race: in guns we trust," *Far Eastern Economic Review*, 12 December 2002.

59. "Declaration of Shanghai Co-operation Organization," reprinted in *Renmin ribao* (*People's Daily*), 15 June 2001.

In the immediate aftermath of 11 September Jiang Zemin called President Bush to offer empathy and co-operation. China then dispatched a vice foreign minister to Pakistan to urge General Musharoff to work with the United States against Al Qaeda and the Taliban. Beijing also actively supported the UN's drafting and adoption of a strong counter-terrorism resolution. Subsequently, Beijing has shared intelligence with Washington and has co-operated in other ways. When America turned its attention to obtaining UN backing for a rigorous new inspection regime on Iraq, Beijing proved helpful in bridging differences between the United States and Britain on one side and France and Russia on the other, and China then voted in favour of Resolution 1441. China as host also acquiesced when President Bush sought to focus the October 2001 APEC leaders' meeting on counter-terrorism, rather than the trade issues that had previously been central to such meetings.[60] US–China co-operation on counter-terrorism since 11 September has been wide-ranging, substantive and important, and the leadership in both countries wants to maintain this record.

There is the potential, however, for counter-terrorism to change from providing the bedrock of US–China strategic co-operation to becoming a source of strategic distrust. Unfortunately, there are many feasible paths to this undesirable outcome.

Despite the co-operation at the UN on Iraq noted above, for example, the Bush administration decided to use military force to bring about regime change without obtaining a second UN resolution specifically authorizing this initiative. Beijing sees potential dangers stemming from America's actions in Iraq. They risk marginalizing the UN Security Council, which China views as its premier forum for playing a serious role on global security affairs. And most fundamentally, Beijing fears they may greatly strengthen the position of the most unilateralist officials in the Bush administration, producing an American foreign policy that China views as potentially increasingly destabilizing and threatening, especially if such attitudes guide American policy towards North Korea.

The evolution of the war on terrorism has the potential, in short, to create pressures for China to try to limit US actions in order to protect China's own interests. But the response in the Bush administration, which believes strongly in drawing clear lines between enemies and friends, could be sharp and negative. It is imprudent, therefore, simply to project ongoing co-operation on counter-terrorism and on North Korea as sources of stability in the US–China strategic relationship. Such co-operation will require focused attention and mutual compromises that may prove very difficult to sustain, despite China's strong desire to maintain constructive ties with the US.

---

60. President Clinton used the 1999 Auckland APEC leaders' meeting in part to discuss and organize action on the unfolding problems in East Timor. This had been the first use of this meeting to address a security issue. The October 2001 Shanghai APEC leaders' meeting was the first to focus primarily on security as versus economic concerns. Craig S. Smith, "Asia session will focus on terrorism and trade," *The New York Times*, 17 October 2001.

Conclusion

US–China relations are in more solid shape that any would have anticipated at President Bush's inauguration in January 2001 and, despite the leadership succession in Beijing, both sides want to maintain the strategic co-operation that has developed. The succession itself poses no clear threat to continued development of US–China relations, although if crises should occur the new allocation of power in Beijing could complicate China's handling of the situation. There are, in addition, serious underlying problems – domestic politics in both countries, cross-Strait relations and the evolution of the war on terrorism – that could produce major change for the worse. Unravelling in any one of these three spheres, moreover, makes unravelling in the other two considerably more likely. It will, therefore, take mutual sensitivity and a serious commitment to the value of the US–China relationship itself to sustain the level of common interest and effort that is so evident at the start of 2003.

Power Transition and the Making of Beijing's Policy towards Taiwan*

Yun-han Chu

ABSTRACT   Few policy domains can come close to Taiwan affairs in exemplifying the way Jiang's reigning authority has been self-extended beyond his official tenure. Fighting for his place in history, Jiang's desire to reset the cross-Strait scoreboard before his full retirement remains strong. Also, the structure of the newly elected SCP clearly reinforces Jiang's ability to cast a long shadow over Hu for some time to come. Hu is thus expected to adhere with great caution to Jiang's updated policy guidelines on Taiwan affairs, as laid out in the retiring general secretary's farewell Party work report to the CCP 16th Congress. Besides, Hu has few incentives not to because the Taiwan affairs portfolio carries excessive risk and a slow return, in addition to being one of the policy areas that he is least prepared for. However, the symbolic significance of the Taiwan issue also means that the generational turnover from Jiang to Hu cannot be considered complete until Hu takes full command over Beijing's policy towards Taiwan.

The making of Beijing's policy towards Taiwan carries two seemingly contradictory characteristics. On the one hand it has tremendous weight as a symbolic mark of leadership within the Chinese Communist Party (CCP). On the other hand, it has become increasingly subordinated to pragmatic consideration of both domestic and external structural dimensions. On the symbolic hand, it remains one of the most exclusive and prominent policy domains reserved for the paramount leadership of the CCP. The top leader of each generation is evidently motivated to carry the torch of the reunification campaign himself, and only himself. Much in the way the CCP elite of the past wanted to leave their personal mark on the Party's evolving guiding ideology, the recent leadership seems motivated to promulgate and pass down their signature guiding documents on the Taiwan issue, such as Deng Xiaoping's "one country, two systems" formula and Jiang Zemin's eight-point proposal of 1995.[1] The interest of these leaders in the stewardship of Beijing's policy towards Taiwan has both symbolic and strategic significance. At the level of symbolic politics, reunifying Taiwan with the motherland is "a task of the century" that defines a leader's place in Chinese history. At the strategic

* An earlier version of this paper was delivered at a conference on "New leaders, new China? Where is China headed after the 16th Communist Party Congress?" co-sponsored by Hoover Institution and Institute for National Policy Research, 24–25 January 2003, Hoover Institution, University of Stanford. I thank Harry Harding, David Mike Lampton, Raymond Myers, Susan Shirk and Julia Strauss for their comments and suggestions.
    1. Jiang Zemin unveiled his historic proposal, entitled "Continue to promote the reunification of China," on 30 January 1995, the eve of Chinese lunar new year.

level, managing the Taiwan issue is a daunting political task of pivotal importance. A mishandling of this potentially explosive issue could conceivably create a series of crises ranging from a major rupture in the PRC's external environment (especially its relationship with the United States), to a cataclysmic outburst of nationalistic lava from below. Under a worst-case scenario, an escalating crisis in the Taiwan Strait could set off a direct military clash with the United States, derail China's ongoing economic reform and, if stretched to its logical extreme, be the iceberg that sinks the Titanic of the CCP regime. The significance of cross-Strait relations means that the generational turnover from Jiang Zemin to Hu Jintao cannot be considered complete until Hu takes full command over Beijing's policy towards Taiwan. However, in the short run it also means that, for an inexperienced and not yet well-entrenched leader, the risk of taking charge of Taiwan affairs might offset its slow-coming symbolic reward.

On the other hand, ever since the dawn of post-Deng era, the structural conditions and institutional arrangements surrounding the making of Taiwan policy have carried more significance than the leadership factor. In stark contrast with the Taiwan policy domain of the 1980s, best characterized by a "Deng-in-command" model, Beijing's policy towards Taiwan in the post-Deng era has become more comprehensible and predictable as it increasingly falls into a strong pragmatic, bureaucratic and consensus-oriented pattern.[2] First, the decision-making mechanism, while still bearing elements of the top leader's personal mark, has on the whole become more institutionalized. Since 1993, the structure of the Central Leading Group for Taiwan Affairs (CLGTA)[3] has consistently involved four systems that carry out essential political, military and intelligence functions in the Taiwan policy domain – namely the foreign affairs system, the united-front work system (which includes an extensive array of Taiwan Affairs offices installed at all levels of government), the PLA system, and the intelligence and counter-espionage system.[4] During the recent re-organization of the CLGTA, with Hu Jintao and Jia Qinglin displacing Jiang Zemin and Qian Qichen as the new head and deputy head, the structure of this decision-making body remains intact.

---

2. For an elaborative analysis of this point, see Yun-han Chu, "Jiang Zemin and the evolution of Beijing's policy towards Taiwan" in Hung-mao Tien and Yun-han Chu (eds.), *China Under Jiang Zemin* (Boulder: Lynne Rienner, 2000).

3. In Chinese, the CLGTA is Zhongyang duitai gongzuo lingdao xiaozu.

4. For instance, the membership of the outgoing CLGTA, that has served since the 15th Party Congress, includes Jiang Zemin (the leader), Qian Qichen (the deputy leader), Wang Zhaoguo, the head of the CCP United Front Work Department, Zeng Qinghong, member of the CCP Central Secretariat, Wang Daohan, the head of Association for Relations Across Taiwan Strait (ARATS), Chen Yun-lin, the director of the CCP/State Council Taiwan Affairs Office, Xu Yongyue, the head of the Ministry of State Security, and Xiong Guangkai, the PLA's Deputy Chief of General Staff in charge of the military intelligence. Most members owe their appointments to their official portfolios in at least one of the four systems. The major exception is Zeng Qinghong, who came in primarily in his capacity as Jiang's chief of staff. Within this small circle, Wang Daohan serves a dual function, being Beijing's top negotiator in cross-Strait political talks as well as Jiang's top political advisor.

The scope of the new membership covers the same four systems as before.[5]

Next, unlike their Party elders, whose revolutionary credentials had empowered them to make decisions simply on the basis of raw intelligence, personal experiences and individual political instinct, Jiang Zemin and indeed all top Chinese leaders of his generation or younger come from technocratic or professional military backgrounds, and have been trained to rely more on policy analyses and recommendations provided by a range of research institutes and departments. Under Jiang Zemin, while the decision-making process involved only a small subset of senior Party and military leaders, they surrounded themselves with an extensive array of think tanks and private advisors.[6]

More fundamentally, during the Reform era a shared commitment among the CCP leaders to certain higher-level national strategic priorities – most importantly the nation's fundamental interests in maintaining a peaceful and stable surrounding environment for the sake of economic modernization – has facilitated the development of intra-Party consensus over the basic policy concerning the Taiwan issue, despite the occasional quibble over operational guidelines and tactics. The forging of this consensus has also been facilitated by a shared assessment, through a largely non-ideological lens, of the constraints and opportunities presented by the international environment, the Washington–Beijing–Taipei triangle, and Taiwan's changing political and economic conditions. It has been widely shared among the CCP leaders that, so long as the prospect of peaceful reunification is effectively preserved, there is neither the urgency nor the strategic imperative to force a final resolution of Taiwan issues before China accomplishes its modernization task. Ultimately, reunification is a mission for the long haul. The only urgency that has become increasingly intense since 1994 is the near-term task to defuse the ticking bomb of Taiwan independence without critically straining China's relationship with the United States, inadvertently prompting Japan to seek rearmament, seriously disrupting the ongoing cross-Strait economic exchanges, or diverting too many national resources. Not an easy task. This means that in the making of Beijing's policy towards Taiwan, room for personal policy predilection is actually quite limited, and these limitations

5. The CLGTA was re-organized soon after the holding of Tenth NPC in March 2003. Four former members, Wang Daohan, Chen Yunlin, Xu Yongyue and Xiong Guangkai, stay on because their official portfolios remain unchanged. There are three new regular members: Guo Boxiong, vice-chairman of the Central Military Commission, Tang Jiaxuan, State Councillor in charge of the foreign affairs, and Liu Yantong, who replaces Wang Zhaoguo as the new head of the CCP United Front Work Department. Their memberships in the CLGTA are evidently tied to their new official portfolio in the PLA, foreign affairs and united front work system respectively. See the report and analysis by Wang Yuyan, *United Daily News*, 29 May 2003, p. 4.

6. For an analysis of the policy research apparatus supporting the CLGTA during the Jiang's era, see Yun-han Chu, "Jiang Zemin and the evolution of Beijing's policy towards Taiwan," and Michael Swaine, "Chinese decision-making regarding Taiwan," in David M. Lampton (ed.), *The Making of Chinese Foreign and Security Policy in the Era of Reform* (Stanford: Stanford University Press, 2002).

will only increase as China becomes more deeply enmeshed in a global-ized world with each passing day.[7]

This article applies this novel bifurcation between the internal direc-tives of leadership and the external conditions of policy to unpack the implications of the power transition that occurred at the 16th Party Congress for the making of Beijing's policy towards Taiwan. It will use this analytical framework to explain why stewardship over Beijing's policy towards Taiwan, much like (and in fact tied to) the chairmanship of the Central Military Commission (CMC), will be one of the last few remaining responsibilities that Jiang Zemin will relinquish before his full retirement. With the countdown clock ticking, Jiang seemed determined not to end his political career with a sour note on cross-Strait relations. During his last one-and-a-half years of official tenure as CCP chief, Jiang and his top advisors invested the bulk of their personal political capital in rejuvenating a reunification campaign that had apparently failed to put the genie of Taiwanese nationalism back into the one-China bottle. On the eve of the 16th Party Congress, Jiang was able to capitalize on China's growing economic and military prowess, in conjunction with economic difficulties and political gridlock under the Chen Shui-bian government and new windows of opportunity opened in the post-11 September world, to reconstruct an intra-Party consensus on how best to deal with Taiwan issues in a post-Kuomintang (KMT) context.

This framework is also used to explain why Hu Jintao, who took over the formal responsibility of managing cross-Strait relations soon after being elected the president of the PRC at the Tenth National People's Congress (NPC), will have neither incentive nor desire to alter his predecessor's basic policy outline, which was first laid out in Jiang's eight-point proposal and then enshrined in his farewell Party work report to the CCP 16th Party Congress.[8] Hu will, in fact, have every incentive to toe Jiang's line, because the Taiwan affairs portfolio carries excessive risk and a slow return, in addition to being one of the policy areas that he is least prepared for. Domestic agenda will be Hu's preoccupation for some time to come, and he will have to invest his limited political capital and exercise his untried leadership gingerly. The delicate power-sharing arrangement construed at the 16th Party Congress left Hu with even less latitude for personal predilections over this sensitive issue area than Jiang had held at a similar stage of power succession in the early 1990s. More fundamentally, even as Jiang Zemin steadily withdraws from the active management of cross-Strait relations, Hu will find himself operating under a very similar set of external and internal constraints. Barring the outbreak of some unforeseen internal turmoil, it is thus inconceivable that Hu Jintao, or indeed the fourth generation leadership as a whole, will in

---

7. This view is also shared by other analysts. See for example, Lampton, *The Making of Chinese Foreign and Security Policy.*

8. As a Beijing's overseas propaganda organ, *Ta kung pao* of Hong Kong, put it "Jiang Report [to the 16th Party Congress] to have 'guiding significance' for work on Taiwan." See *Ta kung pao (Dagong bao)*, 12 November 2002, Editorial, "A guiding document for the work of the Communist Party of China towards Taiwan."

the foreseeable future develop a different set of national priorities on either philosophical or strategic grounds.

Succession Politics and Taiwan Policy

For both its symbolic significance and strategic importance, Taiwan policy has always been one of the most exclusive and prominent policy domains reserved for the CCP's paramount leaders. During the Maoist era, the power of setting the guiding principle on the Taiwan issue rested firmly in the hands of Mao Zedong. Not even Premier Zhou Enlai was in a position to make a final decision on important matters. During the Reform era, Deng Xiaoping exercised the final decision-making authority on all important matters regarding Taiwan (as well as Hong Kong). Neither Hu Yaobang nor Zhao Ziyang were given much chance to weigh in during their tenure as the CCP chief.[9] In the transition to the post-Deng era, for Jiang Zemin, being the designated pivot of the collective leadership of the so-called "third generation," Taiwan policy was one of the torches that he felt he had to carry forward himself. For this reason, after Jiang replaced Yang Shangkun as the leader of the CLGTA around November 1993,[10] and in particular as soon as the collective leadership of the "third generation" was finally fully in charge on the eve of the Fourth Plenary Session of the CCP 14th Central Committee, he wasted no time in taking measures to establish his pre-eminence in this politically salient policy domain and put his personal mark on it.

Formulating a new policy guideline on Taiwan issue, to be known as Jiang's eight-point proposal, was a strong political statement about the coming of Jiang's era. This was probably one of the reasons why he decided to act on Wang Daohan's recommendation to draft a new policy document on Taiwan issues soon after the first Koo–Wang talk in Singapore.[11] Ever since its formal approval by the Politburo around January 1995, Jiang's eight-point proposal has stood out prominently as the guiding document for handling cross-Strait relations. It also immediately superceded an earlier and much more sternly-phrased official document, the "White paper on the Taiwan problem and China's unification," that had been prepared during Yang Shangkun's tenure.[12] The promulgation of this signature document on the eve of the Chinese lunar new year

9. For an analysis of Taiwan decision-making policy during the Mao and Deng eras, see Yang Kai-huang, "Zhonggong duiTai zhengce jieshi yu pinggu" ("An explanation and evaluation of PRC's Taiwan policy"), *Dongwu zhengzhi xuebao* (*Soochow Review of Political Science*), No. 7 (1997), pp. 66–103. For Hong Kong decision-making policy, see Kam Yiu-yu, "Decision-making and implementation of policy towards Hong Kong," in Hamrin and Zhao (eds.), *Decision-Making in Deng's China* (Armonk, NY: M. E. Sharpe, 1995).

10. For the transition from Yang Shangkun to Jiang Zemin, see Yang Kai-huang, "Zhonggong xin lingdaobanzi de duiTai zhengce zhi zhangwang" ("The prognosis of the CCP new leadership's policy towards Taiwan"), *Guojia zhengce luntan* (*National Policy Forum*), Vol. 1, No. 10 (December 2001).

11. On this point, also refer to Lijun Sheng, "China eyes Taiwan: why is a breakthrough so difficult?" *Journal of Strategic Studies*, Vol. 21, No. 1 (March 1998), pp. 65–78.

12. This document was issued in September 1993 in response to Lee Teng-hui's new diplomatic bid for United Nations membership.

clearly signalled that Jiang had staked out Taiwan affairs as his exclusive portfolio and now enjoyed effective control over the setting of agenda.

As soon as the 16th Party Congress was over, Hu Jintao found himself in a situation similar to that of Jiang in his early years holding the position of CCP chief. Like Jiang, who had to consult Deng on all important matters until his mentor's health deteriorated rapidly around late 1993 and early 1994, Hu feels obliged to accord Jiang the status of a quasi-paramount leader. Actually, Hu finds himself in a more precarious situation than Jiang. Jiang had been hand-picked and backed-up by Deng as the pivot of the third generation leadership, while Hu, taking over by Deng's implicit design from a decade ago, is not Jiang's hand-picked successor. For this reason, Hu Jintao is expected to adhere with great caution to Jiang's updated policy guidelines on Taiwan affairs, as laid out in the retiring general secretary's farewell Party work report to the CCP Congress.

For the next few years, it will be politically imprudent for Hu to be perceived as not doing Jiang's bidding in this sensitive policy domain, or to be perceived as being eager to take full command over making policies towards Taiwan. Taiwan affairs can be expected, much like chairmanship of the CMC, to be one of the last responsibilities that Jiang will relinquish, as it provides the major justification for the still-ambitious Jiang to cling to his last official post. It was reported that Jiang's political allies in the Politburo cited the "treacherous Taiwan situation" in asking him to remain in his post of CMC chair.[13] If this is true, it is unlikely that Hu will be able to take over the power in making final decisions on Taiwan affairs, despite the fact that he has already taken Jiang's post in many key decision-making bodies, including the Central Leading Group on National Security (CLGNS).[14] This observation was confirmed in Hu's first substantive public statement on the Taiwan issue in his new capacity of CCP chief. This informal speech, delivered at the NPC "Taiwan delegation" caucus meeting on 11 March 2003, was modest, low-profile and in strict adherence to the existing policy guidelines.[15] Hu also used this occasion to underscore the selling points of Jiang's eight-point proposal, and to compliment Jiang Zemin and the collective leadership of

---

13. It was reported that this orchestrated decision was made by the 25-member Politburo shortly after they had been elected into office at the first plenary session of new Central Committee. See the report by Willy Wo-Lap Lam, CNN Senior China Analyst, on "Taiwan issues keep Jiang in army role," 22 November 2002, Hong Kong, China (CNN).

14. Ching Cheong, "Hu takes charge of national security body," *Straits Times*, 19 December 2002. According to this report, the CLGNS' two vice-chairmen are Zeng Qinghong and Wen Jiabao and Zeng is responsible for day-to-day operations of the group. Members include General Guo Boxiong, vice-chairman of the party's Central Military Commission (CMC); public security minister Zhou Yongkang; national security minister Xu Yongyue; Liu Jing, director of the "601 office" (the anti-*falun gong* office); foreign minister Tang Jiaxuan; Taiwan office director Chen Yunlin; and central office director Wang Gang.

15. For a Chinese excerpt of of Hu's informal speech, see *China Times*, 12 March 2003, p. 13.

the third generation in keeping the development of cross-Strait relations on the right track.[16]

Furthermore, in his post of CLGTA leader, Hu's authority in managing cross-Strait relations will be circumscribed not only by the necessity to operate within the policy parameters laid down by his predecessor, but also because he must share the stage with Zeng Qinghong, reputedly the second most influential member of the newly elected nine-member Standing Committee of the Politburo (SCP), and Jia Qinglin, the new deputy head of the CLGTA. Zeng, Jiang's favourite protégé and most trustworthy trouble-shooter, was apparently groomed by Jiang to be his inner-circle point man on Taiwan affairs. Zeng's credentials in this area date back to the turbulent years between 1994 and 1996 when he served as Jiang's personal envoy in conducting negotiations with Lee Teng-hui's chief of staff, Su Chi-cheng, throughout a stream of secret meetings held in Hong Kong and Macau.[17] Zeng became an official member of the CLGTA in April 1998, shortly after the 15th Party Congress. Jia Qinglin, whose credentials in Taiwan affairs were limited to his tenure as the Party chief of Fujian province, becomes the SCP member in charge of the CCP's united front work. Since Jia owes his controversial promotion to the Standing Committee entirely to Jiang's patronage, it is reasonable to assume that he will faithfully serve as a surrogate of Jiang and Zeng in the CLGTA. Jia's appointment, as well as Wang Daohan's renewed membership in the CLGTA, clearly indicates that Jiang is keen to exert his remaining influence over Taiwan affairs.[18] In contrast to Zeng, Hu has had little exposure to Taiwan issues during his entire political career. His official debut on the stage of Taiwan affairs was his appearance at a ceremony on 24 January 2002 commemorating the seventh anniversary of the launch of Jiang's eight-point proposal.[19] At this bellwether event, sharing the stage with Zeng as moderator, Hu delivered the ceremonial opening remarks preceding Qian's much more elaborate policy speech. The joint appearance of Hu and Zeng at this highly publicized event in a way foreshadowed the delicate power-sharing scheme that emerged about a year later.

While this power-sharing scheme may not be Hu's own choice, nevertheless he should be grudgingly content with holding less than full responsibility in the making of policy towards Taiwan during this early

16. Zhou Mingwei, the deputy director of the Taiwan Affairs Office of the State Council, explained to Taiwan-based reporters at the Tenth NPC new conference that Hu's informal speech re-affirmed the guiding authority of Jiang's eight-point proposal and Jiang's Party work report to the 16th Party Congress. See the report by Wang Mingyi, *China Times*, 14 March 2003, p. 13.

17. *China Times* carried a series of revealing reports about the secret meeting across the Straits through "private envoys" in mid-July 2000. About the secret meetings between Zeng and Su, see *China Times*, 20 July 2000, p 3.

18. Before the Tenth NPC, many observers expected that Zeng would be installed as the deputy head of the CLGTA replacing Qian Qichen. It is speculated that, at the end of the day, Zeng, being politically aware, might not want to carry the direct responsibility of handling the hot potato of Taiwan. He nevertheless can still exercise his influence over Taiwan affairs through Jia Qinglin and Wang Daohan.

19. See a report by Zhu Jianlin, *China Times*, 25 January 2002, p. 13.

stage of his tenure. For his untested leadership, the portfolio of Taiwan affairs carries excessive political risk and minimal prospects for quick political reward. A mishandling of this potentially explosive issue could conceivably break his leadership. At the same time, operating within the existing guiding principles, an opportunity for Hu to engineer a major breakthrough in advancing the goal of peaceful reunification is not yet on the horizon. In this sense, Hu will not mind too much accommodating Jiang's determination not to end his political career with a sour note on cross-Strait relations; by fighting for his place in history, Jiang will inadvertently be holding this hot potato for Hu for extra few years. More specifically, Jiang's retention of the chairmanship of the CMC may help Hu control the strong military personalities in the CMC over the issue of Taiwan.[20] By the same token, it may be a blessing in disguise for Hu to have Jiang's protégés, Zeng and Jia, sharing responsibility as well as potential liability with him in the active management of cross-Strait relations. Thus, regardless of his personal predilections, for the next few years Hu will have little incentive to contest Jiang's supreme authority on the Taiwan issue or to deviate too much from his policy framework. It will be much more rewarding for him to invest his limited political capital in other priorities, in particular to address the issue of growing social and regional disparity by steering a more balanced economic development strategy.[21] However, over the longer term, Hu enjoys a good chance of walking out of Jiang's shadow because Hu enjoys three appreciating forms of political capital: the formal authority that comes with his position in the institutionalized and bureaucratic party-state apparatus, the elite network that stems from his past stewardship of the Central Party Academy, and the well-wishes of the great majority of the Party rank and file as well as great many intellectuals, all of whom welcome a smooth transition and wish him success in this endeavour.

Jiang's Last Effort to Rejuvenate Beijing's Peaceful Reunification Campaign

Towards the end of his official tenure as CCP general secretary, Jiang's position was so well entrenched and he had sufficient strings to pull that he did not have to worry about his record on handling the Taiwan issue being put under close scrutiny by his immediate successor. However, he must have harboured lingering concerns that history might not treat him as kindly. Indeed, as he looked back over his own record, his handling of recurring political crises in the Strait constituted a very frustrating chapter

20. Sources close to the Jiang camp said Jiang had in private expressed doubts about Hu's ability to control the powerful personalities on the new CMC. They included CMC vice-chairmen generals Guo Boxiong and Cao Gangchuan and the newly promoted chief of staff General Liang Guanglie. The trio had in closed-door meetings given vent to hawkish views about the need to "expedite military preparation" to re-absorb Taiwan.

21. It was reported that in his first two months as Communist Party chief Hu Jintao has moved swiftly to create an image for himself as a champion of China's forgotten poor. See Erik Echholm, "China's new leader works to set himself apart," *New York Times*, 12 January 2003.

of his leadership. On his watch, Beijing's peaceful reunification campaign suffered a series of major setbacks. His administration failed to stop Taipei from breaking away from the so-called one-China principle. Also, he learned the hard way to live with, and work around, Taiwan's budding democracy. Repeatedly, Beijing's united front strategies intended to prop up pro-reunification forces in Taiwan, and its intimidating measures intended to arrest the rising tide of Taiwanese nationalism turned out to be futile or even counterproductive. The strategy to exert heavier military pressures on Taiwan might have persuaded Taipei from pursuing outright *de jure* independence, but was not very effective in keeping Taipei's "creeping independence" strategy in check. Additionally, the intended psychological impact of this double-edged strategy was largely nullified by the stream of American sales of higher-grade defensive weapon systems and a step-by-step upgrading of US–Taiwan military co-operation under the Bush administration. The Bush administration also confirmed the American security commitment to Taiwan; "strategic ambiguity," the policy under which Washington for two decades declined to say how it would respond to a PRC attack on Taiwan, was replaced by "strategic clarity." The "three communiqués," the legal pillars that commit the United States to its one-China policy, have increasingly come to look like empty shells, their substance either worn out by the changing circumstances and countervailing precedents, or nullified by the elevated guiding authority of the Taiwan Relations Act. All the above developments made it more difficult for Beijing to hold up the prospect for a peaceful resolution of the issue. The only development that has moved in a direction favourable to Beijing is the intensification of cross-Strait economic ties. But so far Beijing has not been able to find dependable ways to reap its promised political pay-offs.

The most devastating blow to Beijing's reunification campaign was dealt by the electoral victory of the pro-independence DPP in March 2000. This unexpected event virtually shattered Jiang's hope for wooing Taipei back to the negotiation table before the expiration of his official term. Jiang and his top advisors had to hide their frustration behind the empty rhetoric of "listening to his [Chen Shui-bian's] words and watching his deeds," suggesting that they had little choice but to put the DDP government on an extended political probation.[22] Once again, the credibility of his handling of cross-Strait relations was on the line.

Beijing's policy towards Taiwan sat in limbo for almost a year-and-a-half as Jiang and his top advisors sized up the political situation in a post-KMT/post-Lee Teng-hui Taiwan. While waiting for the outcomes of

---

22. This wait-and-see approach was best illustrated by the fact that Beijing's official propaganda organs had refrained themselves from attacking Chen Shui-bian personally for more than two years after his inauguration. This self-restraining measure was lifted only after he assumed the DPP chairmanship in July 2002 and issued controversial statements about "one country on each side of the Strait" on 3 August. See the analysis by Wang Zhouchong, *China Times*, 26 July 2002, p. 11, and the report by Kang Zhangrong quoting a ranking PRC official's remark about why Beijing gave up its hope of Chen Shui-bian after the two-year probation, *Commercial Times*, 1 October 2002, p. 11.

Taiwan's December 2001 Legislative Yuan election, they were scratching their heads for new policy thinking that could help them spot the silver linings in the situation, redefine their tasks and reset their priorities. This convalescing process also entailed a rehashing of the consensus obtaining among members of the Politburo over what adjustments in strategies and tactics were necessary to reverse the losing battle against the "separatist forces" on the island and rejuvenate the moribund peaceful reunification campaign. A reformulated operational guideline began to take shape out of this long convalescing process towards the end of 2001. At the same time, a strengthening of Sino-US strategic co-operation in the aftermath of the 11 September attack and Taiwan's deteriorating economic and political conditions appeared to help restore much of the CCP leaders' confidence in their ability to defuse the ticking bomb of Taiwan independence, along with their faith in the long-term viability of a peaceful reunification campaign.

Emanating from these reformulated operational guidelines came a new round of peace initiatives targeted at the people of Taiwan in general and the pragmatic elements within the DPP camp in particular. Much as in January 1998,[23] Beijing assembled its propaganda machinery around a major policy speech by Qian Qichen at a ceremony commemorating the seventh anniversary of Jiang's eight-point proposal. Most notably, Qian was joined on the stage by both Hu Jintao and Zeng Qinghong, reputedly the two most powerful figures of the up-and-coming leadership. The launch of this new peace overture, definitely the last on his watch, signalled that Jiang was determined not to end his official tenure with a sour note on cross-Straits relations. The unprecedented joint appearance of Hu and Zeng on a Taiwan-centred occasion was designed to send the message that Jiang's best and final offer enjoyed the full backing of the fourth generation. Jiang probably also wanted to use this well-orchestrated policy speech to project a favourable public image, reassuring the CCP rank and file that he and his advisors were again on top of the treacherous situation, and resetting the tone of the internal discussion over the Taiwan issue well before the complicated negotiations over leadership succession due to begin in the next few months.

To elevate the political standing of Qian's policy speech as well as reinforce its message, some of its key elements were subsequently reiterated by top Chinese officials at both domestic and international occasions, including Zhu Rongji's government work report to the NPC in March 2002, foreign minister Tang Jiaxuan's annual address before the United Nations General Assembly in September 2002, and Jiang Zemin's public speech at Texas A&M University during his October 2002 trip to the United States. The crescendo reached its final climax at the 16th Communist Party Congress as certain selling points of the new peace

23. On the eve of Chinese lunar new year, Qian Qichen, through his speech at a seminar in the Great Hall of the People to commemorate the third anniversary of Jiang Zemin's eight-point proposal, sent out Beijing's first official message of its willingness to defrost the big chill in the Straits and reopen political dialogue with Lee Teng-hui after the 1995–96 Strait crisis. See Yun-han Chu, "Jiang Zemin and the evolution of Beijing's policy towards Taiwan."

overture became codified and enshrined in Jiang's Party work report. Also in this report – allegedly the most authoritative guiding document for the next few years – Jiang's eight-point proposal, one of the indelible hallmarks of his 13-year leadership, was reaffirmed as the active policy guideline and elevated almost to the same status as the two fundamental principles laid-down by Deng Xiaoping, peaceful reunification and "one-China, two-systems."

Making Sense of Beijing's Reformulated Policy towards Taiwan

For more sceptical China-watchers, the elaboration on Beijing's policy towards Taiwan contained in Jiang Zemin's report to the 16th Party Congress[24] (as well as Qian's bellwether 24 January 2002 speech and other preambles by leading Chinese figures) amounts to nothing more than a rehashing of Beijing's long-standing policies and strategies, except that Beijing's leaders have now learned how to package their political messages with a subtlety and sophistication that might make the rephrased messages a bit more palatable to their "Taiwan compatriots." For instance, in this report, one can identify the following four new garnishing elements or modifications to earlier formulations.

First, Jiang's report officially codifies Beijing's new formulation of how it defines the one-China principle. The old formula – "there is only one China in the world, Taiwan is a part of China, and the sovereignty and the territorial integrity of China cannot be divided"[25] – has been replaced with a slightly different version: "There is only one China in the world. The Chinese mainland and Taiwan are part of China, and China's sovereignty and territorial integrity can not be divided." This rephrasing is meant to address Taiwan's sensitivity over the issue of pro forma parity.

Secondly, in refreshing its marketing strategy, Jiang's latest peace overture adds some positive footnotes to Deng's "one country, two systems" formula. Thus, on top of the long-standing appeal which had emphasized preserving the status quo,[26] Beijing now tries to promote this master scheme in terms of what might conceivably be a set of values-added to the people of Taiwan.[27]

24. In Jiang's report, the section on Taiwan came eighth under the head of "One country, two systems and complete national reunification." This time, Jiang spent more space on the Taiwan issue than his previous Party work reports to the 14th and 15th Party Congress. See the analysis by Shangli Xue, *China Times*, 9 November 2002, p. 13.

25. In the diplomatic context, customarily the PRC authority would supplement this statement with one additional claim: "The PRC government is the sole legitimate government representing China."

26. In Jiang's words, "After its reunification with the mainland, Taiwan may keep its existing social system unchanged and enjoy a high degree of autonomy. Our Taiwan compatriots may keep their way of life unchanged, and their vital interests will be fully guaranteed."

27. Again, in Jiang's own language, "They [Taiwan compatriots] will enjoy a lasting peace. Taiwan may then truly rely on the mainland as its hinterland for economic growth and thus get broad space for development. Our Taiwan compatriots may join the people on the

Thirdly, to provide Taiwan with positive inducements for coming to the negotiation table, instead of simply repeating an empty promise that "all issues can be discussed under the premise of the one-China principle," Jiang's report is more specific about what can be offered if the two sides enter political talks. For the first time, his report has officially acknowledged that under the premise of the one-China principle Beijing is willing to address Taipei's demand for an expanding international space.[28]

Finally, to project a more conciliatory attitude, Jiang rephrased Beijing's preconditions for the resumption of political talks. While calling for "the leader of the Taiwan authorities to take serious and positive moves to recognize the '1992 Consensus',"[29] he proposed that "on the basis of the one-China principle, let us shelve for now certain political disputes and resume the cross-Straits dialogue and negotiations as soon as possible." This subtle message implies that Beijing wants to leave some leeway for different interpretations of what constitutes the so-called "1992 Consensus," and the new expression, "on the basis of the one-China principle," implies it is not that Taipei has to succumb to a precondition unilaterally imposed by Beijing, but rather the two sides can restart the political talks on a basis that was once mutually agreed upon.

Of course, for the sceptics, none of these rehashing efforts amount to much. In its latest peace overture, the Beijing leadership has essentially reaffirmed its commitment to the two fundamental principles, "peaceful reunification" and "one China, two systems," along with the basic approach to the Taiwan issue laid down by Deng Xiaoping in the beginning of the Reform era, that is, political negotiation is the only route to peaceful reunification.[30] They have remained absolutely adamant about their fundamental position of reserving the right to use military force in order to nullify "the foreign forces' attempt to interfere in China's reunification and the Taiwan separatist forces' schemes for Taiwan independence." Furthermore, Jiang's report reinserted a veiled threat that Beijing would not allow the Taiwan issues to drag on indefinitely.[31] One might credibly argue that, beneath the surface, Beijing is still pursuing its long-standing operational guidelines, that is, "to blockade Taiwan diplomatically, to check Taiwan militarily and to drag along Taiwan econom-

---

footnote continued

mainland in exercising the right to administer the country and sharing the dignity and honour of the great motherland in the international community."

28. The original text in Jiang's report read as follow: "[We] can discuss issues of formally ending hostility between the two sides, Taiwan's space of international activities suitable for its position in the economic, cultural and social fields, and the political position of the Taiwan authorities."

29. For a most authoritative account and documentation on the controversy over what actually constituted the so-called "1992 Consensus," see Su Chi and Cheng An-kuo (eds.), *Yige Zhongguo gezi biaoshu (One China, with Respective Interpretations)* (Taipei: National Policy Foundation, 2002).

30. Deng laid down the basic guideline of peaceful reunification at a CCP high-level meeting held on 8–22 December 1978. *Selected Works of Deng Xioaping, 1975–82.*

31. In a 2000 white paper on "The one-China principle and the Taiwan issue," the PRC authority cited "Taiwan indefinitely refuses to conduct political negotiation" as one of the three conditions that might justify the use of military forces to recover Taiwan.

ically" in order to keep Taiwan within China's political orbit. All the ongoing united front work, diplomatic, military and economic measures targeted at Taiwan simply revolve as two-sided strategic objectives of the same coin: to preserve the prospect for peaceful reunification and to cajole Taipei to the negotiation table.

For some of the more perceptive China-watchers, however, Beijing's carefully crafted policy initiatives revealed that the Beijing leadership has made some meaningful adjustments and adaptations that take into account the new developments across the Strait and opportunities opened in the post-11 September world. Even if their guiding principles are the same, at least there has been some dynamism in their priorities and approaches.

First, Beijing's recent effort to repackage its old messages is significant in its own right. It suggests that members of the CLGTA have finally moved up a steep learning curve in working out how to live with Taiwan's chaotic pluralism and intractable democracy. They have paid more attention to the social pulse of the Taiwanese general public, and exhibited more concern with how Beijing's peace overtures might be received by the great majority of Taiwan's electorate (those who are not diehard supporters of Taiwan independence). The concept of playing the public opinion card is nothing new to the Beijing elite.[32] But for a long while it had not learned how to play the game. In light of Taiwan's deteriorating economic situation and growing dependence on the mainland, Beijing is now gaining points in promoting the view that the Taiwan authority's resistance to direct trade and direct air and sea links is both politically futile and economically counterproductive. Most recent public opinion polls from Taiwan show that the gravity of policy debate over cross-Strait economic relations on the island has shifted increasingly in directions favourable to Beijing.[33]

Secondly, the recent messages suggest that Beijing has reset its short-term agenda. It no longer lays its expectations on wooing Taipei back to the negotiation table under the premise of the one-China principle any time soon. It has probably conceded that there is little chance that the DPP government is going to embrace the so-called "1992 Consensus" or acknowledge the one-China principle in any form acceptable to Beijing. Furthermore, it has recognized that it is unrealistic to expect any democratically elected Taiwanese government to relinquish Taiwan's sovereign status under the rubric of Republic of China. Not even the so-called Pan-Blue camp (comprising the KMT and its offshoot parties) would go that far, its pro-unification orientation, support for the deepening of

32. As early as the 1980s, a CCP internal document called for "to peddle the [domestic] politics through business; to influence the [Taiwanese] government through the people" (*yi shang wei zheng, yi min bi guan*).

33. For example, a public opinion poll conducted by the *United Daily News* on 27 January 2002 showed that 63.6% of the respondents were in favour of "upgrade the trade and economic exchange with the mainland" and only 17.9% were in favour of "downgrade the trade and economic exchange, with 15.7% answering "no opinion" or "don't know." See *United Daily News*, 28 January 2002, p. 11.

cross-Strait economic integration and willingness to embrace the "1992 Consensus" notwithstanding. With dimming hopes for cutting political deals, Jiang and his top advisors are now concentrating all their efforts on promoting the three links in their last effort to improve the record before Jiang's full retirement. To this end, Beijing has considerably lowered the political threshold for establishing the three links. It agreed to applying the negotiation module that helped renew the civil aviation agreement between Taiwan and Hong Kong after 1997 to cross-Strait shipping and air links. Under that module, the difficult issue of who has the jurisdiction over what was avoided by giving private business associations authority to conduct negotiation and sign accords on behalf of their respective civil aviation authorities. Also, in response to inquiries from Taiwan's airlines industry representatives, Qian indicated that Beijing is ready to detach the one-China principle from the three links, meaning that China has dropped its precondition that Taiwan must first accept the one-China principle before direct shipping and airline links can be inaugurated.[34] More recently, Qian clarified before a print media delegation from Taiwan[35] that China agrees to look upon direct transportation links between the island and the mainland as "cross-Strait" rather than "domestic."[36] All the above manifest a marked shift in Beijing's priorities: during much of the 1990s, the top priority had always been tying down Taiwan with the one-China principle and wooing Taipei into political talks; now it chooses to put the horse of three links before the cart of political negotiation.

Thirdly, Beijing has demonstrated new flexibility in applying its united front strategy. It has been trying to reach out to virtually all significant groups across the political spectrum of the island. As Taiwanese politics enters the post-KMT era, Beijing now places emphasis on cultivating goodwill with the pragmatic elements within the DDP. It welcomes virtually all DPP politicians to the mainland in their private capacity, regardless their standing on the independence issue. It is ostensibly trying to drive a wedge between the fundamentalist and the moderate within the DPP. In Qian's words, Beijing recognizes "the distinction between the great majority of DPP members and the very tiny number of inscrutable separatists." It has even proposed that once the DPP takes "Taiwan independence provision" off its party charter it will be possible for the CCP to engage the DPP on a party-to-party basis. To its pleasant surprise, this seemingly disingenuous proposal actually stirred up a series of heated debates within the DPP.

Fourthly, despite the rhetorical sense of urgency in achieving the "complete reunification of the motherland," Jiang Zemin and his top

34. For an official confirmation of the new policy, see a report by Zhu Jianlin, *China Times*, 31 October 2002, p. 13.

35. For the coverage of the meeting, see a report by Kang Zhangrong, *Commercial Times*, 18 October 2002, p. 11.

36. As John Pomfret, the *Washington Post* correspondent, explained it, the semantic distinction befuddled most Westerners, but to Taiwan, worried about losing its sovereignty to Beijing, the distinction is important. See John Pomfret, "China embraces more moderate foreign policy," Washington Post Foreign Service, 24 October 2002.

advisors have obviously dumped the idea of imposing a timetable on the resolution of the Taiwan issue, an idea that was floating around Beijing's policy circles ever since Lee Teng-hui's "special state to state relations" announcement in July 1999. Beijing leaders now seem to consider this idea to be intrinsically destabilizing and potentially counterproductive, and shun discussion of a timetable. Some have argued that the expression in Jiang's political work report to the effect that Beijing "would not allow the Taiwan issue to drag on indefinitely" was probably intended more for a domestic audience than the people of Taiwan. It served the purpose of warding off potential criticism from the hardliners that Jiang has not been able to show them the light at the end of the reunification tunnel. In fact, as a close advisor to Wang Daohan explained, when the CCP enshrined the reunification as one of its three major tasks of the new century[37] it defined the task as a mission for the long term, thus relieving the incumbent of unnecessary time pressure.[38]

Finally, the extent to which pragmatic thinking has permeated Beijing's recent approach to the Washington–Beijing–Taipei triangular relations surprised many observers. More than ever, Beijing is now keen to build up leverage within this triangular strategic relationship. Increasingly it recognizes that, without American co-operation, it alone cannot keep Taiwan's "creeping independence strategy" in check. On one hand, Chinese officials have tried to play down recent American gestures towards Taiwan, including the first trip of a Taiwanese first lady to the United States, the first visit to the Pentagon by Taiwan's deputy defence minister and the fêting of Taiwan's defence minister by American officials in Florida. On the other hand, in the weeks leading up to the summit meeting at Bush's ranch in Crawford, Texas, China moved to establish additional rules controlling the export of missile technology and dual-use biological and chemical agents and has tightened military export regulations, seeking to remove long-standing irritants in relations with Washington.[39] This represents a marked shift in Beijing's bargaining strategy: it used to link co-operation on proliferation issues with American moves to limit arms sales to Taiwan. In contrast to this, Jiang Zemin suggested during his meeting with President Bush in October 2002 that China could reduce its short-range missile deployment facing Taiwan in exchange for a cutback in American arms sales to the Taiwanese military.[40] China's recent move to turn its missile deployment into a strategic lever represents not only a sophisticated integration of its military strategy with its political strategy, but also its earnest subscription to quintessential pragmatism. Previously China had demanded that the United

37. Achieving reunification was upheld alongside advancing modernization and promoting peace and development at the Fifth Plenary Meeting of the 15th Central Committee at the end of 2000. See the report by Lu Zhaolung, *China Times*. 24 July 2002.

38. Based on the comment by Zhang Nianchi, a Shanghai-based scholar, quoted in *United Daily News*, 12 November 2002, p. 13.

39. John Pomfret, "China embraces more moderate foreign policy," Washington Post Foreign Service, 24 October 2002.

40. John Pomfret, "China suggests missile buildup linked to arms sales to Taiwan," Washington Post Foreign Service, 10 December 2002.

States cut its arms sales to Taiwan unilaterally and offered no quid pro quo, always insisting that any issue involving its missile deployments was an "internal matter" and could not be discussed. China's latest strategic gesture is also symbolically significant in the way it suggests that the Beijing leadership has come very close to acknowledging the United States as the de facto custodian over Taiwan, an attitudinal adjustment inconceivable only a few years ago.

In addition to the above five changes in approach, some discerning China-watchers have also detected a shift that may be of deeper importance, a possible shift in Chinese leaders' long-term vision and underlying assumptions. As these leaders update their assessment about the challenges and opportunities brought about by the changing political and economic conditions in Taiwan and new developments taking place in the larger international context, a new confidence and a new perception of China's rising standing in the region can be posited as what accounts for the programmatic adaptability, new flexibility and professed pragmatism identified above. This marked shift has manifested itself not just through their approach towards the issue of Taiwan but also in a score of other foreign policy issues, including the South China Sea, ASEAN–China Free Trade Agreement, nuclear proliferation, terrorism, drug trafficking, environmental issues and the World Trade Organization (WTO). As one observer put it: "Vitriolic condemnation of China's perceived enemies has been replaced with smooth talk. The curious mixture of insecurity and arrogance with which China's government used to view the world has been replaced with a sense of possibility."[41] In the context of cross-Strait relations, Chinese leaders increasingly appear to be approaching the Taiwan issue with a newly acquired confidence in the country's overall capacity to keep Taiwan within its political and economic orbit, and with the implicit underlying assumption that "time is on the PRC's side." Therefore they can afford to be more flexible and patient, more reticent about Taipei's diplomatic venture, and more tolerant of stalemate or even short-term setbacks.

Their new confidence first came from an updated reading of the United States' strategic intentions, especially those of the Bush administration. Beijing's leaders have grudgingly accepted an American dual role in cross-Strait relations. On one hand, Beijing has always felt resentful towards US "interference," believing that Washington's political and security backing constitutes the major obstacle to its reunification ambitions. On the other hand, they are increasingly counting on the United States to restrain Taiwan's separatist tendency. While still harbouring some lingering suspicions, they have become increasingly convinced that Washington is not disingenuous about its pledge of "not supporting Taiwan independence" through witnessing Washington's preventive diplomacy as well as crisis management at work. For instance, the Beijing leadership recognizes that the United States played an important

---

41. Pomfret, "China embraces more moderate foreign policy."

behind-the-scenes role in installing the "five nos" pledge[42] into Chen Shui-bian's inaugural speech.[43] And prompt action taken by Bush's national security team to control the damage caused by Chen's remark on 3 August 2002 before a pro-independence audience that "Taiwan and China, on each side of the Strait, are different countries" was taken as another reassuring sign that the United States will draw the lines out of its own national interests.

Their new confidence also stems from vast improvements over the last few years in the PLA's capacity to wage high-tech warfare, and a new recognition that the cross-Strait military balance has moved steadily in Beijing's favour, given Taiwan's rapidly deteriorating fiscal capacity. Increasingly, its military capacity is becoming more than just a threatening gesture. Sustained increases in defence spending and new high-tech weaponry now give Beijing leaders "an increasing number of credible options to intimidate or actually attack Taiwan" in the event that Taipei crosses the red lines.[44] More significantly, since the 1996 stand-off between two American carrier battle groups and the Chinese navy, the PLA top brass has pressed for an ever-larger budget to acquire a multi-faceted capacity to deter, deny or complicate the ability of the United States and its allies to intervene on Taiwan's behalf.[45] In the four years after 1996, China more than doubled its military spending, and according to the Stockholm International Peace Research Institute, in 2000 it became the world's biggest importer of weapons. Purchases of advanced weaponry from Russia and other former Soviet states, including fighter jets, Kilo-class submarines, Sovremenny-class destroyers and sophisticated air defence systems, are designed to make American commanders pause before they enter a battle on Taiwan's side. At the same time Beijing has developed new ballistic missiles to maintain the credibility of its nuclear deterrent, and it will certainly expand its small inventory of intercontinental ballistic missiles in response to the Bush administration's pursuit of missile defence technologies. The Beijing leadership believes that maintaining a credible military deterrence is an indispensable element in reinforcing Washington's motivation and seriousness in controlling the Taiwanese independence issue.

A further source of Beijing's new confidence stems from its leaders' rereading of the meaning and implications of Taiwan's transition into the post-Lee Teng-hui era. They have spotted quite a few silver linings in the

42. The "five nos" are: no declaration of independence, no alteration of the "Republic of China" name, no referendum on independence, no insertion of a "special state-to-state relations" concept into the constitution, and no need for a renunciation of the national unification guidelines.

43. It became widely known later on that Raymond Burghart, the AIT director, had several intensive consultations with president elect Chen Shui-bian during the drafting stage of his inauguration speech. Also it was alleged that Beijing had obtained the transcript of Chen's speech in advance through US channels.

44. This is the conclusion of a recent comprehensive assessment of China's military aspirations by the Pentagon. See Vernon Loeb, "China buildup said to target Taiwan, US," *Washington Post*, 13 July 2002.

45. John Pomfret, "China to buy 8 more Russian submarines," Washington Post Foreign Service, 25 June 2002.

DPP-reigning sky. First, a new centralist position across the partisan line has emerged from post-Lee Teng-hui politics. For instance, during the 2000 presidential campaign, all three major candidates advocated a cross-Straits policy posture that was demonstrably more moderate and significantly less confrontational than Lee's policy. All three pledged to relax the restrictions on economic exchange and no candidate endorsed or defended Lee's "no haste, be patient" policy. Then, at the accession to the WTO in January 2001, the DPP government decided not to invoke the GATT/WTO's opt-out provision, which permits new members a one-time-only option upon accession to preclude any existing member from the application of GATT/WTO rules. The decision, while well anticipated by all parties concerned, now obliges Taipei to lift the import ban on a wide range of mainland products, putting Taiwan's 50-year trade sanctions against the mainland to a conclusive end. Next, faced with a gloomy economic outlook, rising unemployment, a bleeding stock market, run-away fiscal deficits and a looming threat of Japanese-styled deflation, Taiwan's electorate seem to be so overwhelmed by the deteriorating economic bottom line that they have lost their appetite for lofty diplomatic objectives and outlandish political designs. Finally, and quite ironically, under the Chen Shui-bian administration the tidal wave of Taiwanese nationalism has visibly receded. According to the periodic polls commissioned by the Mainland Affairs Council, the level of support for Taiwanese independence reached an all-time-high of 28 per cent around late 1999.[46] But since then it has stagnated or even gradually declined. On the other hand, there has been a marked shift in popular opinion in favour of further economic integration with the Chinese mainland and the possibility of an eventual political union, especially among the young generation.

Most importantly, Beijing leaders' new confidence is fuelled by the staggering trend of cross-Strait economic integration and its political implications. Mainland China has rapidly evolved into Taiwan's largest export market, an indispensable manufacturing platform for its export-oriented sector, its single most important source of trade surplus and the top recipient of the island's outbound capital flows. Mainland China's share of Taiwan's total exports has risen rapidly throughout the last decade and in 2002 it surpassed the United States for the first time.[47] The mainland now accounts for about 24.9 per cent of Taiwan's total exports, and while the US remains Taiwan's biggest trading partner in terms of total trade, its share of Taiwan's export has dropped to 20.7 per cent. Beyond this, Taiwanese companies have a total investment of at least

---

46. The MAC commissioned this poll in August 1999. I calculated this figure by collapsing the two response categories "independence as soon as possible" (14.3%) and "status quo now, independence later" (13.8%). In the same poll with a sample size of 1067, 39.6% of the respondents chose "status quo now, decision later," 12% favoured "status quo indefinitely," 16.3% favoured "status quo now, unification later," and only 2.1% favoured "unification as soon as possible." See http://www.mac.gov.tw/english/POS/9007/9007e_1.gif.

47. According to Taiwan's official estimation, in the year 2002 Taiwan's trade with mainland China (mostly via Hong Kong) exceeded US$32 billion.

US$70 billion in China, operating more than 60,000 projects and with more than half a million Taiwanese expatriates minding the business on the mainland. More than half of Taiwan's listed companies and virtually all the island's top conglomerates have set up subsidiaries or joint ventures in China.[48] Many of them will soon generate bigger revenues in the Chinese mainland market than Taiwan and thus become more susceptible to Beijing's regulatory authority and goodwill. More significantly, grim long-term prospects have prompted a large number of small business owners and young professionals, believing that Taiwan's economy has passed its prime, to look seriously for career opportunities in the mainland. Many of them began to resettle their families in Shanghai and other metropolitan areas. None of these developments has escaped Beijing's policy makers' observation.

As a result, Beijing has become more confident that the Taiwanese business elite will voluntarily do its bidding out of sheer business interest. Conversely Chen Shui-bian, in his desperate efforts to jump-start Taiwan's sagging economy, has had no choice but to concede more agenda-setting power to the business elite, a trend best illustrated by his holding of the National Advisory Board of Economic Development in the summer of 2001. Upon the recommendation of this board, the DPP government officially dropped Lee Teng-hui's "no haste, be patient" concept and replaced it with "active opening, effective management."[49] Also, caving into mounting pressure from the high-tech sectors, the DPP government has agreed to expand the list of "permissible categories" to include an array of technology-intensive products, including the backbone of Taiwan's high-tech industry, the semiconductor. Lifting the ban on cross-Straits investment in chip plants signalled a significant policy shift, in that the new measure was fiercely opposed by Lee Teng-hui and the Taiwan Solidarity Union.[50] As all presidential aspirants for the 2004 race scramble to reposition themselves in this latest game of redefining the centralist line, Taiwan's leading conglomerates and elite high-tech firms have wasted no time in launching their full-fledged Greater China strategies. Witnessing a new tidal wave of Taiwanese capital outflow looking for new market opportunities after China's WTO entry, many pragmatic-

48. According to the official statistics of the Taiwan Security Commission, at the end of the third quarter of 2002, around 60% of the companies listed on the Taiwan Stock Exchange have invested in the mainland and around 55% of the listed companies in the OTC market have done so. See *China Times*, 19 January 2003.

49. In terms of concrete steps, in November 2001, the Ministry of Economic Affairs unveiled its new approval system for mainland-bound investment. All investments under the permissible categories, and of less than US$20 million, would be regulated under an "automatic approval" system. Under the scheme, officials must decide within 30 days whether to approve new investments, providing the application materials are filed appropriately; otherwise, prospective applications will automatically be approved and become effective immediately.

50. The TSU is a new political party hastily formed on the eve of the December 2001 parliamentary election to defend Lee Tenghui's ultra-nationalistic agenda and to serve as a counterweight against the influence of the pro-China business elite over Chen Shui-bian. Although it received only 7.7% of the popular vote, it enjoyed the status of a strategic veto group that might deprive the DPP of a working majority in the parliament.

minded DPP leaders have grudgingly accepted the view that the trend towards further economic integration with the Chinese mainland is inevitable, despite its complicated social and political ramifications. It is ironic that more progress has been made on loosening up the policy restrictions on cross-Strait economic exchange in the first two years of (an allegedly pro-independence) Chen Shui-bian's presidency than under the eleven years of Lee Teng-hui's tenure.

Conclusion

After taking over as secretary general at the 16th Communist Party Congress and being elected the president of the PRC at the Tenth National People's Congress, Hu Jintao assumed many of Jiang's official titles, but not necessarily his power. Designated as the first among equals of the fourth generation leadership, Hu will be not only obliged to share the stage with many other weighty members of the Standing Committee of the Politburo, but also compelled to toe the Jiang Zemin line, as the structure of the newly elected SCP clearly reinforces Jiang's ability to cast a long shadow over Hu for some time to come. Hu is thus expected to adhere with great caution to Jiang's updated policy guidelines on Taiwan affairs, as laid out in the retiring general secretary's farewell Party work report to the CCP 16th Congress.

Few policy domains can come close to Taiwan affairs in exemplifying the way Jiang's reigning authority has been self-extended beyond his official tenure. Fighting for his place in history, Jiang's desire to reset the cross-Strait scoreboard before his full retirement remains strong. He has demonstrated his political will and capacity to rehabilitate policy consensus and institutionalize his policy legacy over the Taiwan issue. For this reason, Jiang has probably already put forward his best and last offer on cross-Strait relations in his latest policy initiative. Regardless of the shade of his personal predilection, Hu Jintao, navigating in the shadow of still-ambitious Jiang, will have little incentive to alter (either bidding up or bidding down) Jiang's offer for at least the next few years. In a nutshell, while Beijing may be displaying patience, operational flexibility and rhetorical sophistication on an unprecedented scale, its basic bargaining positions are iron-cast for years to come.

With more strategic cards in Beijing's hand, Taipei will be facing an up-hill battle to advance its political agenda. None of Taiwan's major political parties is fully prepared to deal with the spectacular social and political implications of the island's deepening economic dependence on the Chinese mainland. While it remains to be seen if this ongoing trend will load the dice of the national identity issue in favour of cross-Straits political integration in the long term, one should not underestimate the possibility that further economic integration is likely to undermine the social foundation of Taipei's current security preference. Popular aspirations for independent statehood may be dampened under the development of dense social ties and elite networks across the Strait, a convergence of popular culture brought about by an integrated Mandarin-based media market spanning Taiwan, Hong Kong and mainland China, and a refurbishing of Chinese identity among Taiwan's younger generations. For this reason, the American policy elite will soon have to wrestle with the profound implications of cross-Straits economic integration for the US security agenda in East Asia.[51]

51. On this point, see Nancy Tucker, "If Taiwan chooses unification, should the United States care?" *Washington Quarterly*, Vol. 25, No. 3 (Summer 2002), pp. 15–28.

Systemic Stresses and Political Choices: The Road Ahead

Richard Baum

ABSTRACT Although a vibrant market economy and a nascent civil society have begun to emerge in China, the country's Leninist political institutions remain substantially unchanged. The growing disconnect between a dynamic, vibrant economy and society on the one hand and a brittle, anachronistic party-state on the other arguably constitutes a formidable obstacle to China's developmental health and stability. A number of reform-related societal stresses have been allowed to accumulate, their severity masked by continued high rates of aggregate economic growth: rising urban unemployment, a growing urban–rural income gap, widespread official corruption, a teetering banking system and a looming HIV/AIDS epidemic. While the country's new leaders appear committed to dealing pro-actively with these challenges, it is by no means clear that the institutions of governance at their disposal are adequate for the task. What is most urgently needed at present is a serious regime commitment to strengthening the "input institutions" and socio-political feedback mechanisms in Chinese society. This will involve easing present restrictions on unofficial religious, social and occupational groups; expanding the scope of political and intellectual tolerance; enhancing the autonomy of the mass media and organs of public opinion; strengthening the representative functions of people's congresses; and, in general, relaxing Party controls in state administration. While it might be possible for the country's leaders to muddle through for a while longer, the continuing intensification of societal stresses means that time may no longer be on their side.

Now that the changing of the guard is more-or-less complete and China's fourth-generation leaders are settled more-or-less firmly in place, it is possible to step back from the immediate *sturm und drang* of recent events to place the leadership transition in the broader context of China's ongoing political development. Many of the challenges confronting China's new, nine-man ruling directorate, the Politburo Standing Committee, are by now quite familiar. These include, *inter alia*, urban unemployment, income polarization, corruption, a teetering banking system and a looming HIV/AIDS epidemic. Most of these problems were engendered or exacerbated in the course of China's remarkable market transition in the 1980s and 1990s. While the country's new leaders appear committed to dealing pro-actively with these challenges, it is by no means clear that the problems themselves are wholly tractable or that the machinery of governance at the disposal of the leadership is adequate to the tasks. Although a vibrant market economy and a nascent civil society have begun to emerge, China's Leninist political institutions – remnants of a bygone era – remain substantially unchanged. There is thus a growing disconnect between a dynamic, robust economy and society on the one hand and a brittle, anachronistic party-state on the other. This situation – well illustrated by the Chinese government's costly cover-up of the spring 2003 SARS epidemic – poses a formidable obstacle to China's developmental stability. Just how formidable is a matter of ongoing debate among both Chinese and foreign observers.[1]

Jiang's Legacy: A Mixed Picture

This examination of the challenges facing China's new leaders begins with a brief assessment of Jiang Zemin's legacy. With the benefit of hindsight it is evident that most outside observers underestimated Jiang's leadership capacity and survival skills. Despite a notable lack of charisma and a reputation for bending with the wind, Jiang proved to be a competent helmsman. A consolidator rather than an innovator, he kept a steady hand on the wheel as China continued its tortuous transition from Maoism to marketization. Domestically, Jiang dealt effectively with a series of potentially critical problems. These included a strong conservative ideological challenge to the reforms in the early 1990s, following the collapse of communism in Eastern Europe and the Soviet Union; an epidemic of economic overheating and urban hyperinflation in 1992–93; a deepening fiscal crisis in the mid-1990s; and the closure of thousands of inefficient, overstaffed state-owned enterprises at the end of the decade.

With major assistance from tough-talking Premier Zhu Rongji (who is widely credited with engineering the economic "soft landing" of 1994–97, stabilizing the *renminbi* and guiding the subsequent reform of China's ailing banks and SOEs), Jiang managed to avoid the type of spiralling economic disaster that befell post-Soviet Russia in the 1990s. Under his stewardship, average personal income in China more than doubled, foreign direct investment surged and economic growth averaged over 9 per cent annually.[2] In foreign affairs, too, Jiang's accomplishments were far from trivial. Most notably, he managed to preserve a co-operative working relationship with the United States in the face of rising nationalist sentiments in both countries. Under Jiang, China entered the WTO and succeeded in its bid to host the Olympic Games in 2008.[3]

In terms of socio-cultural change, China's progress under Jiang was also impressive. An emergent middle class, currently estimated at more than 10 per cent of the population, took root in China's cities. Its

---

1. See the collection of essays in David Shambaugh (ed.), *Is China Unstable?* (Armonk, NY: M.E. Sharpe, 2000).

2. Estimates of China's GDP growth in the 1990s vary. For a summary of different methods of assessing GDP, and the different results that emerge therefrom, see: "Truth or consequences: China's GDP numbers," *China Economic Quarterly,* No. 1 (2003).

3. For an early assessment of Jiang's leadership, see Bruce Gilley, *Tiger on the Brink: Jiang Zemin and China's New Elite* (Berkeley: University of California Press, 1998). See also Lowell Dittmer's chapter in the present volume; and Richard Baum, "Jiang's steady hand at the helm makes up for lack of charisma," *South China Morning Post,* 27 October 2002. On Zhu Rongji's contribution to China's growth and stability in the 1990s, see Fred Hu, "Zhu Rongji's decade," *Wall Street Journal,* 10 March 2003.

signature material markers – private home ownership (59 per cent),[4] mobile phones (212 million),[5] internet connectivity (60 million), satellite dishes (42 million viewers), travel abroad (16 million sojourners in 2002), private automobiles (10 million), registered lawyers (117,000), and McDonalds and KFC outlets (1100) – have become ubiquitous, if perhaps misleading, symbols of China's emergence from its Maoist cocoon.[6]

Much of China's impressive growth was stimulated by a central government that shifted, first under Deng Xiaoping then under Jiang Zemin, from a Stalinist strategy of centralized planning and tight micro-economic management to one of macro-economic market regulation. In the process, powerful developmental forces were unleashed, most of them localized in nature. By giving provincial and local governments a major stake in promoting economic development through fiscal and administrative decentralization and the downward transfer of residual property rights over profits from state-owned enterprises, the long-dormant genie of Chinese entrepreneurship was released from its captive, bureaucratic-socialist jar.[7]

As the communist party-state has receded from micro-managing every aspect of people's lives, personal freedom and autonomy have grown apace. Personal space has been augmented and a consumer culture has emerged, primarily in urban areas. The growth of this culture has brought with it a dramatic increase in the number of life-style choices available to ordinary citizens. The mass media, while still subject to state censorship and control, are livelier than ever. Civic associations, business groups and professional societies, though subject to state licensing and oversight, have begun to flourish. Non-governmental organizations have also begun to emerge, partially filling the vacuum left by the retreat of the state from its penetrative, paternalistic social role in the Maoist era.[8]

4. Sources for data in this section include *People's Daily* (online, in English), 5 March 2003: http://english.peopledaily.com.cn/200303/05/eng20030305_112717.shtml; *People's Daily* (online, in English), 6 February 2002: http://fpeng.peopledaily.com.cn/200202/06/eng20020206_90042.shtml; *The Economist*, 12 April 2003, p. 58; *The Economic Times*, 25 September 2002; and *People's Daily* (online, in English), 8 July 2002: http://english.peopledaily.com.cn/200207/08/eng20020708_99288.shtml.

5. This figure refers to registered mobile telephone numbers, rather than mobile phones in use. A substantial (but unknown) percentage of these phone numbers belong to people (or firms) who own multiple numbers in different provinces.

6. There is a lack of consensus on both the definition and the size of China's middle class. A CASS report issued in late 2001 estimated that "middle strata" (both urban and rural) included up to 15% of the country's working-age population, or about 110 million people, the bulk of whom lived in large and medium-sized cities. See "China's middle class: to get rich is glorious," *The Economist*, 17 January 2002.

7. On the effects of fiscal decentralization and the shift from micro-management to macro-regulation, see Jia Hao and Lin Zhimin (eds.), *Changing Central-Local Relations in China* (Boulder: Westview Press, 1994). On the downward transfer of property rights see Andrew Walder and Jean Oi (eds.), *Property Rights and Economic Reform in China* (Stanford: Stanford University Press, 1999).

8. The breadth of social change under the reforms is examined in Timothy Brook and Bernie Frolic (eds.), *Civil Society in China* (Armonk, NY: M.E. Sharpe, 1997); also Gordon White, Jude Howell and Xiaoyuan Shang, *In Search of Civil Society: Market Reform and Social Change in Contemporary China* (Oxford: Clarendon Press, 1996). On the tensions and conflicts engendered by social change, see Elizabeth J. Perry and Mark Selden (eds.), *Chinese Society: Change, Conflict and Resistance* (London: Routledge, 2000).

Notwithstanding these impressive developments, Jiang Zemin's legacy remains distinctly clouded. On the economic front, the rapid pace of change over the past two decades has produced, along with near double-digit growth rates, a rash of near-term distortions and dislocations. While the benign genie of marked-based entrepreneurship has been freed, it appears that it has an evil twin: the gini coefficient. As overall incomes have risen in China, income differentials between city and countryside have grown significantly wider, as has the development gap between coast and interior. Reform has produced losers as well as winners. Consequently, the gini coefficient – a crude index of the income gap between the top and bottom 20 per cent of a population – has risen over the past 20 years, from among the lowest in the world (around 0.24) to among the highest (approximately 0.44). While a rise in the gini coefficient is not necessarily indicative of a brewing revolt by the toiling masses (who may, after all, be absolutely better off than before even as their relative share of national income declines), the steep upward slope of the Chinese inequality curve is still worrying to many.[9]

With the closure, consolidation or privatization of thousands of money-losing state-owned enterprises since the mid-1990s, urban unemployment (both open and disguised) has affected an estimated 40–50 million Chinese workers – over 10 per cent of the total – most of whom have no reliable social safety net to cushion the loss of income, health and welfare benefits.[10] While rising unemployment need not in itself prove politically volatile, when combined with growing regional and sectoral income differentials, inadequate or non-existent welfare programmes and public perceptions of rampant corruption by enterprise and local state officials, a potentially combustible political mixture may be created. Since the late 1990s, thousands of labour disturbances have occurred throughout the

9. For a range of estimates on China's changing gini coefficient, see Jonathan Unger, *The Transformation of Rural China* (Armonk, NY: M.E. Sharpe, 2002), p. 171, n. 2. See also *South China Morning Post*, 10 February 2003; Scott Hills, "China scrambles to narrow widening wealth gap," Reuters (Beijing), 11 November 2002; Carl Riskin, Zhao Renwei and Li Shi (eds.), *China's Retreat from Equality: Income Distribution and Economic Transition* (Armonk, NY: M.E. Sharpe, 2001), ch. 2; and Wang Shaoguang and Hu Angang, *The Political Economy of Uneven Development: The Case of China* (Armonk, NY: M.E. Sharpe, 1999), ch. 7. For a cautionary note against reading too much political significance into rising gini coefficients, see Albert Hirschman, "The changing tolerance for income inequality in the course of economic development." *Quarterly Journal of Economics*, Vol. 87, No. 4 (November 1973), pp. 544–566.

10. Wolf *et al.* estimate a total of 43.5 million unemployed urban workers in 1999. See Charles Wolf Jr. *et al.*, *Fault Lines in China's Economic Terrain* (Santa Monica: The RAND Corporation, 2003) p. 13. A group of Chinese economists put the 2002 unemployment total at "over 48 million." See Wang Shaoguang, Hu Angang and Ding Yuanzhu, "Behind China's wealth gap," *South China Morning Post*, 31 October 2002. On the chronic underfunding of enterprise and state-supported welfare systems, see Jane Duckett, "China's social security reform and the comparative politics of market transition," *Journal of Communist Studies and Transition Politics*, Vol. 19, No. 1 (March 2003), pp. 80–101; see also Tang Jun, "The new situation of poverty and anti-poverty," in *The Year 2002: Analysis and Forecast of China's Social Situation* (Beijing: Academy of Social Sciences Institute of Sociology, 2002), trans. in FBIS-CPP20030110000172 (1 January 2003).

country, the largest involving more than 30,000 workers.[11] Moreover, unemployment-related problems may be expected to worsen in the short run, as the effects of China's entry into the WTO begin to be felt. According to one estimate by Salomon Smith Barney, as many as 40 million more workers may be thrown out of work in the next few years, many of whom will be unable to secure alternative employment.[12] And these figures do not include the estimated 80 million or more members of China's "floating population" (*liudong renyuan*) – rural emigrés who have left the countryside in search of urban employment, who often lead a precarious existence as short-term contract workers, day labourers, peddlers or vagrants.[13] Nor do the figures on unemployment-related labour unrest include the more than 150,000 industrial grievances filed with the Ministry of Labour in the year 2001 alone, representing a seven-fold increase over 1994.[14]

Like their urban counterparts, rural dwellers also confront daunting economic problems. For those farmers living in China's fertile coastal deltas and commercialized municipal suburbs, with their ready access to urban markets and infrastructure, the spread of private farming and the proliferation of township and village enterprises since 1980 has on the whole been financially rewarding. For many others, however, including the bulk of the farm population in China's interior provinces, the economic situation has been more stressful and problematic. Based on Chinese government statistics, a 22 per cent drop in farm prices between 1997 and 2000 caused Chinese farmers to lose between US$36 million and $48 million.[15] Personal incomes in rural Guizhou province are estimated, on average, to be ten or twelve times lower than those in Shanghai. According to a recent World Bank estimate, 106 million rural Chinese residents currently live below the poverty line, defined as a per-capita income of less than US$1 per day.[16]

11. Craig Smith, "Workers in China organize to oppose restructurings," *Wall Street Journal*, 7 June 1999; Philip Pan, "Government stifles labor movement," *Washington Post*, 28 December 2002. For extensive documentation of labour disturbances since the late 1990s see China Labour Bulletin (E-Bulletin), http://www.china-labour.org.hk/iso/article_listings. adp?category_id = 3.

12. "WTO cost: 40 million jobs," *Far-Eastern Economic* Review, 5 October 2000, p. 10. On the other hand, some Chinese economists have estimated that the country's WTO accession will lead to a net *increase* of as many as 12 million jobs, leading to a predicted annual GDP boost of up to 3%. See Dorothy Solinger, "Chinese urban jobs and the WTO," *The China Journal*, No. 49 (January 2003).

13. Dorothy Solinger, "China's floating population," in Merle Goldman and Roderick MacFarquhar (eds.), *The Paradox of China's Post-Mao Reforms* (Cambridge, MA: Harvard University Press, 1999, pp. 220–240; also Li Zhang, *Strangers in the City: Reconfigurations of Space, Power, and Social Networks within China's Floating Population* (Stanford: Stanford University Press, 2001).

14. Statistics in Mary E. Gallagher, "'Use law as your weapon': legal development and labor conflict in the PRC" (paper presented to the 2003 Annual Meeting of the Association for Asian Studies, New York, 27–30 March 2003).

15. Wang, Hu and Ding, "Behind China's wealth gap." On the general worsening of economic conditions faced by many (if not most) rural dwellers, see Unger, *The Transformation of Rural China*, esp. ch. 9.

16. Wolf *et al.*, *Fault Lines in China's Economic Terrain*, p. 15. Guizhou–Shanghai comparison by Hu Angang, personal communication to author, 29 August 2003.

With rural villages and townships throughout China facing severe financial hardship, local governments in less well-endowed regions have been forced to rely on extra-budgetary fiscal exactions (including a variety of *ad hoc* taxes, levies and fines) to meet their expenses and provide public services. In the absence of open accounting practices in villages, these off-budget revenues have not infrequently been appropriated by local officials for their own private use. In response to such predatory behaviour, farmers in many provinces have begun to engage in collective protest and resistance, ranging from small, scattered demonstrations to massive acts of defiance and violence.[17] To curb the mounting tide of rural unrest, central authorities have repeatedly warned local officials against imposing unreasonable levies and fees; and in 1997 the State Council issued regulations mandating a "burden reduction" for hard-pressed rural dwellers.[18] Most recently, the central government introduced a "tax-for-fee" system (*feigaishui*), abolishing all unscheduled, *ad hoc* exactions and replacing them with a uniform, moderate agricultural tax. In some areas, village account books have been opened to public scrutiny by local residents.[19]

While urban unemployment and rural poverty continue to confound government efforts at amelioration, China's financial system reportedly hovers near the brink of insolvency. Despite the introduction of tough new banking laws and regulations in the late 1990s, the country's four main central banks remain awash in bad debt. Non-performing loans – remnants of the politically-mandated lending practices of the past – are currently estimated at upward of US$500 billion, equal to more than 40 per cent of China's GDP. Thus far, the regime's strategy of choice for dealing with banking problems has been to combine a partial clampdown on new, non-commercial loans with an aggressive programme of loan write-offs and debt-equity swaps.[20] The hope is that continued high rates of economic growth and a major influx of private capital will eventually swamp the existing debt and thus "fix" the banking crisis. Outside analysts differ widely in their assessment of the probable efficacy of this strategy, and on the consequent likelihood of a full-blown banking crisis.[21]

17. Thomas P. Bernstein and Xiaobo Lu, *Taxation without Representation in Contemporary Rural China* (Cambridge: Cambridge University Press, 2003), ch. 5; and Xiaobo Lu, *Corruption: The Organizational Involution of the Chinese Communist Party* (Stanford: Stanford University Press, 2000.

18. These developments are chronicled in Lu, *Cadres and Corruption*, ch. 6.

19. It is too early to tell if such measures will significantly reduce rural discontent. See Jean C. Oi, Xiaobo Lu and Yawei Liu, *Crisis in the Hinterland: Rural Discontent in China* (Washington, DC: Woodrow Wilson International Center for Scholars, Asia Program Special Report No. 108, March 2003), pp. 6–7, *et passim*.

20. According to official Chinese sources, by the autumn of 2002 over $170 billion worth of non-performing loans had been taken off the books in this manner. See Wang Haijun, "Disposition of non-performing loans in China: progress and challenge" (31 October 2002), http://www.euro-events.com/conf/cfcm2002/pdf/cinda.pdf.

21. Mark Clifford, "Are China's banks caught in quicksand?" *BusinessWeek*, 25 November 2002. The most pessimistic estimate of the seriousness of China's banking crisis is Gordon Chang, *The Coming Collapse of China* (New York: Random House, 2001).

Corruption is another problem that has proven intractable. Despite a series of highly publicized official exhortations and periodic anti-corruption campaigns, bribery, graft and the misappropriation of public property continue to flourish among Party, state and enterprise officials. As revealed by official statistics, such misdeeds have increased dramatically over the past 15 years. In the mid-1980s, for example, the number of officially reported crimes involving corruption averaged around 30,000 cases per year; a decade later the corresponding annual average was over 170,000 cases.[22] And this was evidently just the tip of a much larger iceberg. From 1992 to 1998, over 75 million citizen complaints of corruption were received by Party discipline inspection committees throughout the country.[23] Particularly alarming was the rising incidence of "major" corruption cases (those involving more than RMB 10,000), which mushroomed from just 8 per cent of all reported cases in 1987 to over 44 per cent a decade later. From 1984 to 2001, the average amount involved in all reported cases of corruption rose from RMB 4,054 to RMB 112,492.[24] According to one recent Chinese estimate, economic losses resulting from corruption amounted to as much as 14.5 per cent of GDP from 1999 to the end of 2001.[25] Throughout the last half of the 1990s, public opinion surveys routinely revealed corruption to be the number one concern of most Chinese respondents.[26] In his farewell speech to the 16th Party Congress, Jiang Zemin underscored the severity of the problem. "If we do not crack down on corruption," he warned, "the Party will be in danger of losing its ruling position, or possibly heading for self-destruction."[27]

Finally, if these problems weren't severe enough, since the late 1990s the spread of HIV/AIDS has reached epidemic proportions in some Chinese provinces, most notably Henan and Yunnan. According to UNAIDS officials, the number of people with HIV in China – most infected through tainted blood donations and needle-sharing by intra-venous drug users – was estimated (unofficially) at between 850,000 and 1.5 million in mid-year 2002, with the infection rate reportedly rising by 17 per cent in the first six months of that year.[28] Official unwillingness to acknowledge the severity of the epidemic – including government per-secution of two physicians who first publicized the problem of tainted blood supplies in Henan province – is blamed for the country's late start in developing an effective coping strategy. And it has been predicted that unless dramatically more effective response mechanisms are put rapidly

22. Statistics compiled by Melanie Manion, "Corruption by design: bribery in Chinese enterprise licensing," *Journal of Law, Economics and Organization*, Vol. 12, No. 1 (April 1996), pp. 167–195.
23. Lu, *Cadres and Corruption*, p. 222, Table 6.3.
24. See Andrew Wedeman, "The intensification of corruption in China," *The China Quarterly*, forthcoming 2004.
25. Wang *et al.*, "Behind China's wealth gap."
26. Survey results cited in Lu, *Cadres and Corruption*, pp. 221–22.
27. "Jiang's stark warning on corruption," *CNN.com*, 8 November 2002.
28. See "China gets poor UN review of AIDS policies," *Far Eastern Economic Review*, 1 January 2003; also http://www.unchina.org/unaids/index.html

in place, a total of 10–12 million Chinese will acquire HIV by the end of the decade.[29]

In a recent study of problems confronting the Chinese economy, a group of RAND Corporation analysts concluded that the existence of these (and other) socio-economic fault lines constitutes a potentially serious drag on China's future economic growth.[30] They estimate the potential downward pull of massive urban unemployment and rural unrest on future GDP growth to be 0.3 per cent to 0.8 per cent per year; rampant corruption, 0.5 per cent per year; a deepening bank crisis, 0.5 to 1.0 per cent; a severe HIV/AIDS epidemic, 1.8 to 2.2 per cent; and various other domestic dangers (including critical water shortages and environmental degradation), 1.5 to 1.9 per cent. These estimates – which exclude the anticipated down-side economic costs of possible exogenous crises such as conflict with Taiwan, spiking global energy costs or a sharp contraction in foreign direct investment – add up to an endogenously-driven, "worst case" growth-rate reduction of 4.6 to 6.4 per cent per year, which would dramatically cut into the 7 to 8 per cent annual growth predicted by China's economic forecasters. If exogenous variables are factored into the equation, the potential growth loss could be as great as 8 to 10.6 per cent annually – which would mean a net shrinkage of China's GDP. [31] And these estimates were made before the onset of the 2003 SARS epidemic, whose down-side economic cost has been estimated at around 0.5 to 1.0 per cent of GDP.[32] The authors of the RAND report are careful to point out that the probability of these several calamities occurring together is very low; and thus the actual growth-rate decline would probably be significantly less than their worst-case scenario. Nevertheless, they foresee a strong probability of significantly decelerated economic growth in the near future.

Political Fault Lines: The Leninist Heritage

Facing a wide array of pressing – and potentially growth-impairing – socio-economic problems, China's new leaders have reason enough to be deeply concerned. But there are serious political fault lines as well. Throughout the 1990s Jiang Zemin, Li Peng and other third-generation Chinese leaders maintained tight control over the nation's political life. Fearful of renewed popular unrest in the wake of the 1989 Tiananmen upheaval and subsequent Soviet collapse, they indefinitely postponed major system-wide political reforms, opting instead for cautious, incremental innovations such as village elections. Even this limited reform

29. Bates Gill, "China's HIV/AIDS crisis: implications for human rights, the rule of law and US–China relations," Testimony before the Congressional-Executive Commission on China, Roundtable on HIV/AIDS, 9 September 2002: http://www.csis.org/china/HIV_crisis.htm.

30. Wolf *et al.*, *Fault Lines in China's Economic Terrain*.

31. *Ibid.* p. 6.

32. See Neil J. Beck, "What does SARS mean for China?" (National Bureau of Asian Research: NBR Briefing Paper No. 13, 9 May 2003): http://www.nbr.org/publications/briefing/no.13-SARS/beck.html.

was carefully controlled from above, however; and nowhere was anything resembling authentic political pluralism permitted to take root.[33]

Jiang's failure to implement meaningful institutional reform means that gross abuses of Communist Party power persist. As mandated by Deng Xiaoping's constitutionally-embedded "four cardinal principles," the CCP is, in effect, above the law.[34] Top Party leaders remain unaccountable to all but a small group of their equally unaccountable colleagues. The national legislature lacks autonomous authority. Elections to people's congresses and Party committees at all levels are carefully controlled from above. Multi-party competition and institutionalized checks and balances are eschewed as "bourgeois liberalism." "Rule of law" remains a distant, elusive goal, as courts at each level, far from being independent, are politically and financially beholden to local governments, which are in turn dominated by Party committees.[35] Transparency in Party and governmental affairs is minimal. Major print and broadcast media, while livelier and more diverse in content than ever before, remain subject to state censorship and control. Freedom of worship is limited to five officially sponsored religions. Despite a substantial increase in the degree of personal freedom and autonomy enjoyed by most Chinese citizens most of the time, public expressions of political dissent routinely meet with state suppression.[36]

The combination of rapid socio-economic change and minimal political-institutional reform highlights a central paradox confronting Leninist regimes as they attempt to accommodate new social forces and pressures unleashed in the process of economic reform. Charles Lindblom once observed that Leninist systems are particularly well suited to inducing social change from above; that is, they have muscular, well-developed statist "thumbs" that can exert highly concentrated pressure on society. By the same token, however, Leninist systems have weak, insensitive "fingers," that is, they have great difficulty accurately gauging and responding to dispersed societal signals.[37] In contrast, Lindblom

33. On the limited democratic efficacy of village elections, see Erik Eckholm, "China's villagers vote, but its party rules," *New York Times*, 4 November 2001. See also the collection of documents posted on the Carter Center's website, http://www.chinaelections.org. On the limitations of civil service reform in the 1990s, see K.T. Liou, "Issues and lessons of Chinese civil service reform," *Public Personnel Management*, No. 26 (Winter 1997), pp. 505–514.

34. The four principles, which mandated individual allegiance to CCP leadership, Marxism-Leninism-Mao Zedong thought, socialism and the people's democratic dictatorship, were written into the preamble of the PRC constitution in 1982. See Richard Baum, *Burying Mao: Chinese Politics in the Age of Deng Xiaoping* (Princeton: Princeton University Press, 1996), pp. 149–150.

35. For contrasting views on the development of a Chinese "rule of law," cf. Stanley Lubman, *Bird in a Cage: Legal Reform in China after Mao* (Stanford: Stanford University Press, 1999); and Randall Peerenboom, *China's Long March Toward Rule of Law* (Cambridge: Cambridge University Press, 2002).

36. For a cogent summary of the developmental difficulties engendered by a rigid, unresponsive Chinese party-state, see Merle Goldman and Roderick MacFarquhar, "Dynamic economy, declining party-state," in Goldman and MacFarquhar, *The Paradox of China's Post-Mao Reforms*, pp. 3–29.

37. Charles Lindblom, *Politics and Markets: The World's Political-Economic Systems* (New York: Basic Books, 1977).

observed, pluralist democracies have relatively weak thumbs, rendering them incapable of generating concentrated coercive force; but they have well-developed, sensitive fingers, enabling them accurately to gauge and respond to changing environmental stimuli. In short, Leninist systems excel in mechanisms of force, while market democracies excel in mechanisms of feedback.

As Chinese society becomes more complex, differentiated, and information-rich, the need for enhanced sensitivity in the system's political receptors, or "input institutions," increases greatly.[38] The market mechanism – Adam Smith's "invisible hand" – performs this function in the economic sphere, enabling producers and consumers to respond quickly and effectively to shifting market signals. But there is a growing need for equally sensitive feedback mechanisms in the political sphere. In democratic polities this function is normally performed by interest groups, a free press, public opinion and competitive elections. Lacking such autonomous, well-articulated input institutions, however, China's Leninist polity remains seriously insensitive and unresponsive. In effect, it suffers from being "all thumbs." The consequences of such insensitivity were well illustrated during the early stages of the 2003 SARS epidemic, when the government's lack of candour and blockage of vital information combined to prevent the timely implementation of effective countermeasures.

In an effort to gain added political sensitivity without at the same time ceding political initiative to independent social or political forces, the CCP has adopted various "united front" techniques. Designed to link the Party more closely with important non-Party socio-economic constituencies and occupational groups through "mutual consultation and supervision," united front organs have traditionally included the Chinese People's Political Consultative Conference, mass organizations such as the All-China Federation of Trade Unions and the All-China Women's Federation, and the eight officially recognized "democratic parties." The problem with such organizations is that, despite their nominal commitment to mutual supervision and consultation, they are almost entirely creatures of the Communist Party. Closely controlled and supervised by Party officials, such corporatist bodies are ill-suited to perform the vital input/feedback functions needed to foster effective governance. Indeed, because of their careful cultivation, tending and weeding by the CCP, these organizations are often cynically referred to as "flowerpots."[39]

Implicitly conceding the inability of the CCP's traditional united front bodies to incorporate and represent the interests of all sectors of China's increasingly complex society, Jiang Zemin lobbied hard in his final years

---

38. On the importance of input institutions in China's political modernization, see Andrew Nathan, "Authoritarian resilience," *Journal of Democracy*, Vol. 14, No. 1 (January 2003), pp. 13–16.

39. On the inability of state-sponsored corporatist bodies to promote and protect the interests of their own members, see Jonathan Unger and Anita Chan, "China, corporatism, and the East Asia model," *The China Journal*, No. 133 (January 1995), pp. 29–53.

as China's top leader to broaden the CCP's socio-economic base and thereby "keep abreast of the times." In February 2000 he stated that "Only if the Party [represents] the development of China's advanced social productive forces, the forward direction for China's cultural advancement, and the fundamental interests of China's vast population will the Party always be able to maintain an invincible position."[40] This rather awkward formulation was subsequently refined and repackaged by Jiang's chief of staff, Zeng Qinghong, as the "three represents" (*san ge daibiao*). A year later, in July 2001, Jiang enlarged the scope of the "three represents," urging his comrades to embrace the aspirations and "advanced culture" of middle-class businesspeople and *nouveaux-riches* entrepreneurs.[41] Reversing almost five decades of doctrinal hostility to capitalism, Jiang now called for co-opting successful entrepreneurs into the Communist Party. In so doing, he triggered an intense backlash from a vocal minority of Party traditionalists, who viewed this as a sellout of the CCP's revolutionary birthright.[42] Notwithstanding such opposition, Jiang secured an important victory at the 16th Party Congress when the "theory of the three represents" was enshrined in the Party constitution alongside Mao Zedong Thought and Deng Xiaoping Theory.

Perforce, the constitutional incorporation of the "three represents" reflects the CCP's growing recognition of the urgent need to strengthen its societal "fingers." But it is only a first step. And while the "three represents" will arguably permit a greater diversity of interests and opinions to be incorporated within the Party, in the absence of corresponding institutional changes this will do little to empower ordinary citizens vis-à-vis the Party; nor will it necessarily grant a more autonomous, authentic voice to the Party's rank-and-file. Because the "three represents" neither guarantees accountable, responsive governance nor ensures greater transparency in policy-making and administration, the verdict on Jiang's controversial theory remains undecided. Much will depend on what concrete structural reforms, if any, follow from this ideological opening wedge.

Politics: The Art of the Plausible

Faced with a variety of deepening fault lines, but averse to potentially destabilizing macro-political reforms (such as multi-party elections and a constitutional separation of powers), China's new leaders would appear to have a limited range of political options at their disposal. Politics is (or

40. Quoted in Yu Yunyao, "fully strengthen Party building in the new era in accordance with the requirements of the 'three represents'," trans. in FBIS-CPP20010824000143 (24 August 2001).

41. These developments are analysed in Joseph Fewsmith, "Rethinking the role of the CCP: explicating Jiang Zemin's Party anniversary speech," China Leadership Monitor, Vol. 1, No. 2 (December 2001).

42. Willy Wo-lap Lam, "The Jiang protégés and the Jiang theory," *China Brief*, Vol. 2, No. 11 (23 May 2002), http://china.jamestown.org; "CPC leftists send letter to Central Committee on Jiang's retirement," *Yomiuri shimbun* (Tokyo), 30 August 2002. trans. in FBIS-JPP20020830000191, p 7.

should be) the art of the possible – or at least the plausible. Given China's current circumstances, what political pathways are available? How can greater state sensitivity, responsiveness, accountability and transparency be engineered without threatening the very survival of the regime?

Short of a system-threatening breakdown of social order, a fundamental democratic breakthrough in the near future can probably be ruled out. Lingering memories of the political chaos of the Cultural Revolution, the 1989 Tiananmen crisis and the collapse of the Soviet Union gravitate against expectations of a bold, top-down political transformation. For more than a decade, the regime's fear of instability has precluded all but the most non-threatening political innovations. Even the one significant reform that appears to contradict this observation – the widespread introduction of direct village elections – was designed less to promote genuine democratic governance than to head off a brewing peasant revolt against corrupt, predatory local officials.[43] The central government's failure to authorize direct elections in China's 50,000 townships tends to confirm the suspicion that elections are intended more as a tension-relief mechanism than an instrument of genuine self-governance.[44]

Since the Tiananmen crisis, "muddling through" has been the regime's political strategy of choice. Steady, high rates of economic growth in the 1990s, underpinned by a massive influx of foreign direct investment, helped make this strategy viable, taking the edge off socio-political discontent. When problems arose that could not be ignored – farmers protesting against excessive extractions, laid-off workers demanding payment of embezzled wages and pensions, outraged parents demanding investigation of a fatal fireworks explosion in a primary school – they were handled on an *ad hoc*, individual basis. So long as such incidents were localized, isolated and unorganized they could be dealt with by a paternalistic government determined to keep the lid on social disorder. If necessary, village elections could be held to remove corrupt rural cadres; government officials could launch high-profile investigations into the causes of a school fire (or coal-mine disaster); and money could be found to pay off angry workers and pensioners.[45]

In this connection, Andrew Nathan has observed that the regime has at least partly succeeded in shoring up its fragile popular legitimacy by "encouraging individual rather than group-based inputs" and by "focusing complaints against specific local-level agencies or officials," thereby "diffusing possible aggression against the Chinese party-state."[46] Such a strategy of localized anger displacement and redirection is most effective

43. See Lianjiang Li and Kevin O'Brien, "The struggle over village elections," in Goldman and MacFarquhar, *The Paradox of China's Post-Mao Reforms,"* pp. 129–144.

44. On the chequered history of township elections see Lianjiang Li, "The politics of introducing direct township elections in China," *The China Quarterly*, No. 171 (September 2002), pp. 704–723.

45. According to a recent report by researchers at the CASS Institute of Sociology, the central government made one-off, *ad hoc* transfer payments totalling US$3.1 billion to aggrieved urban workers in 1999, up almost 65% from the 1998 level (Tang Jun, "The new situation of poverty and anti-poverty").

46. Nathan, "Authoritarian resilience," p. 15.

when discontent is small in scale and widely dispersed, and when communication among aggrieved groups is difficult. What began happening in the late 1990s, however, was the mobilization and aggregation of discontent by disadvantaged groups possessing modern means of communication: mobile phones, pagers, personal computers, fax machines and the internet. As socialized manifestations of discontent became larger in scale, their potential political danger to the regime became greater.

A massive non-violent sit-in by 10,000 followers of *falun gong* in Beijing in April 1999 was a turning point in the socialization of discontent. The fact that the authorities dealt with this incident in harsh, repressive fashion – detaining thousands, torturing hundreds (with 93 deaths reported in custody) and launching an intensive nation-wide propaganda campaign denouncing *falun gong* as an "evil cult" – bespeaks the leadership's deep fear of contagious protest.[47] Similar suppression, albeit on a much smaller scale, had occurred a year earlier, following an attempt by organizers of the nascent China Democracy Party to use the internet to build support for political-institutional reform.[48] More recently, in 2002, the mobilization and co-ordination of a massive labour protest involving tens of thousands of laid-off workers and unpaid pensioners from dozens of industrial enterprises in and around Liaoyang city in north-east China was followed by the arrest and imprisonment of the movement's leaders.[49] As these and other examples – including a series of audacious hijackings of China's SINOSAT satellite TV signal by supporters of the *falun gong* – amply illustrate, the "information revolution" has created new possibilities for the socialization of discontent, making it possible, amongst other things, for political activists quickly and effectively to publicize labour disturbances, acts of official misconduct and human rights abuses.[50] In response to such rapid, uncontrolled information flows, the Chinese government has employed upwards of 30,000 "cyber police" to monitor and censor the content of some 300,000 China-based internet websites, with varying degrees of success.[51]

With the scope and scale of socio-economic discontent rising, it was hardly coincidental that Hu Jintao, in his first major act of national leadership following the 16th Party Congress, made a pilgrimage to the

47. These figures are taken from Amnesty International, "Report 2001: China" (online), http://www.web.amnesty.org/web/ar2001.nsf/webasacountries/CHINA?OpenDocument. The best short analysis of the rise (and fall) of the *falun gong* is Ian Johnson, "China's blind-eye helped, then hurt, *falun dafa* movement," *Wall Street Journal*, 13 December 2000.

48. See *Nipped in the Bud: Suppression of the China Democracy Party* (New York: Human Rights Watch, 2000).

49. *China: Paying the Price: Worker Unrest in Northeast China* (New York: Human Rights Watch, 2002); also Philip Pan, "Jail, betrayal and fear: government stifles labor movement," *Washington Post*, 28 December 2002.

50. On the satellite hijacking incident, see the Chinese government's London embassy website, http://www.chinese-embassy.org.uk/eng/35172.html. Also Robert Marquand, "One lone voice fights for human rights in China," *Christian Science Monitor*, 18 April 2002.

51. Xiao Qiang and Sophie Beach, "The great firewall of China," *Los Angeles Times*, 25 August 2002; Li Xiguang, "Internet transforming China's media," *South China Morning Post*, 27 September 2002.

CCP's old revolutionary base of Xibaipo, where he reaffirmed his commitment to the Party's traditional egalitarian ethos of "plain living and hard struggle." A month later, on the eve of the Chinese New Year, Hu Jintao and Premier-designate Wen Jiabao travelled to the interior provinces of Inner Mongolia and Shanxi, respectively, where they paid "comfort visits" to hard-pressed farmers, herdsmen and coal miners. Displaying empathy for the poor, the marginalized and the dispossessed, Hu and Wen sought to enhance their – and the CCP's – public image as upright and caring.[52] A similar, if belated, effort by China's top leaders to deal resolutely with the worsening SARS epidemic and assuage mounting public fears was very much in evidence during the middle stages of the epidemic in the late spring of 2003.[53]

Notwithstanding such episodic displays of leadership compassion and determination, however, China's myriad socio-economic problems are unlikely to prove amenable to *ad hoc*, paternalistic solutions. Sporadic acts of *noblesse oblige* by concerned state leaders certainly count for something; but they are not, ultimately, a viable substitute for sound institutions.

Needed: A Transition to "Soft Authoritarianism"

What is most urgently needed at present is a serious elite commitment to strengthening the institutions of socio-political inclusion and interest articulation. This would involve a number of concrete steps that go well beyond the limited objectives of Jiang Zemin's "three represents" and Hu Jintao's "comfort visits." Such steps include the easing of present restrictions on unofficial religious, social and occupational organizations; expanding the scope of political and intellectual tolerance; enhancing the autonomy of the mass media and organs of public opinion; strengthening the representative functions of people's congresses; and, in general, relaxing Party control on governmental administration. Such "soft authoritarian" reforms would not, in and of themselves, ensure governmental transparency, accountability or the rule of law; still less would they solve the country's economic problems. But they would, at a minimum, help to strengthen China's congenitally weak input institutions and thereby revitalize its frail, malnourished socio-political "fingers."[54]

Preliminary movement in the direction of soft authoritarianism first occurred in the late 1980s, under Zhao Ziyang. In his political report to

---

52. John Gittings, "Mind the gap," *The Guardian* (online), 21 January 2003, http://www.guardian.co.uk/elsewhere/country/story/0,7792,879323,00.html; also Erik Eckholm, "China's new leader works to set himself apart," *New York Times*, 12 January 2003.

53. See "China feels side effects from SARS," *Washington Post*, 2 May 2003, p. A1.

54. The term "soft authoritarianism" was originally coined with reference to the combination of paternalistic, executive-dominated government and pluralistic socio-political inclusion displayed by South-East Asia's "little dragons." Later it was adapted by Minxin Pei and others to describe a possible political trajectory for post-reform China. See Pei, "China's evolution toward soft-authoritarianism," in Barrett McCormick (ed.), *What If China Does Not Democratize* (Armonk, NY: M.E. Sharpe, 2000), pp. 74–98.

the 13th Party Congress in 1987, Zhao outlined a programme of partial political reform that included a number of significant proposals: removal of the Communist Party from state administration; delegation of governmental authority and responsibility to lower levels; reform of the personnel system to minimize political patronage; enhancement of the supervisory authority of representative bodies and mass organizations; and strengthening of the rule of law. Perhaps the most radical proposal of all, however, was Zhao's call for the party-state to recognize the legitimacy of diverse interest groups – the first step toward authentic political pluralism: "Different groups of people may have different interests and views," he said; "they too need opportunities for the exchange of ideas." Zhao further affirmed that "socialist society is not a monolith ... special interests should not be overlooked. Conflicting interests should be reconciled."[55]

If adopted, Zhao's reforms would have taken the first significant step toward easing the endemic state–society separation in China. In the event, however, Zhao's proposals were stillborn, stopped in their tracks by the Tiananmen crackdown. Zhao himself was purged for "splitting the Party." Thereafter, fear of social instability and chaos, reinforced by the sudden, startling disintegration of the Soviet Union, prevented China's third-generation leaders from renewing the call for enhanced political pluralism and feedback. To date, neither Zhao nor his 1987 proposals have been rehabilitated.

More serious than the threat of a sudden, Soviet-style collapse of Communist Party rule, however, is the prospect of a continued erosion of CCP authority and popular legitimacy. Political cynicism and alienation run high throughout Chinese society. The regime's Marxist-Leninist philosophical underpinnings have been diluted virtually beyond recognition by 25 years of market reform and rationalization; and the Party is no longer able to offer an inspiring vision of China's future. Increasingly, the CCP is seen as irrelevant to many people in their daily lives – an annoyance to be avoided where possible and endured when necessary. Indicative of growing popular indifference to the Party's leaders and policies, ordinary Chinese often laugh and roll their eyes upward when asked about Jiang Zemin's "theory of the three represents." And many ordinary Chinese expressed their displeasure – occasionally in the form of organized protests – over the government's crude, heavy-handed attempts to prevent the spread of the SARS virus.[56] As a measure of institutional alienation, a recent poll commissioned by the Chinese Academy of Social

---

55. Traditionally, Leninist systems have asserted as a matter of principle the complete identity of public and private interests, denying the very possibility of any legitimate discrepancy between the two. During the Cultural Revolution the hegemonic dominance of the public interest reached its apotheosis with Mao Zedong's injunction to "destroy the self, promote the public" (*posi, ligong*). Zhao Ziyang's proposals for enhanced political pluralism and reform are analysed in Baum, *Burying Mao*, pp. 220–22.

56. See Rupert Wingfield-Hayes, "SARS threat to Communist Party," BBC News (online), 8 May 2003: http://news.bbc.co.uk/2/hi/asia-pacific/3011739.stm.

Sciences revealed that 80 per cent of respondents would prefer to elect their government officials directly, if given the choice.[57]

Under such circumstances, and given the relative improbability of a sudden, radical democratic breakthrough from above – which would undermine the very foundations of Communist Party rule in China – China's new leaders might reasonably be expected to begin to experiment with more inclusive, hybrid forms of soft authoritarian governance. Though the reform measures outlined by Zhao in 1987 were neither fully elaborated nor quintessentially democratic in nature, they nevertheless identified a plausible way to narrow the gap between an overbearing party-state and a congenitally enfeebled society. In this respect, they could be seen to constitute important first steps in China's transition to political modernity.

Perhaps the biggest barrier to soft authoritarian reform is the formidable factor of political inertia. Other things being equal, and short of a large-scale systemic crisis, China's fourth-generation leaders, like their third-generation predecessors, may well opt to take the path of least resistance, choosing to "muddle through" with only modest, incremental tinkering and minimal structural adjustment. Perforce, muddling through is the default political strategy preferred by most entrenched political elites, most of the time. But China's leaders may not have this luxury for much longer. Given a deepening of the socio-economic and political-institutional fault lines discussed above, time may not be on their side. Although the country's extraordinary record of near double-digit economic growth since the Tiananmen disaster has enabled the regime to weather the transitional shocks of marketization and "opening up" without undergoing serious, systemic political upheaval, the good times may not last. Stopgap measures such as controlled village elections, leaders' "comfort visits," ubiquitous rural "letters-and-visits stations" (*xinfang ju*) and the 1989 Administrative Litigation Law (which permits individual citizens, but not groups, to sue government agencies), are arguably steps in the right direction insofar as they permit some political stress reduction.[58] But they are only baby steps, a "hard authoritarian" regime's minimal concession to the need for more robust input/feedback institutions.

So long as the economy continues to grow, China's leaders may be able to delay the onset of necessary institutional reforms further. But there are two big drawbacks to such a strategy: first, it makes the regime a captive hostage to global (and local) economic forces that it cannot readily control; and secondly, it compounds the political risks posed by an increasingly restive, cynical population. Far better, it can be argued,

57. For an analysis of recent trends in Chinese public opinion, see Joseph Fewsmith, "China's domestic agenda: social pressures and public opinion." *China Leadership Monitor*, No. 6 (Spring 2003), http://www.chinaleadershipmonitor.org/20032/jf.html.

58. On the efficacy of "letters-and-visits stations" in dealing with rural grievances, see Bernstein and Lu, *Taxation without Representation*. On the implementation of the Administrative Litigation Law, see Minxin Pei, "Citizens vs. mandarins: administrative litigation in China," *The China Quarterly*, No. 152 (December 1997), pp. 832–862.

pro-actively to initiate institutional reforms while the economy remains relatively robust, than to wait until the system is in crisis and "regime failure" becomes a real (rather than merely a hypothetical) possibility. The need for more sensitive socio-political "fingers" has never been greater in China. The Leninist "thumb" needs to relax its grip while it still commands sufficient public authority to do so.

Some observers take issue with this view. Nathan, for example, suggests that the Chinese party-state has already made a successful transition from "totalitarianism" to a "classic authoritarian regime," one which "appears increasingly stable."[59] Others, however, argue that the Chinese polity has decayed to the point where nothing short of a major democratic overhaul would be sufficient to prevent the further erosion of political and social stability.[60] The question appears to boil down to whether the CCP, by tinkering with the state's input institutions (and thereby bolstering the instruments of soft authoritarian rule) could forestall indefinitely more radical changes associated with free, democratic elections, power sharing and limited government.

Beyond the 16th Party Congress: Plus ça Change?

Grappling with the question of China's "authoritarian resilience," Minxin Pei has suggested that the Chinese party-state currently contains elements conducive both to political renewal and political decay. The important question for him is "which process will ultimately overtake the other?"[61] For Pei, the soft authoritarian pathway – involving enhanced press freedom, improved village (and township) elections and more representative people's congresses, among other things – would, if implemented, tilt the balance decisively in the direction of political renewal, enabling the government "to respond more effectively to the needs of China's increasingly dynamic and diverse society." The problem, in his view, is that "under current circumstances, the CCP is unlikely to take these steps since they would require the Party to exercise its power in untried ways, even to risk giving up some power (albeit in the name of governing more effectively)." And he concludes, somewhat pessimistically, that, "as things stand, those predicting the regime's political renewal may have the harder case to make." Just so.

Searching for clues to the shape of things to come, scholars and other outside observers have carefully parsed the words and deeds of China's new leaders and scrutinized the official and unofficial media for telltale signs of political intent. Thus far, no clear, coherent picture has emerged, only tantalizing – and often contradictory – bits and pieces of information. Immediately following the 16th Congress, for example, Hu Jintao stressed the twin themes of constitutional governance and rule of law,

59. Nathan, "Authoritarian resilience," p. 16.
60. See, for example, the essays by Wang Shaoguang, Bruce Gilley, He Qinglian and Bruce Dickson in *Journal of Democracy*, Vol. 14, No. 1 (January 2003).
61. Minxin Pei, "Contradictory trends and confusing signals," *Journal of Democracy*, Vol. 14, No. 1 (January 2003), pp. 73–81.

calling for greater openness and transparency in the operations of leading Party bodies, including the Politburo.[62] Along similar lines, in late December 2002 the mayor of Beijing told a meeting of the municipal Party committee that henceforth Beijing would expand the "orderly participation" of residents in politics, enlarge "the people's right to know," and "transform the will of the Party into the will and action of all Beijing residents."[63] Less than four months later, however the mayor was summarily sacked for lying to the people of Beijing, denying that there had been a severe outbreak of SARS in the nation's capital.[64]

In a move designed to increase local governmental transparency, officials in several counties in Guangdong province have reportedly started to open their budgets and hiring practices to public scrutiny.[65] Going a step further towards official accountability, local authorities in Siyang county, Jiangsu, conducted a public referendum early in 2003. Residents were asked to name the county's worst-performing officials in each of several administrative spheres. Private entrepreneurs voted for the most inefficient commercial cadre; taxi drivers chose the worst traffic cop; and fisherman selected the most incompetent fishery official. Altogether, nine local cadres were suspended for six months. Their salaries were halved and they were forced to undergo self-criticism.[66]

In selected urban districts of Ningbo and Beijing municipalities, direct elections for neighbourhood committee leaders were held early in 2003.[67] Meanwhile, in the Shenzhen Special Economic Zone, local officials openly discussed their intention to adopt a rudimentary separation of powers, under which the Party's right to intervene in day-to-day governmental affairs would be sharply curtailed, its role limited to advising on strategy.[68] Thus far, however, the Shenzhen reforms have failed to materialize.

Another important barometer of institutional reform is the progress of direct township elections. The first such elections were held spontaneously, without higher-level government sanction, in a handful of districts in Sichuan province and elsewhere beginning in 1998.[69] To date, however, there have been no signs of a broad expansion of these experiments, as central leaders reportedly remain deeply concerned about

62. Ching-ching Ni, "New Chinese leader looks like own man," *Los Angeles Times*, 4 March 2003, p. A3.

63. Quoted in *Taipei Times*, 2 January 2003, p. 8.

64. John Pomfret, "SARS coverup spurs a shake-up in Beijing," *Washington Post*, 21 April 2003, p. A1.

65. Bruce Gilley, "Guangdong leads China toward reform," *Wall Street Journal*, 24 February 2003; Joseph Kahn, "Democratic hopes test China's political limits," *New York Times*, 2 March 2003

66. "Nine Chinese officials suspended in landmark vote," Reuters (Beijing), 20 January 2003.

67. "A qualified vote," *The Economist*, 5 April 2003, p. 42.

68. *Economist Intelligence Unit*, 14 January 2003.

69. See Lianjiang Li, "The politics of introducing direct township elections in China."

the Party's ability to control the processes of nominating and screening candidates.[70]

On the media front, a few local newspapers began to publish articles calling for accelerated democratic reform in the run-up to the Tenth National People's Congress in March 2003. But when one paper printed an essay by Li Rui, Mao Zedong's 85-year-old former political secretary, criticizing both Mao and Deng Xiaoping for their failure to introduce political democracy, the offending journal, the *21st Century World Herald*, was temporarily shuttered by the Party's propaganda department. Reportedly, only Hu Jintao's personal intervention prevented the newspaper from being permanently closed.[71] Similarly, in the aftermath of the SARS epidemic of spring 2003, a few newspapers and magazines that had boldly exposed the government's lack of candour in failing to inform the public of the magnitude and severity of the burgeoning health crisis found themselves subject to renewed state censorship – or worse.[72]

Finally, in a clear sign that tight restrictions on the topics of acceptable political discourse still exist, the CCP propaganda department in August 2003 issued new regulations to universities, newspapers and think tanks banning public discussion of the so-called "three impermissibles" (*san ge burang*) – political reform, constitutional revision and re-evaluation of the 1989 Tiananmen crackdown.[73] Evidently, scattered, piecemeal experiments in incremental reform are permissible at the grassroots level – but only insofar as these serve to enhance state legitimacy. On the other hand, critical debate over the regime's central political institutions, principles and practices remains strictly off limits.

Radical Democratization: A Postscript

These developments further point to the conclusion that a radical, top-down democratic breakthrough is not likely to occur any time soon.[74] Nevertheless, a few tantalizing international precedents do exist. These involve cases where "hard authoritarian" dictators, faced with mounting systemic stresses, unexpectedly opted to initiate broad, sweeping institutional changes. Who, for example, would have predicted early in 1986

70. Tony Saich and Yang Xuedong, "Township elections in China: extending democracy or institutional innovation?" paper presented at the international seminar on "Local Governance in India and China: Rural Development and Social Change," Kolkata, 6–8 January 2003, pp. 2, 30 *et passim*.

71. John Pomfret, "Chinese newspaper shut after call for reform," *Washington Post*, 14 March 2003; Ray Cheung, "Hu stepped in to stop closure of controversial newspaper," *South China Morning Post*, 8 April 2003.

72. Nailene Chou West, "Radical magazine a no-show in capital," *South China Morning Post*, 24 June 2003; also Susan V. Lawrence and Kathy Chen, "Media reforms in China betray contradictions, *Wall Street Journal*, 25 June 2003.

73. See Reuters (Beijing), 20 August 2003; also John Pomfret, "China orders halt to debate on reforms," *Washington Post*, 27 August 2003, p. A1.

74. In an earlier attempt to assign rough probabilities to various alternative political outcomes in post-reform China, I reckoned the odds against a "democratic breakthrough from above" to be approximately 12:1. See Richard Baum, "China after Deng: ten scenarios in search of reality," *The China Quarterly*, No. 145 (March 1996), pp 153–175.

that Mikhail Gorbachev – a loyal apparatchik in the Soviet Union's post-Stalinist party machinery – would shortly launch democratic reforms with such profound transformative potential? Was there anything in Gorbachev's personal history or career path prior to becoming general secretary of the CPSU that prefigured his startling post-Chernobyl policy of *glasnost*, culminating in the constitutional termination of the Communist Party's 70-year monopoly on political power? And what of Chiang Ching-kuo, the Moscow-trained son of Chiang Kai-shek and former head of Taiwan's much-feared secret police, who succeeded his father as president of the Republic of China in 1975? Shortly before his death in 1988, Chiang Ching-kuo unilaterally rescinded the politically repressive martial law regulations imposed by his father in 1949 and agreed to permit electoral competition by the *dangwai* (non-Kuomintang parties) – measures that culminated, within a few years, in the near-complete democratization of the Taiwanese polity. Such examples serve to confound the conventional wisdom which holds that Leninist-style one-party regimes are inherently incapable of meaningful self-reform because their leaders will never voluntarily relinquish their monopoly of political power. These examples also serve as a reminder that bold, visionary leadership can – and sometimes does – emerge in the most unexpected places.[75]

It should be noted, however, that neither Mikhail Gorbachev nor Chiang Ching-kuo is likely to be a source of inspiration to China's new leaders. Gorbachev's reforms brought about not only his own downfall but the collapse of the Soviet Union, while Chiang's democratic opening eventually culminated in the decline and fall of Taiwan's ruling Kuomintang. An even more unpleasant fate met the architects of South Korea's democratic opening in 1987. Less than a decade after they set in motion Korea's stunning democratic transition, military strongman Chun Doo-hwan and his presidential successor, Roh Tae-woo, were convicted and imprisoned for crimes of treason, mutiny and corruption committed during their tenure in office. For those hoping for an early democratic breakthrough in China, the lesson here is not a particularly salutary one. Nor is this lesson likely to be lost on China's fourth-generation leaders as they search for a secure, viable pathway to political renewal, gingerly "groping for stones" in the turbulent, fast-flowing stream of social change.

75. These cases are discussed in Richard Baum, "To reform or to muddle through?" in Gang Lin and Susan Shirk (eds.), *The 16th CCP Congress and Leadership Transition in China* (Washington, DC: Woodrow Wilson International Center for Scholars, Asia Program Special Report No. 105, September 2002), pp. 39–44.

Glossary of Chinese Terms

The following is a glossary of Chinese terms used in the main text of all articles and research reports. All characters have been supplied authors.

Romanization	English equivalent	Chinese characters
Bai Enpei		白恩培
Bai Keming		白克明
Beidaihe		北戴河
Bo Yibo		薄一波
bumen	ministries	部門
Cao Bochun		曹柏純
Cao Gangchuan		曹剛川
cha'e	margin of elimination	差額
chanye gongren	industrial workers	产业工人
Chen Bingde		陈炳德
Chen Jianguo		陈建国
Chen Kuiyuan		陈奎元
Chen Liangyu		陈良宇
Chen Shui-bian		陳水扁
Chen Xitong		陈希同
Chen Yun		陈云
Chengdu		成都
Chi Haotian		迟浩田
Chiang Ching-Kuo		蔣經國
Chiang Kai-shek		蔣介石
Chu Bo		储波
cunguansuo	village management office	村管所
da guanjia	big manager	大管家
daguo zhanlüe	great power diplomacy	大国战略
Dai Bingguo		戴秉国
Dalian		大连
dang he guojia lingdao zhidu de gaige	reform of the leadership system of the Party and the state	党和国家领导制度的改革

dang zhongzhi	Party general branch	党中支
dangwai	non-Kuomintang Parties	党外
danwei	work unit	单位
Deng Changyou		邓昌友
Deng Xiaoping		邓小平
Diaoyutai		钓鱼台
Ding Guangen		丁关根
Ding Henggao		丁杭高
Du Tiehuan		杜铁环
erxian	second front	二线
falun gong		法轮功
feigaishui	tax-for-fee reform	费改税
Fu Quanyou		傅全有
gangyao	directives	纲要
Gao–Rao		高－饶
Ge Zhenfeng		葛振峰
genben liyi	fundamental interests	根本利益
geti gongshanghu	private industrialists and merchants	个体工商户
guangda renmin	"the overwhelming majority of the people"	广大人民
Gui Quanzhi		桂权致
Guo Boxiong		郭伯雄
Guo Jinlong		郭金龙
Hanchuan		汉川
hangye zonghui	business councils	行业总会
He Guoqiang		贺国强
He Yong		何勇
Hefei		合肥
heping gongchu	peaceful co-existence	和平共处
hexin	core	核心
hongguan tiaokong	macro adjustment	宏观调控
Hu Angang		胡鞍钢
Hu Jintao		胡锦涛
Hu Yaobang		胡耀邦
Hua Guofeng		华国峰
Huang Ju		黄菊

Huangshan		黄山
huanjie	term change (reshuffle)	换届
Hui Liangyu		回良玉
Jia Qinglin		贾庆林
Jia Wenxian		贾文显
Jiang Futang		姜福堂
Jiang Qing		江青
Jiang Zemin		江泽民
jiang zhengzhi	mindful of politics	讲政治
jianshe xiaokang shehui	"build a moderately well-off society"	建设小康社会
Jinan		济南
Jing Zhiyuan		靖志远
jingguan zhan	economic management station	经管站
jingzheng duoyuan	economic and political multipolarity	经政多元
jizi	fund raising	集资
Kaifeng		开封
Koo–Wang		辜 – 汪
Kui Fulin		隗福临
Kunming		昆明
kuo zhao sheng	"expanded enrolled students"	扩招生
Lanzhou		兰州
lao daxuesheng	university graduates prior to the cultural revolution	老大学生
laosanjie	1966, 1967 and 1968 middle-school and high-school graduates	老三届
Lao Shan		老山
Lee Teng-hui		李登辉
Lei Mingqiu		雷鸣球
Li Andong		李安东
Li Changchun		李长春
Li Jianguo		李建国
Li Jinai		李继耐
Li Keqiang		李克强
Li Lanqing		李岚清
Li Peng		李鹏
Li Qianyuan		李乾元

Li Rui		李锐
Li Ruihuan		李瑞环
Li Wenhua		李文华
Li Xiannian		李先念
Li Zhaoxing		李肇星
Liang Guanglie		梁光烈
liang zhong zhidu	two systems	两种制度
Liao Xilong		廖锡龙
Liaoyang		辽阳
licai xiaozu	fiscal oversight small group	理财小组
Lin Biao		林彪
Liu Dongdong		刘冬冬
Liu Huaqing		刘华清
Liu Huaqiu		刘华秋
Liu Jiulong		刘久龙
Liu Qi		刘淇
Liu Shaoqi		刘少奇
Liu Shunyao		刘顺耀
Liu Shutian		刘书田
Liu Yahong		刘亚洪
Liu Yongzhi		刘勇致
Liu Yunshan		刘云山
Liu Zhenwu		刘镇武
liudong renyuan	floating population	流动人员
Lu Xueyi		陆学艺
Luo Gan		罗干
Luoyang		洛阳
Meng Jianzhu		孟建柱
Meng Xuenong		孟学农
Nanjing		南京
Nankai (daxue)	Nankai (University)	南开（大学）
nanshui-beisong	planned central canal between the Chang (Yangtze) and the Huang (Yellow) River	南水北送
nanxun	southern inspection	南巡
nianqinghua	rejuvenation	年轻化
Ningbo		宁波

nongmingong	peasant workers	农民工
Pei Huailiang		裴怀亮
Qian Guoliang		钱国梁
Qian Qichen		钱其琛
Qian Shugen		钱树根
Qian Yunlu		钱运录
Qiao Qingchen		乔清晨
Qiao Shi		乔石
Qimen		祁门
Qinghua (daxue)	Tsinghua (University)	清华（大学）
Qu Fanghuan		瞿方煥
quandi	enclosure	圈地
quanmian jianshe xiaokang shehui	build a well-off society in an all-round way	全面建设小康社会
Renmin ribao	*People's Daily*	人民日报
san ge burang	"three impermissibles"	三个不让
san ge daibiao	"three represents"	三个代表
sanxin weiji	three faith crises	三信危机
shengchanlun	"productive forces theory"	生产论
Shenyang		沈阳
shi	strategic advantage	势
Shi Yunsheng		石云生
shijie duojihua	global multipolarization	世界多极化
shuang daiguan	double substitute management	双代管
Song Defu		宋德福
Song Wenhan		宋文汉
Song Zhaosu		宋照肃
Su Chi-cheng		蘇志誠
Su Ge		苏格
Su Rong		苏荣
Sun Liping		孙立平
Sun Zhiqing		孙志庆
taishanghuang	"emperor behind the scenes"	太上皇
Tan Yuexin		谭悦新
Tang Jiaxuan		唐家璇
Tang Tianbiao		唐天标

taoguang yanghui	hide one's capacities while biding one's time	韬光养晦
tekunhu	"especially poverty stricken"	特困户
Tian Chengping		田成平
Tianjin		天津
tiliu	village-retained fees	提留
tixi	regime	体系
tongchou	township unified fees	通抽
tuixiu	retire	退休
Tunxi		屯溪
Wan Li		万里
wan yan shu	10,000- word document	万言书
Wang Daohan		汪道涵
Wang Gang		王刚
Wang Hongwen		王洪文
Wang Jianmin		王建民
Wang Lequan		王乐泉
Wang Qian		王乾
Wang Ruilin		王瑞林
Wang Taihua		王太华
Wang Xudong		王旭东
Wang Yunkun		王云坤
Wang Zhaoguo		王兆国
Wen Jiabao		温家宝
Wen Shizhen		溫世震
Wen Xisen		溫熙森
wending ya dao yiqie	"stability over all"	稳定压倒一切
women de dage	our elder brother	我们的大哥
Wu Bangguo		吴邦国
Wu Guanzheng		吴官正
Wu Quanxu		吴铨叙
Wu Shengli		吴胜利
Wu Shuangzhan		吴双战
Wu Yi		吴仪
Wuhan		武汉
Xi Jinping		习近平

xia hai	"plunge into the sea" (of commerce)	下海
xiagang zhigong	laid-off staff and workers	下岗职工
Xibaipo		西柏坡
xibu da kaifa	develop China's western region	西部大开发
xin yi jie lingdao jiti	a new term of leadership collective	新一届领导集体
xinfang ju	"letters-and-visits" stations	信访局
Xing Shizhong		邢世忠
xinren weiji	crisis of faith in the party	信任危机
Xinxiang		新乡
xinxin weiji	crisis of faith in socialism	信心危机
xinyang weiji	crisis of faith in Marxism	信仰危机
xinyongshe	credit co-operatives	信用社
Xiong Guangkai		熊光楷
Xu Caihou		徐才厚
Xu Youfang		徐有芳
yanda	"strike hard"	严打
Yang Baibing		杨白冰
Yang Deqing		杨德清
Yang Guoliang		杨国良
Yang Huaiqing		杨怀庆
Yang Shangkun		杨尚昆
Yang Zhengwu		杨正午
Ye Aiqun		叶爱群
yi bian yi guo	one country on each side	一边一国
yi ge shijie	one world	一个世界
yixian	first front	一線
yiyuanhua	unanimity	一元化
Yu Yongbo		于永波
Yu Zhengsheng		俞正声
Yuan Shoufang		袁守芳
yushi jujin	"keep up with the times"	与时俱进
Zeng Peiyan		曾培炎
Zeng Qinghong		曾庆红
Zhang Dejiang		张德江
Zhang Dingfa		张丁发

Zhang Li		张黎
Zhang Lichang		张立昌
Zhang Shutian		张树田
Zhang Taiheng		张太恒
Zhang Wannian		张万年
Zhang Wenkang		张文康
Zhang Wentai		张文台
Zhang Yuzhong		张郁仲
Zhang Zhen		张震
Zhao Leji		赵乐际
Zhao Ziyang		赵紫阳
Zheng Shenxia		郑申侠
Zhengzhou		郑州
Zhenning		镇宁
Zheying Shan		赭英山
zhili zhengdun	retrenchment policy	治理整顿
Zhong Shengqin		种胜钦
Zhongnanhai		中南海
Zhou Enlai		周恩來
Zhou Yongkang		周永康
Zhu Fazhong		朱法重
Zhu Qi		朱啓
Zhu Rongji		朱镕基
Zhu Wenquan		朱文泉
zhua da fang xiao	"grasp the big, drop the small"	抓大放小
zuzhibu	Organization Department	组织部

Index